HOW TO GET STARTED IN
COIN
COLLECTING

No. 1495
$19.95

HOW TO GET STARTED IN
COIN COLLECTING

BY BOB LEMKE

TAB TAB BOOKS Inc.
BLUE RIDGE SUMMIT, PA. 17214

FIRST EDITION
FIRST PRINTING

Copyright © 1983 by TAB BOOKS Inc.
Printed in the United States of America

Library of Congress Cataloging in Publication Data

Lemke, Bob.
How to get started in coin collecting.

Includes index.
1. Coins—Collectors and collecting. I. Title.
CJ81.L45 1983 747.4′075 82-19316
ISBN 0-8306-0495-2
ISBN 0-8306-1495-8 (pbk.)

Contents

Preface

YOU'VE MADE THE RIGHT DECISION IN PICKING up this book. Like too many other beginning coin collectors—when I first discovered the hobby nearly a quarter of a century ago—I was too eager to spend my money on coins. It was only later that I learned the wisdom of the hobby adage: Buy the book before you buy the coin.

If there had been a book like this available when I got started, I would have saved thousands of dollars that were spent on bad deals before I learned the ropes. I hope this book will enable you to get started on the right road to full enjoyment of numismatics from the beginning.

In my job as a numismatic journalist, I deal with coins every day. More importantly, I deal with coin collectors, coin dealers, investors, and speculators. I see more of the inside workings of this fascinating hobby/industry than all but a handful of the most active numismatists. The experience gained from more than eight years of this daily involvement has gone into the making of this book. I want you to get the right start—to make a lifelong pastime of what I consider to be the greatest hobby in the world—because it offers entertainment, education, and the potential for huge profits all at the same time.

Enjoy the book and the hobby.

FIRST AND FOREMOST, THIS BOOK IS DEDICATed to my wife, Mary, and my little girl, Crystal. The many evenings and weekends during which it was written came out of their time.

Appreciation is also due to my employer: Krause Publications. Besides paying me for participating in my hobby everyday, they also provided all of the photos in this book.

Special thanks to my parents and Aunt Corrine. Their gifts of coin books helped me get where I am today.

This book is also dedicated to my fellow hobbyists—friends among the ranks of collectors and dealers; around the office, around the town, around the state and around the nation. Without such people, numismatics would be a cold hobby.

Introduction

THIS BOOK INTRODUCES ONE OF THE NATION'S most popular and profitable hobbies to the beginning collector. The emphasis is on collecting United States coins, but all areas of numismatics are examined. Opening with a history of numismatics as a hobby and as a means of investment, this book puts the current state of the hobby into perspective for the reader who is just getting involved. A survey of specialized numismatic literature offers you a chance to get off on the right foot by acquiring the necessary reference tools to maximize enjoyment and potential profitability from coin collecting.

You are given solid how-to advice on the often confusing topics of buying and selling coins. Included is valuable information on avoiding costly pitfalls. To assist the collector in choosing what to collect, this book provides an easy-to-understand history of U.S. coins and related numismatic collectibles. To help the new numismatist feel at home in the hobby, part of this book deals with the different ways in which people collect, the care and display of coins, getting involved in coin clubs at all levels, and the whole range of personal, educational, and social benefits to be derived from numismatics.

This book is intended as a first numismatic book for the potential or fledgling coin collector. It is written to be clearly understandable to all ages, but it is probably best suited for the teenage or young adult reader. It is written to provide the novice numismatist with everything he should know before diving too deeply into coin collecting. The principal aim of this book is to foster the enjoyment of numismatics by insuring that persons with a budding interest have a source to which they can turn for honest, accurate, current information about all aspects of coin collecting and avoid potential problems that would turn them away from a potential lifelong hobby.

A special feature of this book is the viewpoint from which it is written. My 23 years of numismatic hobby experience—the last eight years as a professional numismatic journalist—have provided an insider's look at a complex hobby/industry that is available to very few people who are not full-time coin dealers. Yet, most books written by coin dealers are not impartial enough to be of maximum benefit to the collector. The dealer/author always has a vested interest in writing, and that is to sell himself as a coin dealer. The various buy, sell, and investment recommendations given in such books have to be viewed with an eye toward the dealer's motive.

With this book, I want to promote the welfare of coin collecting and to encourage new collectors to join the fold. Being daily involved in all aspects of the numismatic world, I am able to pass on valuable information about the current status of this hobby.

Another special feature of this book is the coverage of the U.S. paper money field. Virtually every coin collector also collects some type of paper money. The paper money field is one of the fastest growing specialties in the numismatic hobby. Yet, because it is highly specialized, few other books do more than briefly touch upon it. This book presents a wide range of information on what to collect (and why) in U.S. paper money.

Also of special interest are the tips on protecting the beginner's pocketbook from outright crooks who hang around the fringes of the hobby. One of the greatest dangers to the continued enjoyment of the coin collecting hobby is the potential for being ripped off in a bad deal. This book gives specific advice on how to safely buy and sell coins and participate in hobby activities.

Chapter 1

History of Numismatics

I T SEEMS LOGICAL TO ASSUME THAT THE WORLD'S first coin collector appeared on the same seventh century B.C. day that the Greeks in Lydia created the first coin by stamping a lump of silver/gold alloy with a pictograph inscription of a lion, bear, and bull. It is appropriate, then that the hobby/science/industry that has evolved over the past 2500 years takes its name from the Greek word *numis*, meaning money. The term for the hobby is *numismatics* and the hobbyists are *numismatists*. For the benefit of the novice who wants to avoid embarrassment the first time he has occasion to pronounce the word in public, I'll provide a short lesson. Pronounced phonetically, the name of the hobby is *new-miz-MEH-tix*. The accent is on the third syllable. For no good reason, the term for a coin collector is pronounced *new-MIZ-meh-tist*. The accent is on the second syllable.

Getting past the name is probably the toughest part of joining the coin-collecting fraternity. That tongue twister has been known to stump many hobbyists, new and veteran. A self-effacing line sometimes heard in hobby circles goes like this: "Six months ago I couldn't spell numismatist; now I are one." Heaven only knows what those who collected coins before the word numismatist was coined called themselves. Probably just plain ol' coin collector.

Little is known about the early days of coin collecting. It can be reasonably speculated that it must have been a pastime confined exclusively to the very wealthy. Besides being the only persons who could afford to keep a coin for its aesthetic or curiosity value, the rich—right up until the last half of the twentieth century, and then only in America and other relatively affluent countries—were the only persons with the time to have a hobby.

The Renaissance in Italy and Western Europe, from the fourteenth to the sixteenth centuries, seems to have marked the true birth of coin collecting on a wide scale. The art of the great masters spawned in that period includes paintings showing gentlemen of the leisure class in the examination and enjoyment of coins and medals (Fig. 1-1). During the great age of exploration in the latter part of this period, the first books devoted to numismatic themes appeared. Like all books in those pre-Gutenberg days, they are extremely rare today and command handsome prices from coin collectors who compete with bibliophiles for each available volume.

In seventeenth-Century Europe, as in 1980s America, coin collectors focused their attention on the numismatic items of the past. In today's world in which most hobbies are little more than fads that often pass in a few years' (or even months') time, it is satisfying for the

Fig. 1-1. This Renaissance-era painting shows an Italian man of wealth with an ancient Roman medal.

there was a premium value placed on gold and silver coins) made it unlikely that few collections would survive intact.

One noteworthy exception was the sixth President of the United States, John Quincy Adams, who formed a collection in the early decades of the nineteenth century (Fig. 1-2). Even as recently as the late 1970s, coins whose pedigree can be accurately traced to that collection could be found at public auction.

The United States Mint also began a coin cabinet in the 1830s, which it maintained and enhanced through the striking of "limited edition" specimens for itself and to trade with private collectors; eventually the mint turned the collection over to the Smithsonian Institution, where it continues to grow (Fig. 1-3).

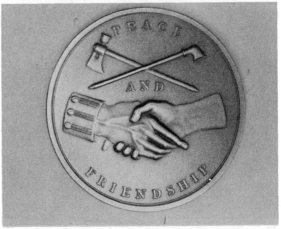

Fig. 1-2. John Quincy Adams was an avid coin collector. Collectors can obtain copies of his official Indian Peace Medal directly from the U.S. Mint.

numismatist to reflect on the permanence of his chosen pursuit. The same silver staters of the ancient Greek republics and gold commemoratives marking the succession of Caesers in Imperial Roman times that we collect so enthusiastically today were being collected by equally devoted numismatists 500 years ago on the other side of the world.

Early numismatists were especially fond of commemorative medals—if the details of old paintings and books can be relied upon—probably because their larger size gave the original coiner more room to produce a lavish design and embellish with a detailed inscription. It is no exaggeration to say that much of what modern man knows of the ancient world is the result of the legacy unwittingly passed on by the coins of the day. Such a legacy seems to be all too often ignored by those who choose coinage designs today. This is true in the United States and around the world.

Coin collecting as a hobby did not begin in this country until the late 1860s, after the Civil War. The hard times that marked the emerging years of this nation saw so many coin shortages and monetary emergencies (when

Fig. 1-3. The United States Mint, shown here in an 1830s engraving, collected coins of the world. The mint's cabinets later went to the Smithsonian Institution where they are maintained today.

Perhaps the finest collection of American-related coins ever assembled, the Garrett Collection, was started in the early 1860s by T. Harrison Garrett of the Baltimore and Ohio Railroad Garretts. Subsequently, the collection was willed to Johns Hopkins University. It remained intact until a series of public auctions, conducted in 1979-1981, that amassed a total price in excess of $22 million (Fig. 1-4).

Many other famous American families of the 1800s had a scion or two who was known to squander the family fortunes on rare coins. In many cases, the great collections thus founded have made their way into relatively public hands through donation to libraries, universities, and other organizations. The collection of United States coinage assembled by Josiah Lily (founder of the pharmaceutical firm that bears his name), is now on indefinite public exhibit at the Smithsonian Institution (Fig. 1-5).

Besides building date sets of the relatively recent, but already challenging United States coinage, many of these early collectors turned their efforts to the coins and monetary tokens of Colonial and pre-Federal days. Other very popular collecting items were the myriad commemorative medals struck in honor of George Washington. Surprisingly, and thankfully for modern-day collectors, a great number of the nineteenth century numismatists made an effort to keep their collections current by obtaining specimens of such things as the private gold coinage being minted in the Western states and territories.

Great coin cabinets were also being formed in Europe and the Mideast during the nineteenth Century. Nevertheless, the hobby was still confined to the very rich or to governments and mints.

By the waning years of the nineteenth century, the coin-collecting hobby had reached such a level of popularity that the United States government issued its first coins intended solely for collectors: the Columbian half dollar of 1892 and the Isabella quarter of 1893. Both coins marked the 400 anniversary of the discovery of America by Columbus and the Columbian Exposition world's fair

Fig. 1-4. T. Harrison Garrett, scion of the great American railroad family, began a collection that sold in 1979-1981 for $22 million.

held in Chicago in 1893. The coins were sold for $1 apiece and the profits were used by the fair committee to help fund the extravaganza.

In the 1880s, collectors saw the rise of professional coin dealers dedicated to bringing monied collectors together with the coins they wanted (while making a profit for themselves). As early as the 1870s, frequent auctions of rare coins were being conducted in New York and other Eastern metropolitan centers.

The last half of the nineteenth century also saw the foundation of organized numismatics. The small informal circles of collectors were giving way to national societies. The American Numismatic Society, founded in 1858 as a largely New York City collectors' club, and the American Numismatic Association, founded in 1891, began to attract members from all parts of the nation.

The first national convention of coin collectors was held in 1894 in Detroit, Michigan, under the auspices of the American Numismatic Association. The association continues to hold the largest and most prestigious coin convention in the world.

The last half of the nineteenth century also saw the first publication of widely circulated numismatic literature in this country. Catalogs such as Dr. M. W. Dicke-

Fig. 1-5. Curators of the Smithsonian Institution at work on a display of part of the famous Ely Lilly collection on exhibit there.

son's *American Numismatic Manual* of 1859, and Director of the Mint James Ross Snowden's 1861 *The Medallic Memorials of Washington in the Mint of the United States* helped stimulate collector interest.

In May, 1866, the nation's first numismatic periodical, the *American Journal of Numismatics,* published its first issue. In late 1875, the New York coin and stamp dealer firm of J. W. Scott & Co. began publication of what has been called the first commercial numismatic periodical: *The Coin Collector's Journal.* The premiere issue of *The Numismatist* came out in 1888; the magazine was later adopted as the official journal of the American Numismatic Association. *The Numismatist* continues to be mailed to members each month. It is the longest continuing numismatic periodical.

The dawn of the twentieth century saw a continued trend toward expansion. Following the war with Spain at the turn of the twentieth century, the Panic and depression of 1907 and World War I, the prosperity of the 1920s made an absolute fad of coin collecting in the upper classes. The hobby continued to draw the attention of persons with fabulous wealth. Colonel E. H. R. Green, who managed at one time to squeeze ownership of all five specimens of the 1913 Liberty nickel into his eclectic collection of such useful devices as bejeweled chamber pots and railroads, was typical of many men of money who have turned to coin collecting. For some it is a passing fad; for others it is a lifelong and serious avocation.

A Lithuanian immigrant transplanted to Texas, B. Max Mehl became the first coin dealer to use modern advertising methods to popularize the hobby and promote his services as a coin dealer. For more than 50 years, his advertisements in nationally circulated magazines such as *Collier's* piqued the public's curiosity with such things as his standing offer to pay $500 for a 1913 Liberty nickel. In reality, Mehl knew full well there were only five specimens of the coin, and where each was located at any given moment. His real aim was to sell copies of his *Star Rare Coin Encyclopedia* (Fig. 1-6). This combination buying and selling list made Mehl the richest and best known coin dealer in the nation for more than half a century. It was Mehl's advertisements that got an entire generation of Americans searching their pocket change for valuable finds and brought countless numbers of those optimistics souls into the hobby fold.

The hobby became quite quiet in the 1930s as the Great Depression forced many people to give up saving coins in favor of eating. For those who managed to maintain their spending power in the latter-1930s, the U.S. Government obliged with continuing issues of commemorative coinage that seemed to please no one except

Fig. 1-6. Texas dealer B. Max Mehl did much to popularize the coin collecting hobby in the 1930s with nationwide distribution of his "Star Rare Coin Encyclopedia."

the speculators who sometimes virtually controlled entire issues and the politicians whose pet causes the profits from the coins furthered.

During World War II, the nation's attention was focused more on survival than on hobbies. Many of today's coin collectors, however, credit their travels abroad in military service, or the coins brought back by a father or other relative, with the beginnings of their interest in coin collecting. Portraits of foreign monarchs from coins obtained at Allied bases all over Europe, coins with undecipherable script from North Africa and the Orient, scrap-metal coins bearing the swastika and other fascist symbols from Germany and Italy, and bundles of "Mickey Mouse" money from Pacific territory liberated from Japanese occupation all worked to create a postwar generation of coin collectors.

It was also in the postwar years that the coin collecting hobby became a business and then an industry. The striking of commemorative coins by the U.S. Mint continued into the early 1950s. Each new issue garnered new collectors and big profits for private promoters until President Harry S. Truman banned special-issue coins in 1954.

In 1952, Chet Krause founded *Numismatic News,*

the hobby's first newspaper, as an evening and weekend project. He worked on his kitchen table in a rural Wisconsin farmhouse in time left over from his "day job" of building homes and churches (Fig. 1-7). In 1960, the Sidney, Ohio, daily newspaper spun off the hobby's first weekly periodical, *Coin World*. Today, both publications flourish as weekly newspapers. By the early 1960s, monthly magazines dedicated to the coin collecting hobby were being sold on national newsstands, where they provided a continuous exposure for new collectors.

During the 1960s numismatics began to split into hobby and investment functions. Speculators and would-be plungers drove prices on certain items to dizzying heights in an incredibly short time. Those who were manipulating the market made a killing; those who were just along for the ride were liable to find themselves "buried" in certain coins at prices that have yet to allow them to recoup their "investment."

The ranks of average coin collectors continued to grow and prosper while the big boys were playing market games. The ever-present hobby aspects of numismatics continued to lure new collectors while the solid investment that a well-planned coin portfolio represents began to draw the attention of a new force in the hobby—the investor who is in it solely for the money.

Inflation throughout the 1970s forced people to look beyond the traditional savings account and stock market for a means of holding onto or inspiring growth in their capital. For many, this turned out to be the field of tangible collectibles: art, stamps, gems, Oriental rugs, and, especially, coins.

In 1974, the lifting of a United States government ban against private citizens owning gold helped fuel the interest of collectors. Nations from around the globe began to capitalize on the American public's gold hunger by striking commemorative gold coins strictly for collectors. Almost all of these *noncirculating legal tender* gold pieces, as they are known in the hobby, were produced by private mints in the United States and marketed to American collectors by Madison Avenue promotions firms. Few, if any, of the coins ever saw the native soil of their "issuing" country and about the only people in those nations who ever saw the coins were those who had the power to authorize their issue and who received the profits.

Still, these issues were generally of the highest quality in design and striking. And they helped popularize the hobby of world coin collecting in the United States, if not abroad.

As the new coin investors become more sophisti-cated, they begin to avoid this type of coin and seek out the more traditional numismatic items—rare coins. A new market factor was the insistence on purchasing only the finest-condition coins available. The investors had discovered what had heretofore been the best-kept secret in American numismatics: Top grade coins appreciate faster in value than the same pieces in lesser states of preservation.

A veritable buying frenzy of this type of material—coupled with speculative demand on gold and silver (coins as well as bullion) as a hedge against continued inflation—sent prices skyrocketing throughout the closing years of the 1970s.

By 1978, all of the traditional "rules" of coin investing had gone out the window. Virtually any top-grade rare coin bought one day could be sold the next day for a fat profit.

As 1979 drew to a close—and it looked as if coin collecting was going to be taken over by the man in the three-piece suit and the corporate investor—the whole speculative market collapsed. Gold and silver prices peaked at $800 and $50 an ounce, respectively, and then plummeted in the face of rising interest rates. The rising interest rates also captured the attention of the investor who was now able to lock his funds into vehicles paying double-digit interest rates that were guaranteed. At the same time, many investors were finding they had been swindled in their numismatic speculations. Those who hadn't bothered to learn anything about coins or to find a reputable coin dealer were discovering the "gem" coins they had purchased were overgraded or doctored and worth only a fraction of what they had paid. Some investors who had chosen their dealer unwisely found their entire portfolio had been misappropriated as some of the new breed of instant coin dealers began to go belly up.

The 1980s opened with the numismatic hobby/industry as quiet as it had been in more than 20 years. Only at the beginning of 1982 were the first signs of life beginning to stir. And they are good signs because it is not the big-dollars investor coming back for another go-around, but rather the average coin collector who has been there all along. Laying low while prices on the big-ticket items rose and fell, continuing to collect and study the vast base of numismatic material that was beneath the gaze of the condition-conscious investment client, the grass-roots hobbyist is once again making himself felt in the marketplace.

While so many investors lost their shirts playing a game about which they knew almost nothing, the traditional collector, in many cases, enters the 1980s with a

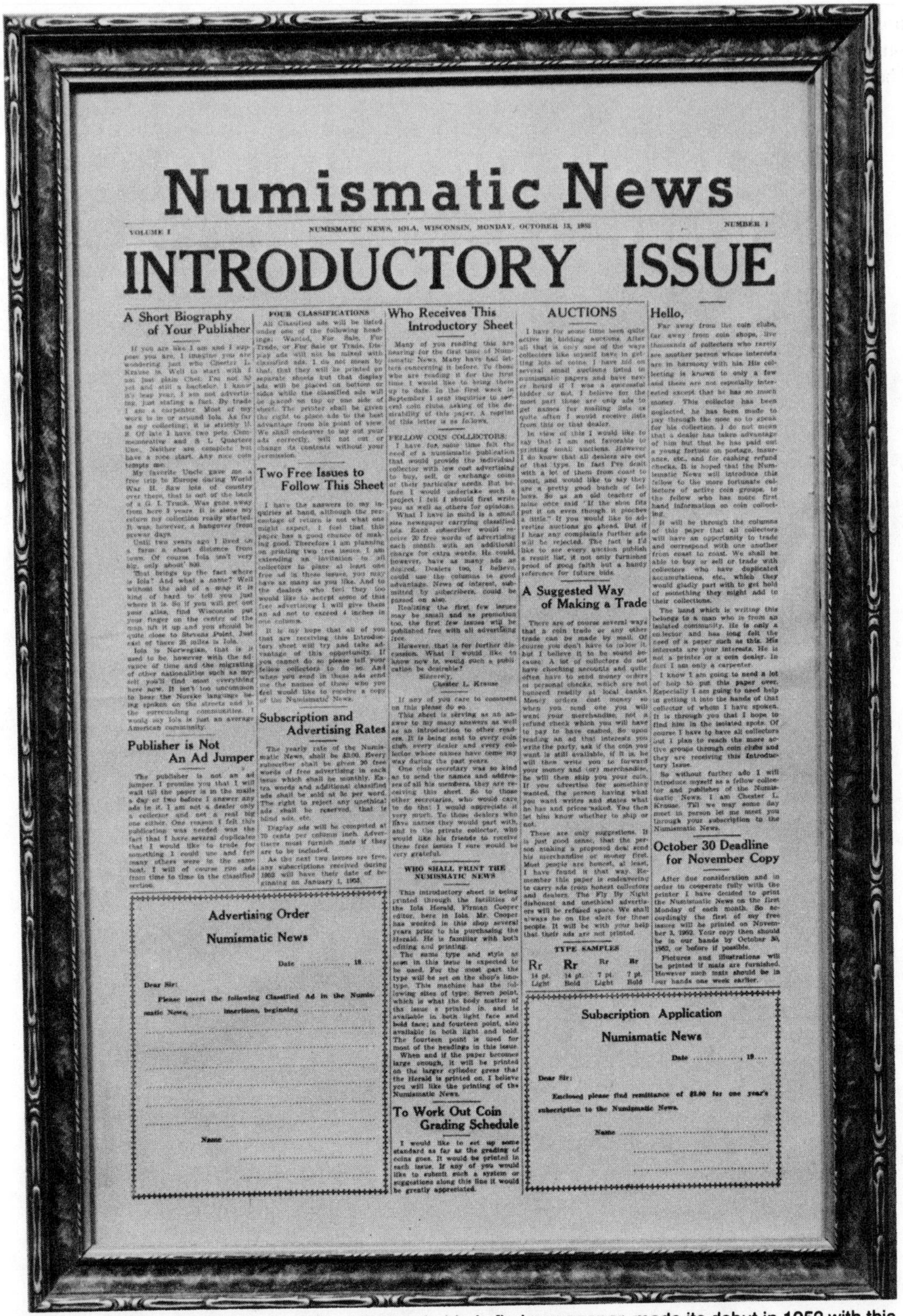
Numismatic News

VOLUME I — NUMISMATIC NEWS, IOLA, WISCONSIN, MONDAY, OCTOBER 13, 1952 — NUMBER 1

INTRODUCTORY ISSUE

A Short Biography of Your Publisher

FOUR CLASSIFICATIONS

Who Receives This Introductory Sheet

AUCTIONS

Hello,

Two Free Issues to Follow This Sheet

FELLOW COIN COLLECTORS:

A Suggested Way of Making a Trade

Publisher is Not An Ad Jumper

Subscription and Advertising Rates

WHO SHALL PRINT THE NUMISMATIC NEWS

October 30 Deadline for November Copy

TYPE SAMPLES

Advertising Order

Numismatic News

Date ...., 19....

Dear Sir:

Please insert the following Classified Ad in the Numismatic News, ... insertions, beginning

Name

To Work Out Coin Grading Schedule

Subscription Application

Numismatic News

Date ...., 19....

Dear Sir:

Enclosed please find remittance of $1.00 for one year's subscription to the Numismatic News.

Name

Fig. 1-7. *Numismatic News*, the coin collecting hobby's first newspaper, made its debut in 1952 with this premiere edition.

portfolio that has appreciated in value—just as it has traditionally done in good times and bad throughout history. The wild roller coaster of numismatic speculation aside, there are good sound reasons for pursuing coin collecting as a hobby, as an investment, or as a combination of the two.

Chapter 2

Numismatics as a Hobby

THERE ARE PROBABLY AS MANY REASONS FOR being a coin collector as there are coin collectors. What motivates each of us to seek out, acquire, study, enjoy, and even profit from numismatic items? In my work I come into daily contact with coin collectors of all levels of sophistication. I meet thousands every year and know several hundred of them well enough to begin to understand what has brought them to this great hobby of ours.

First and foremost, numismatists collect coins because they are *collectors*. (Fig. 2-1). If there were no coins, paper currency, medals, or tokens to satisfy their collecting urge, they would all be collecting something else. Indeed, every coin collector I know *does* collect something else. I collect baseball cards and so does a southern Illinois collector who is one of the nation's leading numismatic exhibitors. A veteran numismatic couple in Wisconsin also owns a nationally famous antique doll collection. My boss collects antique cars and trucks made in Wisconsin. A southern California coin dealer has one of the most unusual collecting interests; he saves the airsickness bags from the many different airlines he flies on each year in the course of his business. Many, many others collect stamps.

The point is that all coin collectors are collectors first and coins just happen to be what they collect. I'm sure the psychologists have many studies on what makes one person a collector, and another not one. And I'm not sure I'd want to be told what drives me—and about 10 million other people in this country—to collect coins and other numismatic items. My observation would be that the two major noneconomic factors that make a collector are the thrill of the hunt and the pride of ownership. But I'm sure that doesn't adequately explain why we collect.

Perhaps the collecting urge can be boiled down to simple terms. No matter how it is viewed, collecting is a challenge. It might just be that coin collectors, and all other collectors as well, are the type of people who enjoy and thrive on a challenge. For some, the challenge might be to amass the largest collection in terms of quantity (whether it's coins, sea shells or just tin foil). Other dyed-in-the-wool collectors are challenged to accumulate the collection with the greatest monetary value or aesthetic value.

In the coin-collecting hobby, it is not uncommon to find collectors who are attempting to collect the worst specimens in a particular specialty. One such popular area is among U.S. Commemorative half dollars. Originally sold at two or more times face value, most commemoratives were preserved in their original uncirculated condition. Yet, I have encountered several different

Fig. 2-1. The coin collector holds history in his hand. Who can look at this assortment of old coins and not wonder where they have been, what they have seen, and whose lives they have touched?

collectors who are trying to collect the most worn example of each of the commemoratives that they can find. This might be a reaction to the collecting trend of recent years that has caused the prices of U.S. commemoratives in the highest grades to soar into the stratosphere.

What might or might not be an unfair stereotype of the average coin collector holds that he is merely a person who makes a pastime of the simple joys of plugging coins into holes of cardboard folders. Certainly this is over simplified, but the basic premise might be accurate. Maybe collectors believe that "there is a place for everything and everything in its place," and that we are the people who must put things where they belong.

As with all aspects of the hobby of coin collecting, the challenge of hunting out the numismatic items needed to fill a collection is a very personal thing. I'm sure the coin dealers don't share my opinion, but it is my observation that, for all too many coin collectors, the thrill of the hunt is limited to hunting up the money to spend. While that is certainly a primary consideration in numismatics (and in all other hobbies) it does not have to be the last word in coin collecting.

Some examples might help. For the sake of continuity, I'll discuss choice, brilliant uncirculated Morgan silver dollars. This is a set of about 100 dates, mint marks and major varieties issued between 1878 and 1904, and again for one year in 1921. Morgan dollars have been one of the hottest United States coins for a number of recent years, both with collectors and investors.

For too many collectors, the entire thrill of pursuing the Morgan the silver dollar series in choice B.U. grade (MS-65 in American Numismatic Association grading standards) consists of scanning the ads in a coin paper and sending off a check to the dealer who advertises the lowest price for each date and mint mark. Unfortunately, those collectors are likely to learn someday that the coins they bought are overgraded, altered, or otherwise misrepresented. Because they were only hunting for a way to spend money, and probably know little about the coins they were buying, they will be satisfied right up until the moment they discovered the coins they bought are worth far, far less than their purchase price.

The more knowledgeable numismatist will hunt for his MS-65 Morgan cartwheels by making the effort to buy only those specimens that he determines to live up to their advertised grade. This could mean checking out the grading standards of a large number of mail-order coin dealers, traveling to many coin shows, or bidding in many auctions. But the collector who has done his grading homework and can accurately rate Morgan dollars will be able to take great pleasure in his collection. He will know that the hunt has paid off for him in an outstanding set of accurately graded and priced coins that will pay handsome profits should the time ever come to sell.

Still another type of numismatist might find the thrill of the hunt in the Morgan series to consist of buying scarce varieties at the price of common coins. Now in most cases there is not enough of a demand for the varieties to significantly affect their price in the market, but they are often undeniably rarer than the common example of the same date and mint mark. This collector is hunting for coins that have special meaning to him. For him, the greatest thrill in the hobby is "cherry picking" a variety from among a roll of common specimens, and then perhaps haggling the dealer down a bit from his asking price.

If I wanted to collect Morgan silver dollars, my hunt would involve seeking out and purchasing only those specimens that exhibit the multicolored natural toning that some silver dollars acquire over the years under different storage conditions. This patina is considered extremely desirable by a large number of collectors, but it is looked upon as an unsightly blemish by at least an equally large segment of the fraternity who prefer their silver dollars to be as bright, white, and shiny as the day they left the mint a century ago.

That's quite a tall order, given storage and handling conditions of 75 to 100 years ago, but an order that certain unscrupulous persons are willing to fill through the application of chemical or mechanical means. That is not to say that a beautifully toned silver dollar hasn't been tampered with either. Spectacular coloring can be imparted to an otherwise drab silver coin by exposing it to the fumes of certain sulphur compounds for even as short a period as several minutes. This chemical coloring is often used to hide flaws on a coin in hopes that the colors will take the buyer's eye off the problem area.

I think the most visually striking numismatic exhibit I have seen in many years was a recent coin show display of a veritable rainbow of Morgan silver dollars. They were laid out on a glass-and-mirror base that allowed the reverse—which may tone a different color or intensity than the obverse, or even not tone at all—to be viewed at the same time. For me, the challenge of assembling a collection of multihued Morgan dollars would be the only

way to collect the series. Besides, if it's color the collector is looking for, he can often buy cheaper coins by disregarding the scarce date or mint mark for the common.

Collectors who might be inclined to follow suit and follow the rainbow of toned Morgan dollars should be advised at the outset of their hunt that a naturally and attractively toned coin will almost always carry a premium price in excess of what the average specimen in the same condition would bring.

Because many advanced numismatists soon come to feel that too many collections can be built on money alone, they often turn to the lesser traveled roads of numismatics for the real challenges they seek. This often takes the form of paper money or *exonumia* (tokens and medals) specialties.

In these areas, the collectible items are far less extensively cataloged—if they are cataloged at all—and there are far fewer collectors and dealers to draw on for assistance. All of this makes them generally more challenging than most areas of coin collecting. The pride of ownership is probably what separates the coin collector most decisively from the investor (and certainly from the hoarder). Breathes there a coin collector with soul so dead that he does not inwardly beam as he views and handles each of the items in his collection? And most collectors will be excused a small amount of gloating if that pride of ownership shows as they display their coins to a close friend or relative at home or to hundreds or thousands of fellow hobbyists at a coin show. I (and most real collectors I know) am proud of each and every item in my collection. After all, if it wasn't special to me, I would not have bought or kept it in the first place. Even the coins that I tell myself are strictly for investment purposes raise the same feelings of satisfied possessiveness. They are, of course, coins that I have determined have great profit potential and which I took considerable time and effort to select. I'm afraid, though, that the pride of owning those items might someday be a bit too strong and that I will have a hard time selling them when the price is right.

Each time I visit my safety deposit box, the investment items receive the same contemplative gaze and handling that my favorite collectors items do. That's the main thing about pride of ownership for a numismatist; he can be as proud of a ratty old bank note from his home town as he is of the proof gold piece that is the *pièce de résistance* of his holdings.

That raises another strong point of the purely hobby side of coin collecting: it is truly a hobby for all budgets. Certainly the general public has the impression that coin collecting is a rich man's game. After all, they *do* call it the hobby of kings (for good reason, I might add, the Kings of Italy and Egypt were two of this century's best-known coin collectors).

There is a young man in New Jersey who has been written up in the hobby press and general press for his unusual coin collection. Because he can't afford to collect real U.S. coins, he collects pictures of them as they appear in the various magazines, newspapers, and auction catalogs. Like many other collectors, he collects by date and mint mark. He has photos of all the great rarities because they appear often in hobby literature. His unique collection usually lacks pictures of the more common coins simply because they are rarely pictured. Yet, this young man is more of a numismatist than many who spend thousands of dollars a year (or even hundreds of thousands). He has made a true hobby of it by reading, studying, and learning.

Suppose you cannot afford to collect Morgan dollars such as the MS-65 graded specimens. The lowest price for such a coin is currently in the area of $60, and many run into five figures—as high as $70,000. If collecting MS-65 Morgans is beyond your budget, you can always collect them in MS-60 grade. These have the same luster and absence of wear, but just a few more natural blemishes or weaker presentation of design details. Prices begin at $45, and they can reach as high as $30,000. Still too much? How about circulated Morgan dollars that have been used for the purpose they were made—as money. You can buy average circulated Morgan silver dollars for little over the value of the silver they contain, around $15-20.

To use the most extreme example in the Morgan cartwheel set, let's compare prices of the 1892-S (San Francisco Mint) coin. If your budget can stand the strain, you can have a near flawless MS-65 specimen for about $24,000. If you can stand a few bag marks (abrasions on the coin's surface from being bumped by other coins in the original bags as they came from the mint), but your budget can't stand an MS-65 coin, you can always opt for the MS-60, average uncirculated, specimen at a bit under $7,000.

Too high yet? How about a well-circulated, but still respectable piece with a good deal of the design intact and no damage—what collectors call a solid, very good condition—for $23. That's right, a coin that costs $24,000 in top grade can be found relatively easily in average condition for about 1/1,000th that price. While this is, admittedly, a very unusual example, it does illustrate that being a coin collector is not dependent on spending great sums of money.

But what about those of us who don't want to spend even $15 per coin? Well, in that case you're probably out of luck as far as Morgan dollars go, but much of the rest of the hobby is wide open to you.

Don't scoff at one of the hobby's principal building blocks: plugging coins into holes in an album. Some might consider me an advanced collector, or at least a knowledgeable numismatist, but one of my greatest hobby joys is a yearly exercise I began nearly a decade ago. I try to compile a complete date and mint set of Lincoln Memorial sets from circulation. Even discounting that I don't try to find the scarcer proof coins struck at San Francisco each year since 1975 and sold only in special sets to collectors, I have yet to complete that 50-plus coin set from pocket change in a year's time. I once came up one shy of the 1968 version and then found one in February the next year.

Sure, I could probably complete the set by picking up a few rolls of cents every day and searching through them, and I could easily buy each and every coin in the group for a total investment of about $5, but that's not the point. The point is to have fun with one of the simple hobby challenges at almost no cost beyond a cardboard coin folder each year and 1 cent apiece for each coin I pull from circulation.

Between the face-value penny and the $70,000 silver dollar, there is a wide range of coin prices. Such a range insures that anyone who wants to be a coin collector, *can* be a coin collector.

Choosing how much money you are going to spend on your hobby is one of the first big decisions you have to make. The bottom line is to keep it comfortable. The collector who spends his children's school lunch money on numismatic pursuits has missed the real meaning of a hobby. Like all aspects of numismatics, you set the parameters and make all the decisions. There is no "right" or "wrong" way to be a coin collector.

One of the greatest benefits of coin collecting is the hobby's well-deserved reputation as a tool for learning. Pick up an ancient Roman silver denarius. The fat man on the coin's obverse can't speak to you, nor can the figure of a woman on the back, but you can learn from them. For most coin collectors, the acquisition of an unfamiliar coin compels them to make tracks for the library. Do the inscriptions on the ancient Roman piece have you baffled? Your first step is a trip to the English Latin dictionary. Besides discovering which Caesar you are looking at, you will have learned at least several Latin words and abbreviations commonly found on coins.

You're liable to pick up some mathematics practice trying to discover the denomination of your coin. Ancient coins were valued principally by weight. You'll also learn something about weights and measures in the ancient world as you convert the coin's gram weight to an older system.

A mythology education awaits you as you attempt to find out which goddess is portrayed on the back—and why. The brief, glorious and usually violent life of a Roman emperor will be unfolded as you study ancient history in an effort to find out something of the life of the man whom this coin honors. Perhaps you will even find out why it was struck. Many ancient coins were commemorative in nature. In the ancient world, coins were a good source of news. At the speed with which money changed hands and traveled, citizens in outlying countries of the Roman empire might first learn that they had a new Caesar when they found his image staring up at them from the coin in the palm of their hand.

For many collectors, a coin, a bank note, a medal or a token is just an excuse to get lost in a stack of books while searching for knowledge and even entertainment. If your children show signs of budding numismatic interest, you can't go wrong by encouraging them. You will be astounded at what they learn as a by-product of their involvement in the hobby. And so will their teachers at report card time.

Still another of the many intangibles that make numismatics interesting as a pastime is the mysterious quality of which all numismatic items are possessed that can best be summed up by the phrase "history in your hand. See Fig. 2-2. To return to the same example of the ancient Roman silver piece, reflect for just a moment on its history. After all, such a coin is 2000 years old.

Whose hands has this silver coin passed through. Think of the good it has done for its countless owners over 20 centuries, and how much evil has been done in it's name. Did Jesus Christ hold this coin in his hand when he spoke the parable about rendering unto Caesar those things that are Caesar's? Or did Judas hold this coin in his hand, along with 29 others, when he sold out?

Moving ahead more than 1500 years, to early

Fig. 2-2. The collecting urge is a common bond among all numismatists.

eighteenth century America, consider a currency note you hold gently in your hand. The paper is thick, but brittle after more than 200 years of handling. Imprinted on the back of the note—along with a death threat aimed at counterfeiters—is the name of the man whom the colony of Pennsylvania commissioned to produce its paper money; the very note you hold in your hand was printed by Benjamin Franklin. Did the same note later pass through the hands of other patriots to pay for food, powder, or clothing for the colonists fighting for independence? Or did it remain in Tory hands and pass from British soldier to Hessian mercenary? As the Revolutionary War made the note worthless, did it become a children's plaything?

You cannot look upon an old coin or a piece of paper money without imagining dramatic historical scenarios in which it has been involved. At least you can't if you are a true coin collector. To hold these items in your hand is to become part of that coin's or note's history. Just as you now hold it, chances are that centuries from now the very same piece will be held in the palm of another coin collector who will feel the very same sense of awe and mystery.

As you hold that coin in your hand, don't you also feel something undefinable? You might not feel it if you held a geological specimen, a piece of antique glassware, or even a rare postage stamp. It is a powerful feeling that perhaps is a very potent unconscious influence on many people that makes them coin collectors. For lack of words to describe this vague sensation, let's just call it the "feel" of money.

That coin in your hand was, is now, or might again become legal tender. It is the stuff that drives mankind. It has been slaved for, sweated for, stolen for and slain for. To most it was merely a vehicle to buy the things they needed or wanted. For you it is more. Or is it? Do you collect it only for its aesthetic value, its historical value, or its curiosity value? Or do you feel it, too?

Rub your fingers slowly over the coin's surface (if it is not an uncirculated specimen). Turn it this way and that in the light to catch the glint of the reflection off its surfaces. It is almost hypnotic. There is a very special property about silver coins. This is even more true with gold. They are deceptively heavy for their size. The density of the precious metals in their composition makes them feel intrinsically important.

While a lump of pure gold or silver ore also feels heavy, it does not have the same appeal as if it were stamped into coin form. There is something about the intervention of human hands that deepens the lure of these coins. It is the urge to be a creator? We take a raw natural element—you can't eat it, wear it or live in it—and turn it into a thing of value.

It might be that coin collectors as a group can be explained away as simply being misers in disguise. Certainly the coins we collect can, in many cases, no longer be spent as money. We have certainly paid far more than their stated face value or intrinsic metallic value to acquire them, but it might be that we are simply legitimizing the accumulation of money. The veil of respectability we give it by turning it into an organized hobby makes the world less suspicious, less jealous, and less likely to view us as eccentric or dangerous.

On the brighter side of human nature, there is another aspect of the coin collecting hobby that is also powerful and pervading. Felt by nearly all who collect and cited most often as a principal reason for collecting, numismatic items have an aesthetic appeal. Coins and paper currency (at least most of it) have a beauty that transcends mundane considerations.

While each era's coinage usually exemplifies the epitome of the skills and craft of that age and geographic area, it is probably best to look no further than our own borders in the nineteenth century, or to the modern world, to discuss this aspect of the hobby's appeal. I'm afraid that because most of us aren't art appreciation majors, we will never fully recognize the aesthetic beauty of ancient and medieval coinage, and most of what was coined around the world in recent times. Before you dismiss a coin of middle Europe in the middle ages as being unprofessional or unattractive, consider that such coins were produced without the automated engraving and minting equipment that has been around only in the past century. In their own way and for their time and place, each of these coins is a masterpiece of three-dimensional art.

When looking at the vast majority of U.S. coins and paper money produced since 1800, we need to make no such apologies. After the first hurried coinage issues of 1792 were rushed into production and into the citizens' hands to reaffirm the newly won identify of the nation, great attention has traditionally been shown to the design and method of minting of United States coinage. The coinage travels the world and spans the centuries as a fitting representation of the country.

The U.S. Treasury Department—often at the behest of the president—has usually commissioned the nation's finest sculptors to prepare coinage designs. At other times, design competition has been introduced with a panel of the nation's top artists judging the entries. To this day, the United States Fine Arts Commission passes on all coinage design proposals for their aesthetic merit.

The Treasury Department retains the final word.

Limited (as American coinage design often is) by legislation that mandates the use of a representation of Liberty on certain coins, an eagle on others, and prescribed inscriptions on most, the design of American coins has been traditionally excellent. Nevertheless, there has been much controversy in recent years about the use of staid, 50-year-old portraits for many of our coins.

The use of the image of Liberty was mandatory on all coins. It has appeared in many guises—an Indian princess of the cent of 1859-1909, and several gold coins; wearing a Mercury—like winged cap on the dime of 1916-1945; and as a symbol of Peace on the silver dollars struck between 1921-1935. She has been shown seated at the Pacific shore; presiding over international trade that made our country strong in the nineteenth century (Trade dollar); standing in a defensive posture at the nation's portal (25¢ of 1916-1930); and walking (50¢ of 1916-1947 and $20 gold 1907-1933).

The bald eagle—which by law must appear on all silver and gold coins—has been with us since the eighteenth century when it looked more like a plucked chicken than the majestic bird that graces the back of the Peace dollar. The bald eagle comes down to us in modern times as the symbol of the Apollo moon exploration program, landing on the lunar surface (Eisenhower and Anthony dollars).

America's paper currency, (my personal favorite), provided artisans with an even larger "canvas" on which to display their craftsmanship. The larger format of the currency note has allowed the same ideals that our coinage represents to be more fully and grandly explored by the artists who have worked at its creation.

Unfortunately, the United States must currently take a back seat to many other nations in terms of coin and currency design. We are virtually trapped in a monetary style that passed by the rest of the world years ago. The many vibrant, bold, and live designs of some nations' coins and currency are the envy of a great number of this country's coin collectors who have seen the same face of Abraham Lincoln on the one-cent coin for over 70 years, and the same basic design on our paper money for the past half century.

Although U.S. Mint Chief Engraver Elizabeth Jones' popular new design for the George Washington commemorative half dollar has brightened the scene for most collectors, it remains to be seen whether the influence will spill over into new coinage designs for our regular issue pieces.

Another area of coin collecting encompasses fraternism. All numismatists belong to the same hobby community. We share many of the same collecting goals, aspirations, and fears. If a casual acquaintance turns out to be a fellow coin collector, we have an immediate common ground. Though there is no way to know for certain, informed observers say that the most accurate guess as to the number of persons in the United States who consider themselves coin collectors is 10,000,000.

Many collectors have gone into a sort of hobby semiretirement. They are generally older numismatists who have long ago completed their collections or determined that they will never be able to find or afford the remaining items they want. They are still seen at local club meetings, weekend coin shows, and even traveling around the country to the bigger events. Even though they might have sold their holdings down to the last penny in the safe deposit box, they remain active and interested because they enjoy the company and friendship of other coin collectors.

Today there are too few common denominators that so many persons of such differing background and personality can meet under and communicate. One of these is the hobby of coin collecting. For whatever reasons we collect—whether we are young or old, rich or poor, city or country—we share the numismatic hobby.

Chapter 3

Numismatics as an Investment

I DON'T KNOW WHEN OR WHERE IT BECAME CRASS for a numismatist to admit he made, is making, or expects to make a bundle of money on his pastime, but until recently—if you dared to sully a numismatic conversation with something so commercial as profitability—you were treated to the same type of looks you'd get if you sneezed all over the salad bar.

Not me! As much as I love the aesthetic and historical aspects of coins, currency, medals, and tokens, I'm in numismatics for the money. If I want pretty pictures, I can cut them out of the *National Geographic*. If I want to hold history in my hand, I can collect old newspapers. Nope, I collect what I collect because I know that, by pursuing this hobby intelligently, I can make it pay off in a big way.

I'm already making it pay off. During a few years of my youth, I pursued the hobby and its lore. I combined this background with some natural instincts and a journalism degree to land a job as a numismatic writer. I put in eight hours a day at a job that most coin collectors would give their last silver dollar for. I write about coins, coin collectors, and coin collecting.

Being steeped in the hobby/business 40 or 50 hours a week, I soak up a lot of knowledge that pays off in other ways. Besides being able to write this book, I also rub elbows with some of the sharpest investment minds in

numismatics. I'm confident that I've learned how to wisely invest money in numismatics to make it pay sizeable dividends later. I've also been made aware, sometimes at rather high cost, that there are pitfalls for the unwary. In this chapter, I'll present an overview of numismatics as an investment to place it in its proper context with the other rewards of the hobby, but by no means demeaning its importance.

Every night when I walk in the front door of my home, I can't help giving a little smile; my earlier numismatic investments made it possible for me to buy that house. Taking advantage of a lull in the real estate market, I was able to come up with a quick down payment at the opportune time by selling off some of my coin and paper money investment items. Now a true numismatist doesn't sell off his holdings without experiencing some pangs of loss, but I had told myself—when I was buying these items—that they were for investment purposes, and that I could not afford to collect such things as a hobby.

I also proved to myself one of the greatest investment advantages of numismatic items—their liquidity. With my house deal deadline pressing closely, I was able to take a small notebook full of U.S. coins and paper money to a major winter coin show and come up with the necessary cash. On some of my investment items, I only broke even, but these were items that had been held only a short time. On most of the rest, I made a decent profit, and on a few I made almost obscene profits.

Maybe I was lucky in picking the right items for investment in the first place. Maybe I was lucky in picking the right time and place to sell. But it couldn't have been all luck. I proved to myself that numismatics is a sound investment medium. And I think I can prove it to you. Also, I'm sure that nearly every other serious collector can cite personal instances where numismatic investments have paid off, or could be made to pay off.

The whole secret, as far as I'm concerned, is that you have to make informed decisions when buying for investment before you can expect to profit. Even if a numismatist does not consider himself an investor—if he is building his collection on solid ground—he is also unwittingly building an investment. While he wasn't thinking of numismatics when he said, "Look after the pennies and the dollars will take care of themselves," Ben Franklin was right on with that appraisal. You don't have to attend investment seminars, buy your coins from a guy in a three-piece suit, or subscribe to expensive tip sheets to realize a profit from numismatics. A good collection takes care of itself on this score.

Fortunately, one of the primary collecting urges—true in the coin hobby as elsewhere—is that collectors generally want to obtain the finest examples they can afford. Rather than buying a handful of lower-grade, inexpensive coins, most numismatics will opt to spend that same amount of money on a single-, high-grade specimen. While their collections will build more slowly in this manner, they will also be more attractive and pleasing to own. Happily, the collector who pursures his hobby in just this manner is also doing the wise thing from an investment standpoint. When it comes time to sell, choice-condition coins are more highly sought after and they have appreciated in price more greatly than low-grade coins.

Similarly, it is a basic tenet of coin collecting that because you can't collect everything, you eventually specialize. Instead of buying everything in sight, you make the conscious decision to limit your collecting to certain areas, series, types of coins, etc. This makes your holdings a true collection rather than an accumulation. You probably also have built your collection carefully in terms of correctly graded and genuine, unaltered specimens. These will stand you in good stead when the time comes to sell.

As for timing, if you were serious about your collection, you probably pursued it for a long period of time rather than jumping around the entire world of coin collecting, buying and selling on the basis of passing whims. This satisfies the principal rule of successful numismatic investment.

Distilled to its basics, good coin collecting strategy is now, always has been, and always will be, good investment strategy. The rules are the same, the game is the same, only the attitude differs. The principal law of numismatic investment is that numismatics is a long-term investment. Of course, like every other law, you can break it sometimes. If you do it often enough, you are going to get caught and you will have to pay the price. The great precious metals boom of 1979-1980 seemed to disprove this precept. You could seemingly buy virtually any decent U.S. collectible coin and sell it the next day for a profit. But that was an aberration of the long-term law brought on by near hysteria from non-collectors and the Wall Street community who seized upon numismatics (actually gold and silver bullion) as the answer to continuing double-digit inflation.

Many unknowledgeable persons who got caught on the late end of the frenzy are left holding the coins on which they expected to turn a fast profit. The gold and silver market dropped nearly as fast as it rose and, unfortunately, many of the first-time investors bailed out early—taking their lumps and their losses—forever soured on numismatics as an investment and as a hobby. Had they sat back and held their purchases for the more traditional waiting periods, I'm confident they could have recovered their original investments, and probably something more.

For a variety of reasons, those who expect to profit from numismatic investments should expect to hold their purchases from three to five years. Because nearly all your purchases are at retail prices, and all your sales will generally be at the wholesale level, you must expect some time to elapse before that spread is covered. The spread on common bullion coins can be as little as 5 percent. Highly popular series of high-grade coins will generally have a 20 percent buy/sell spread. Some of the lesser appreciated items will have a wholesale/retail differential of as much as 40 percent—or more. You can't ignore the wholesale/retail structure that governs the coin market.

Some of the more useful coin-pricing guides will spell out the buy/sell prices on each item they cover. This allows you to see at the outset what percentage you're going to have to overcome. The basic reason for the oft-quoted three- to five-year turnaround time is to let the good ol' law of supply and demand take hold. Like Will Rogers said about investing in land, they aren't making old coins any more—at least genuine ones. New collectors and investors enter the field every day. It's the same thing that causes overall economic inflation. Too many people trying to buy a limited number of anything will drive the price up.

Each time a new numismatist joins the ranks of silver-dollar collectors, he increases the competition for the limited number of collectible silver dollars that exist from the original limited mintage. If you and he decide you want the same silver dollar in an auction or a mail bid sale, you can easily see why the price of the coin is going to go up. If there were two examples of the same coin, you might each get one, for example, at its current $100 retail price. If you're both going after only one piece, though, it might hit $110, $120, or more before one buyer is discouraged. The next time an example comes around, the losing bidder might well pay the same $110 for it—even if he is the only buyer. More likely, however, he will be competing for that second example with another new buyer who has already heard that the price of such a coin, in the last auction, hit $120. And so the prices climb.

While some collectors decry this sort of thing, saying too many new collectors are just driving prices out of reach for them, they change their tune when it comes time to sell their coins. Rising coin prices demand a constant influx of new buyers, and this also accounts for the long-term investment requirement you must be prepared to make in coins. When the national economy is slow and when there are investment vehicles like All-savers certificates and IRA plans (offering a guaranteed interest percentage far above what the American public is accustomed to), there are going to be fewer new collectors or investors making their presence felt in the coin market. This is all part of the cyclical nature of the rise and fall of coin prices, and it is a well-known factor to seasoned numismatic investors. For several well-documented decades, that cycle has been about a five-year roller coaster; peaks and valleys have occurred about every half decade.

All of these factors, and others that are as complex as international economics, influence the coin market and the way you invest in it. A numismatic strategy that takes all of this into account, and is widely followed by those who consider themselves collector/investors, is to separate their collecting activities from their investment activities. You buy some coins for your personal collection and you buy some coins for your investment portfolio.

I suppose a peek into my safety deposit box will provide as good an example of this philosophy as any. I consider myself a true collector as well as an investor. My holdings are probably much more sharply defined along collection/investment lines than most. Simply stated, most of what I collect as a collector has little intrinsic value; I collect it because of its historic, aesthetic or personal interest value.

An example is my collection of Brooklyn bridge medals issued in the 1880s in conjunction with the opening of the bridge. I have been infatuated with this great American landmark ever since I first laid eyes on it in 1976. Since then, I have sought out the nearly century-old souvenir medals that depict the bridge. I research the medals and the bridge, and consider this one of my favorite collections. As an investment it is a loser. None of the medals are struck in gold or silver so they have no intrinsic value. While several of them are genuinely rare, there is so little demand for them that prices have never been, are not now, and probably never will be high. I would be very lucky to get my money out of them should I ever decide to sell. In short, I collect them for their own sake.

Next to the bridge medals is a MS-65 example of the 1913 Buffalo nickel (the first year of issue). It was purchased about 1978 for $100 or so in surplus funds that I had in a regular bank savings account (making perhaps 5 percent interest). Today, I could easily sell the coin for nearly $400. That coin is strictly an investment. I bought it with funds not needed for anything else (in contrast to some of my Brooklyn Bridge medals for which I have gone without lunch to buy). It was bought with great attention to proper grading and in consideration of its nice golden toning. It was bought because I know the Buffalo nickel series will remain a popular collector favorite and that as a first-year coin it enjoys added demand above and beyond later coins in the series of similar mintage. As a collector, I don't collect the Buffalo nickel series. Therefore, I will have no problem about selling the coin when I feel the time is right to put that money into another coin or note. My Brooklyn Bridge medals, on the other hand, will probably be buried with me.

The same goes for my paper money. I have a collection of late 1870s-1935 national bank notes issued in my home town of Fond du Lac, Wisconsin. Each note has the name of the issuing bank on it. Some of the banks still stand, but others have long since gone bankrupt or been merged. The signatures of the bank's officers on the bottom of the note are names that now grace streets and parks in and around the city.

As national bank notes go, they are hardly investment items. They are relatively common as far as Wisconsin Nationals go and they are in lower grade than is commonly preferred. It was a conscious decision on my part, when I began the collection, not to buy uncirculated notes. As I handle each of my Fond du Lac notes, it is easy to imagine that the 1902 $10 bill, for example, once went into my grandfather's wallet as a week's profits from his chicken hatchery or that the small-size $5 might have represented a night out on the town spent by my father when he was dating my mother. This is history in your hand, but no great investment item.

The next note in my album is a different story. Although it is in the same condition as some of my Fond du Lac Nationals, it is one of the better surviving examples of the National Gold Bank notes issued in California from 1870-1878. For these rare, beautiful, and historic notes, fine condition is considered high grade. The example in my lock box is a solid, bright fine note. As such, I paid more for it when I bought it and I expect to get a premium, when I sell it, over and above the price of an average fine note of the type.

I can no more afford to collect 100-year-old National Gold Bank notes than I can afford to light candles with $100 bills, but this note represents a solid numismatic investment. When my wife left her job at the veterinary clinic to have our daughter, she received a lump sum from her retirement program. Part of that money went to buy this note. Our thoughts were that the note would be held for retirement. Considering the steadily upward price curve on National Gold Bank notes in this condition, I expect that the original $1,100 investment of 1979 will be but a paltry fraction of what the note sells for in another 30-40 years—even considering the ravages of inflation.

These are examples of how collecting and investing strategies differ for one numismatist. One group of items, the collection, is for hobby purposes. The other is for maximum future appreciation. But this is not to say that the two have to be mutually exclusive. For example, if an early (1875 series) national bank note from one of Fond du Lac's issuing banks were to come on the open market, I would feel entirely justified in merging my hobby budget with my investment budget to chase the note. I know that, as much as I would like to have it for my personal collection, it is also an excellent numismatic investment vehicle. My studies of Wisconsin National Bank notes indicate such early notes from that city are extremly rare (if they even exist at all). As such, and given the relatively constant demand for scarce nationals, I know the price will continue to appreciate on a truly rare note like that.

You'll notice that buying strategies differ on items purchased for a collection and on items bought for investment. They must because of the different purposes for which they are acquired. For a personal collection on which a numismatist realistically expects to obtain little profit, he can feel free to buy whatever meets his other—strictly hobby-oriented—criteria. For invest-

ment purposes, items added to a portfolio should meet the well-delineated standards in terms of popularity, condition, and current price.

I have so far limited my discussion to buying coins and other numismatic items either as collectors items, long-term investment vehicles or a combination of the two. But what of short-term numismatic investment? For openers, there is no such thing as true short-term numismatic investment. What that term really means is speculation.

Depending on how you play the game, speculation can be fun (if you make out financially) or a downer (if you lose your shirt). Because of that, I'm going to give you the same advice a broker would give you. Speculating in the coin market, just as much as speculating in pork bellies, is a high-risk proposition that should only be undertaken with capital you can afford to lose. In other words, don't bet the rent money on a short-term numismatic speculation. The market is too unpredictable and the influences on it are too mysterious to the ordinary observer.

While speculating on a large scale in numismatic items—we won't even concern ourselves here with gold and silver bullion, or futures—can be dangerous to your financial well being, a little small-scale speculation seldom hurts.

There's a fellow here at the office who orders the maximum number (five) of U.S. proof sets each year even though he only needs one for his collection. His goal each year is to order the five sets at the issue price and then sell four of them upon arrival to finance the fifth set which he keeps as his own.

This collector is speculating based on his experience and knowledge of the past performance of the U.S. proof set program in recent years. He knows that the U.S. Mint receives about 4 million proof set orders a year and that it takes most of that calendar year (sometimes even longer) to complete delivery of them. He also knows that a great many collectors do not want to tie their money up for so long a period and wonder when they will receive the set or sets they ordered. These people prefer to buy their sets directly from a coin dealer, who has, in turn, purchased them from the lucky collectors who were among the first to receive the new sets.

Our office speculator is often one of those lucky collectors. For example, this year he ordered the maximum five sets, at $11 each. The $55 investment, while not insignificant, represents money he can reasonably afford to have tied up even for the long term. When he received his sets, within the first several weeks after the first deliveries were made, the wholesale price had already risen to $14 a set. Selling four of his sets, he was

19

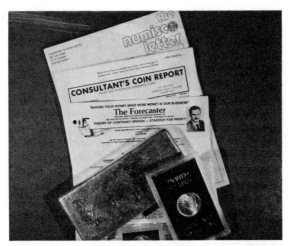

Fig. 3-1. For the prospective numismatic investor or speculator, there is no shortage of newsletters and tip sheets to help map your strategy. None take the place of experience and common sense.

able to recoup $56. Therefore, his own set was "free" and he had $1 for his efforts.

This is certainly not foolproof, however, because some years the sets never move upward in price. A person buying a quantity on speculation can be left holding them for a considerable period of time. Small-scale "speculation," with money you can afford to tie up or even lose, is an interesting side of the investment angle of coin collecting, but it is not to be confused with the type of speculation that is best left to the brokerage houses.

Most of the hobby periodicals carry ads from publishers of numismatic investment newsletters (Fig. 3-1). For a subscription fee that can run well over $200 a year, these newsletters offer advice on many aspects of coin market investment. They are often prepared by experienced market observers and professional coin dealers. The advice they give might be as general as "buy silver dollars," or as specific as "we recommend the purchase of MS-60 1898-S Morgan dollars at the current retail price levels because . . ."

They otherwise run the gamut from the ridiculous to the sublime. Some newsletters offer good, sound, precise investment information and have a proven solid and consistently high level of accuracy in their predictions and recommendations. Others are not worth the paper they are printed on. Unfortunately, it is hard to tell at first glance which is which.

If you think you would like to have a little bit of guidance along the road of coin investments, you might consider taking a look at the various newsletters offered

in the coin papers. Write to each one that catches your eye. All should be willing to provide you with a recent sample copy for either free or for $1 or so to cover handling. Any newsletter that is hesitant about letting you see their product before plunking down $45, $90 or $200, should be written off. They're obviously more interested in getting your subscription dollar than in helping you with your investment portfolio.

Next, study the sample copies you receive. You'll notice that some of them use more space trying to sell you their books, seminars, private telephone services, and even their own coins, than in giving you the advice and tips you are looking for. If I was paying that kind of money for a newsletter, I'd darn sure want *news*—not a sales pitch.

After you've weeded through the newsletters that way, you're on your own as far as picking subscriptions. Go with your instincts. If one of them strikes you as sounding reasonable and giving you what you want, you are probably in agreement with the publisher's basic investment strategy and you might well prosper by following the advice therein.

Fig. 3-2. Harry Forman is a well-regarded coin dealer. His book is popular with beginning collectors and advanced investors.

The coin market boom of 1979-80 spawned a remarkable number of entries into the newsletter field. When every coin in sight was going up in price on a weekly basis, it was difficult to sound stupid in making investment suggestions. The 1981 market adjustment shook out quite a number of the "instant experts" and the field is basically back to the same eight or 10 proven newsletters that have withstood the cycles of the coin market.

My own experience with the newsletters has been pleasant. They make interesting reading. The one time I did follow a "buy" recommendation, I was very pleased. In 1978, John Kamin's newsletter *The Forecaster* recommended the purchase of MS-65 1928 Oregon Trail commemorative half-dollars at the then-current retail level of $95. I liked Kamin's reasoning that this particular coin was a rarity among a series of coins that are generally considered common (the Oregon Trail series as a whole), and I bought one. The *Numismatic News* "Coin Market"

today says I should be able to sell my 1928 Oregon commemorative to virtually any dealer in the country for $495. That's 100 percent profit a year on my original investment. I'm not too proud to admit that I never would have thought of making that purchase without the advice given in the newsletter.

There is so much to the field of numismatic investment that it would take another book to begin to cover it adequately (Fig. 3-2). A good, rounded education in the fundamentals of coin collecting will be necessary if you decide to delve into the investment world at a later date. Consider this book your first numismatic investment and try to learn from it. Whether you are a beginner, or have had some coin collecting experience, there is always something new in numismatics for you to pick up on. By keeping abreast of the changing coin market and making the effort to learn all you can about your chosen areas of specialty, you can't help but come out ahead on the dollars and cents aspects of the hobby.

Chapter 4

The Future of Coin Collecting

NOBODY CAN PREDICT WHAT CHANGES WILL BE wrought in our hobby within our lifetimes, but I think that most of us can reasonably expect to see the day when coins become strictly a collectors item when paper money is only an unsanitary relic of fiscal history. We are fast entering the cashless society. If you don't believe it, think about how you paid for the last collectible coin you bought or even this book. Chances are that it was paid for by check or credit card. Certainly the store or mail-order dealer who sold you this book paid for it by transfer of funds from his bank account to that of the publisher or distributor.

What will happen to coin collecting when money becomes nothing more than electronic debit and credit impulses in a central computer? Some people believe that day, when the cashless society becomes a reality, will spell the beginning of the end for the coin collecting hobby. After all, they point out, in these days of zippers, snaps and Velcro closures, few people collect buttons anymore; yet, that used to be a thriving hobby.

While that might be true, it is my belief that, for the many reasons spelled out in Chapter 1, coin collecting has a much broader appeal than any other hobby. After all, the ancient silver and gold coins of the Greeks and Romans ceased to be legal tender centuries ago, yet they are still avidly collected. You can no more buy a loaf of bread with an ancient coin than you can with a handful of buttons, but we still collect coins.

It's my guess that, even if coin collecting does not survive as a viable hobby in the centuries ahead, the curiosity value of these things we collect will persist until we, our children, and their children are long in our graves.

Certain signs in the hobby today point to the eternal appeal of collecting money. One of the most active areas of the paper-money-collectible field currently is the collecting of old checks. Until every home has a personal computer tied into the bank, we will continue to transact business with paper demand deposits (checks), and they will continue to be collectible.

The same is true for stock certificates. Large, beautifully executed examples of the engraver's art, stock certificates represent a store of wealth as surely as a jar of buried gold coins did in the last century. Numismatists are beginning to find these areas of money substitutes to be interesting collecting avenues.

There are even people collecting old, invalidated credit cards. From the metal charge plates of the early decades of the twentieth century to the bright, little plastic rectangles that stuff our wallets, these forms of instant money are finding devotees among the ranks of traditional numismatists.

It's my guess that the eternal lure of whatever happens to pass for money is such that collectors will always find a way to derive hobby pleasure from it. I look for numismatics to remain the king of hobbies far into the future.

Chapter 5

Buy the Book
Before You Buy the Coin

AN OFTEN-HEARD ADAGE IN THE COIN-COLLECT-ing hobby that is as true today as it was when it was first uttered, probably in the late nineteenth century, advises the collector to "buy the book before you buy the coin." In other words, look before you leap. There is no substitute in this hobby for experience. It doesn't matter whether it's experience gained at coin club meetings, conventions and exhibits, at the elbow of a veteran collector or dealer, or from the pages of a book.

There is so much enjoyment that can be derived from coin collecting and, at the same time, so many pitfalls to be avoided if you are to maximize that enjoyment. We should all be willing to give ourselves a headstart by soaking up the wisdom of more than a century of rich hobby experience in this country by availing ourselves of the countless books, catalogs, monographs, magazines, and papers that are the legacy of those who have gone before us.

There are four basic types of numismatic literature, each with a specific purpose. For openers, there is the type of book you now hold in your hands: general volumes on coin collecting. They can be thought of as background, basic hobby educational materials, or merely a pleasant book with which to curl up with on a long winter night.

You'd think that, in a hobby that has been around for as long as coin collecting, there would be nothing new to write about. Not true. This is a growing and changing hobby and the literature reflects that. For better or worse, the fast-paced market conditions of today's hobby have a way of very quickly making literature obsolete. This is true for at least any literature that is aimed at quoting specific values or giving investment advice.

During the early 1980s, I see an interesting trend for those of us who like nothing better than to read about our hobby. This trend indicates that a very rich vein of numismatic lore is about to be explored and that we will be the beneficiaries. I'm referring to the several recent books written by retired or soon-to-retire coin dealers. Many of these old pros have half a century or more of experience living and breathing numismatics. Their memoirs make fascinating reading. We are just now reaching the stage where great numbers of the coin dealers, who rose and fell with coin collecting in the U.S. from the 1930s and 1940s, are in a position to share their experiences with us. Some of these books offer collections of anecdotes and others are investment oriented. All of them can enrich your involvement in numismatics.

A second reason to buy a coin book is to allow you to know what you are looking at. For this purpose, there are hundreds of catalogs available at any one time. While most of the catalogs include some type of pricing information (for our purposes), that is secondary. The main purpose of a catalog is to help you identify your coin, bank note, or medal.

Virtually all catalogs are geared to visual identification. From the earliest coin catalogs of the nineteenth century—which first offered line drawings of coins and detailed written descriptions, then later began the use of photographic plates—to the most recent cataloging efforts, with their tens of thousands of photos, the emphasis has been on allowing the reader to match the coin in his hand with one in the book.

Catalogs usually provide such data as history of the coin's issue, mintage figures, and perhaps some background on the who, what, when, where and why of the item. Even if the catalog is outdated, the reader can get an idea of relative value of a coin and if the coin he holds is worth more, less, or the same as similar coins from one country or other countries.

To really find out what your numismatic items are worth, you will need to refer to one of the many types of coin price and grading guides. For most world coins, paper money, tokens and medals, etc., the basic grading guides that most catalogs provide is sufficient to properly grade the piece in question. While this also used to be true of U.S. coins, it is no longer the case. The recent demand for strict and exact grading has led, in the past 15 to 20 years, to the development of special coin-grading guides that provide line drawings or photos to allow the coin in question to be tagged with a grading appellation that will be acceptable to the potential buyer.

With shades of grade so often worth hundreds or thousands of dollars in the U.S. coin market, it is senseless to talk about pricing coins until they have been properly graded. At that point, the various price guides step in to provide the bottom-line figure. Current market conditions have given rise to a whole new generation of coin-pricing literature. Where for so many years all that was needed was an annual updating of the famous "Red Book" *(A Guide Book of United States Coins)*, the scene today calls for new price information at least weekly for the average collector. Modern technology has even given the coin dealer—and those collectors who can afford it—electronic "literature" that provides pricing information virtually by the minute. Each of these price guides is aimed at a different segment of the hobby/business.

Combining virtually all of these functions—some better than, or at least different than, others—are the coin-collecting periodicals. In the United States, three weekly newspapers and two monthly newsstand magazines provide the bulk of the regularly published and timely information to keep collectors abreast of the hobby. Additional organizational and commercial papers and magazines are aimed at specialty segments within the collecting fraternity.

There is also a good bit of "digested" numismatic news available to the public and the casually interested collector through weekly coin columns in the general press and an occasional article on investment topics in the nation's many business papers and magazines.

It might surprise some people to learn that one of the world's top-10, best-selling, nonfiction books is a coin collectors' catalog. It might surprise them even more to learn that few coin collectors or dealers can tell you the correct name of the book.

The book is R.S. Yeoman's *A Guide Book of United States Coins,* but it is universally known to everyone associated with the coin-collecting hobby/industry as the Red Book. That appellation is the result of the bright red covers that have identified the world's best-selling coin book since its introduction in 1947.

Now in its 35th edition, for 1982, total sales figures for the Red Book remain a trade secret of the publisher, Whitman Coin Products division of Western Publishing Company (itself a division of Mattel, the toy giant). It is reliably estimated that printing of the book in recent years has been at about the 10-million-copy level. Industry insiders say that only Dale Carnegie's *How to Win Friends and Influence People,* the *Betty Crocker's Cookbook,* and Dr. Benjamin Spock's book, *Baby and Child Care,* have outsold the Red Book in the nonfiction department over the years.

The Red Book's author, R.S. Yeoman, is often credited with shaping the modern coin-collecting hobby, and particularly for bringing it to the grass-roots base of popularity it now enjoys nationwide (Fig. 5-1). Yeoman entered the field of numismatics in 1940 when he designed the first coin folder, the little blue book of holes, that millions of Americans of all ages and walks of life have spent over 40 years trying to fill. The popularity and wide distribution of those folders quickly convinced Yeoman that the American public was very interested in coin collecting. Why couldn't they find certain coins needed to fill holes in their folders? Where did they turn after filling their folders?

An authority on U.S. coins, Yeoman recognized the need for a comprehensive listing of accurate information and values that would be readily available to the general public. The result was that first Red Book in 1947. The succeeding 35 editions have expanded from the basic coverage of United States government-issued coinage to include many related American coinage issues. These

Fig. 5-1. R.S. Yeoman, author of one of the 10 best selling nonfiction books in the world, *A Guide Book of United States Coins* (better known as the Red Book) with the first edition (1947).

range from the early coins and tokens of the Colonies to the private, state, and territorial coins that marked the expansion of the country at a rate faster than the U.S. Mint could follow.

All of the basic data any U.S. coin collector needs can be found in the pages of the Red Book. There are photos for identification purposes, mintage figures, tables of weights and measures and fineness for each type coin, grading basics, and listings of all popular varieties.

So pervasive is the Red Book's influence on collectors that an error coin or a minting variety is not recognized by most dealers and collectors until it is listed in the Red Book. An example is the 1943-P, 3 over 2 nickel. This overdate, caused by striking a new numeral 3 over the existing 2 on a die to conserve material during the war

years, was known to large numbers of collectors for many years. It was strictly a $5 item in circulated condition because of limited demand by collectors. Once it was listed in the Red Book, just a few years ago, it suddenly became a "legitimate" error coin. Demand (and price) skyrocketed. The 1982 Red Book lists the 1943/2 overdate nickel at $65 in circulated grade. Yet, several similar overdate coins, because they have not been recognized in the pages of the Red Book, languish at the $5 price level.

Until a few years ago, the Red Book also had the reputation as *the* ultimate retail price guide. Most dealers priced their stock according to the values listed in the Red Book, and most collectors knew they could expect to pay about Red Book prices for coins they purchased.

Tremendous gains in the speed at which the market

moves have rendered the pricing function of the Red Book somewhat obsolete. No book that is published only on an annual basis can expect to keep current with the fast-moving price structure of today's coin market. Still, in some of the slower-moving areas of the market, such as colonial coins, territorial gold, and some of the rare varieties, the Red Book is held to be a good source for a ball-park figure with which to work.

The Red Book was a groundbreaker in its manner of presenting coin values. Until the publication of the first edition, there was little reference material for the collector concerning coin values. The ads in the periodicals and the buy-and-sell lists of coin dealers could be reasonably expected to reflect each particular dealer's view of the market—taking into consideration his own stock.

Yeoman's book presented a radical approach to pricing. A survey of respected coin dealers was made. He averaged their input and came up with an accurate reflection of each coin's premium value. Over the years, it has become a mark of distinction for a coin dealer to be asked to serve on the Red Book pricing panel. Many dealers so chosen will make note of that honor in their advertisements.

The Red Book is the first book that most coin collectors buy, and it is the one book that many advanced collectors continue to buy each year. Because of its lengthy publishing history and reliability, the Red Book makes an excellent reference tool for the collector or investor who wants to chart the past popularity of a coin or series in order to determine the advisability of a current purchase.

A companion volume—not nearly as great a seller, but one that actually predates the Red Book—is R.S. Yeoman's *A Handbook of United States Coins*. It is popularly known as the Blue Book because of the color of its cover (Fig. 5-2). First published in 1942, the Blue Book is essentially a wholesale price listing of U.S. coins. Not quite as full of historical data as its companion, the Blue Book lists the price a collector could reasonably expect a coin dealer to pay for a coin.

It used to be said that all anybody needed to become a coin dealer was a handful of cash and copies of the Blue Book and the Red Book. By buying at Blue Book prices and selling at Red Book prices, the "dealer" could be assured of his profit margin without having to know anything about coins. While the reality was never that simple, this oft-told tale does speak well of the respect held for these books—and their author—for over 40 years.

Copies of the Red Book and the Blue Book can be purchased at virtually every coin or hobby shop and at most book stores across the nation. While acquisition of

Fig. 5-2. The Blue Book offers wholesale prices as a companion volume to the Red Book.

the latest edition of the Red Book gives the coin collector a handle on most of the U.S. coins he will encounter, there are several other catalogs that each deal with a specialty area of U.S. coinage. Not published annually, they might be given to slight obsolescence. This is especially true if they attempt to present value information. Nevertheless, the educational and entertainment value of each of these catalogs makes them useful reference tools for the collector—especially the beginner.

The books, catalogs, newspapers, magazines and other literature mentioned in the remainder of this chapter are my preferences as a numismatic collector, investor, writer, and editor. They do not represent, by any means, the only literature available on the subject. They are not necessarily the best particular book on each selected topic. They are merely my recommendations.

Two other basic catalogs on U.S. coinage that I feel are essential for the serious collector are *United States*

Commemorative Coinage by Arlie R. Slabaugh and the *United States Pattern Experimental and Trail Pieces* by Dr. J. Hewitt Judd (Fig. 5-3).

I recommend the Slabaugh commemorative book simply on the basis of price and suitability for the beginner. There have been several other reference catalogs written in recent years that are more thorough, more comprehensive, more detailed, and more expensive than the Slabaugh book. But unless you are planning to specialize exclusively in the commemoratives, the other books are more than you will ever need to know about U.S. commemorative coins.

Because it was last published in 1976, Slabaugh's commemorative book does not provide data on the 1982 Washington commemorative half-dollar or the 1984 U.S. Olympic commemorative coins. It is possible, however, that a new edition will be forthcoming. Certainly the pricing information provided by Slabaugh at that time is obsolete, but combined with the prices he also cites from 1962, that information can be valuable in charting the progress of these coins' value.

The principal benefit of Slabaugh's commemorative book is that it provides the beginner with all the essential information about the coins, their designs, their reasons for being, the number originally minted, the number actually issued, and much more—all in an inexpensive package. You can't fully appreciate the U.S. commemorative coinage series without a book such as this.

While U.S. pattern coins are generally collected only by the more advanced numismatist, the Judd catalog is a useful reference for every collector. There is much to learn in it concerning the ancestors of the regular-issue coinage that we collect. Probably of greater interest to most collectors is the look at coinage that might have been. With pricing information provided in the latest edition by Bowers and Ruddy Galleries, the book became a valuable market tool. Previously, the price structure of pattern coinage was a highly speculative matter and it was one not easily followed by the novice.

The Judd catalog is well illustrated. This helps the collector identify coins that are unlike those he might be familiar with. Although it might be something of a "wish book" for the average collector, the Judd catalog can answer a lot of questions about nonstandard U.S. coinage.

World coin collectors have a single reference catalog they can turn to for virtually all of their needs. It is the

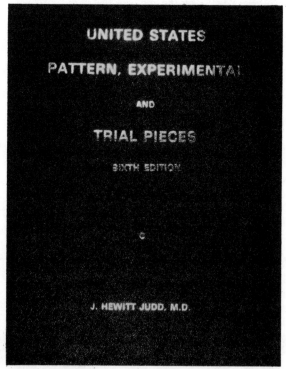

Fig. 5-3. Highly recommended books for the serious U.S. coin collector are Slabaugh's *U.S. Commemorative Coinage*, and Judd's *U.S. Pattern, Experimental and Trial Pieces*. Both are hobby standards.

Standard Catalog of World Coins by Chester L. Krause and Clifford Mishler (Fig. 5-4). The Standard Catalog is published annually by Krause Publications. I have contributed to the last several editions by loaning photos, doing price survey evaluations, even opaquing page negatives as deadline approaches.

Retailing at about $30, the SCWC (as we call it) is not inexpensive, but it is not a small book—at 2048 pages. During the nearly 10 years that the book has been published, it has supplanted every other world coin reference book and become, truly, the standard catalog for that area of the hobby.

Because of its size and physical make-up, the book has come to be known throughout the hobby as the "telephone book." This is not without just cause. The only printing company in the United States capable of handling a print job of this magnitude is R. R. Donnelly in Illinois. Donnelly prints about 90 percent of all the metropolitan phone books in the country.

Unequaled in scope, size, or detail by any other coin book ever published, the SCWC embraces more than 230 years of the world's coinage history. It details the various date and mint listings of the authorized coin issues of legally constituted governing authorities from the 1750s to the present. The book features not only the complete date and mint mark listings for each coinage type, but accurate pricing data in up to four grades of preservation. Unlike the U.S. coin market, the world coin scene is not extremely volatile. Prices presented in the SCWC are generally "good" from one volume to the next. Like the Red Book, the Standard Catalog obtains its prices from a panel of hundreds of dealers and collectors worldwide.

Especially valuable for the beginner are the more than 40,000 photographs, an "instant identifier" guide, and the comprehensively cross-indexed, country-name list. By using the identifier section, the collector can usually find which country issued any coin he might be holding in his hand. By turning to that nation's listing in the catalog, he can match the coin with the photos to find out what he has and what it's worth.

Besides cataloging the coins, the book provides a wealth of background data in compact form for each issuing authority. There is generally a map of the nation, a listing of its rulers, and a summary of its monetary system. Other introductory material offers guides to international date systems, grading terminology in several languages, and a key to abbreviations and designators found on foreign coins. Some 75,000 coins are listed and priced (from more than 1300 coinissuing authorities). Included is a pretty good summary of U.S. coinage.

If that's too much catalog for the beginning world coin collector, there is a new (1982) volume out called the *Standard Catalog of 20th Century World Coins,* by the same authors and publisher. Considerably smaller, less expensive ($12.50), and less extensive than the "telephone book," the twentieth century world coin catalog fills a void for the collector who wants to specialize in modern world coins. Rather than listing coins by date and mint mark, the catalog concentrates on type listings.

This specialty book retains the emphasis on photography, for identification, and contains much of the same introductory and educational material found in the larger catalog. The *Standard Catalog of 20th Century World Coins* is especially useful for the typical collector.

While either of these two volumes is a good general reference for the world coin collector, there are about as many other world coin catalogs as there are countries that issue coins. If you are going to specialize in only the coins of one nation or continent, there are specialty catalogs available to guide you along such narrow paths. The American Numismatic Association, as one benefit of membership, offers each new member a comprehensive library catalog of the ANA library holdings (available by mail to members). This library catalog serves as the hobby's most extensive bibliography of easily obtainable

Fig. 5-4. The "telephone book" is the nickname given the *Standard Catalog of World Coins*, a one-volume reference library that no numismatist should be without.

reference books and catalogs. It is invaluable to the collector trying to find books of his specialty.

World coin specialty catalogs can be as narrow as a monograph on the coinage issues of the independent state of Croatia, from 1941-45, or as broad as a catalog covering all known coin, currency, and monetary token issues of a nation dating back many centuries. Because many of them represent real labors of love by dedicated collectors with long experience in the particular area, they are the last word in specific reference. A drawback to most of these, however, is that they can be hard to obtain and they do not usually contain pricing data. For the student specializing in one area of world coins, however, they are an essential addition to the bookshelf.

The best way to approach a world coin library would seem to be to buy one of the general reference books first. After some time, when you have refined your collecting goals (you can't collect the whole world, after all), you should begin considering in what areas you want to specialize. Then begin accumulating the pertinent literature. In many cases, the search for some of these specialty catalogs is as exciting and challenging as the search for the coins themselves.

Unlike the field of collectible United States coins, there is no single widely accepted reference catalog in the field of U.S. paper currency. Paper money has simply not been collected for as long a time or by as many people, as U.S. coinage. Consequently, little research was published in this area until relatively recent times.

The newest reference catalog on U.S. paper money is the *Standard Catalog of U.S. Paper Money* (Fig. 5-5) by Krause Publications. I may be accused of even greater bias in recommending this book because I am the co-author with Chet Krause. First published in 1981, and expected to be issued on an annual basis, the SCUSPM is primarily a practical guide to the commercial aspects of collecting U.S. paper money. The focus is on prices.

While the book presents enough historical and economic data to enable the collector to understand the when and why of note issues, its primary purpose is to tell him what his notes are worth. For this reason, the nation's top experts in the several specialty areas of U.S. paper money provided pricing input. The result is a catalog that can provide realistic information about current market conditions.

In putting together the *Standard Catalog of U.S. Paper Money,* it was the authors' intention to cover every specialty within the broad field of paper money items issued under the auspices of the federal government. That gives the catalog the widest possible range for maximum utility to the collector.

The biggest advantage to the collector is that this catalog is the first attempt in some 30 years to correct errors that have appeared in other catalogs and been fostered throughout the hobby. Many notes that have never existed have been wrongly listed in other references. This has caused some collectors much aggravation as they sought to complete collections that could never be completed. By using the resources of the nation's top experts, the listings in the SCUSPM were purged of all known erroneous listings.

The catalog provision of the first alphabetized listing of note-issuing National Banks by city within state has also been hailed by collectors as a major breakthrough in this popular specialty. The computer technology that made such a listing popular is a specialty of Krause Publications' cataloging efforts. The firm prides itself on being able to put computers to work for the collector.

The longest-running catalog of U.S. paper money is titled *Paper Money of the United States,* by the late Robert Friedberg. Published in its 10th edition in 1981, the book has been around since 1953. It is given much credit throughout the paper-money hobby as being the volume that helped popularize the collecting of U.S. cur-

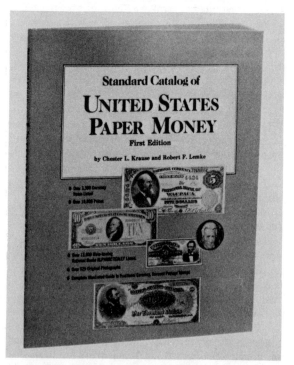

Fig. 5-5. For collectors who want to become involved in U.S. currency, the *Standard Catalog of U.S. Paper Money* is recommended.

rency for the average numismatist. When compared to the monographs that had made up the bulk of previous U.S. currency cataloging, the Friedberg book (it is almost unknown by its true title; collectors usually refer to it as "Friedberg") put into one set of covers a comprehensive listing of the most popularly collected types of U.S. paper money. Because it was based on on-going research, it did tend to foster some misconceptions about the collectibility of certain notes.

As with the Krause-Lemke catalog, the emphasis in the Friedberg book is on market valuations. Because it is published on an erratic schedule, it is difficult for the book to keep abreast of changing price structures.

The third principal reference catalog that attempts to cover virtually the entire field of U.S. paper money is Gene Hessler's scholarly volume titled *The Comprehensive Catalog of U.S. Paper Money*. The emphasis in this volume is on the facts, figures, and history of all types of U.S. currency. Price information is provided, but because the book is published only every several years, the information on value is soon outdated.

The reference value of the book is never obsolete. Few collectors have done as much original research on this topic as Hessler and the results are evident in the pages of his book. He presents data on total numbers of notes printed that can be found nowhere else but the archives of the U.S. Treasury. His book is replete with photos of specimen and trial notes (about which he published a companion catalog) that few collectors will ever see outside the book's pages.

The background data provided for each note issue can be matched by none of the other existing catalogs. For educational purposes, Hessler's catalog is a valuable resource for every collector.

Certain specialty areas of U.S. paper money collecting have also been the subject of major catalogs. For those who would specialize in the modern currency issued since 1928, Chuck O'Donnell holds the key to understanding this aspect of the hobby with his book *The Standard Handbook of United States Paper Money*. While the new edition was published in 1982 by Krause, the company did little more than arrange the printing of the book. The research was done or coordinated by O'Donnell. He is the nation's leading authority on small-size (the current standard in use since 1928) U.S. currency.

The O'Donnell book is a formidable compilation of official statistics and data regarding the issue of all types and varieties of modern U.S. paper money. Whether a person is collecting only the six basic types of small-size notes or the thousands of variations on those themes, the O'Donnell catalog provides the necessary information to collect intelligently. This catalog is also the only book to attempt to provide market price information for some of the more obscure varieties.

For collectors of Confederate currency, there is Col. Grover C. Criswell's *Confederate and Southern States Currency*. Criswell is the world's leading expert on Southern fiscal paper of the Civil War era (or, as he prefers to call it, The First War for Southern Independence). Often featured on television programs in connection with his specialty, Criswell's book is one that a novice collector can easily enjoy and understand. Only enough of the complex and convoluted economics of this troubled time is provided to give a general background. The basic thrust of the book is in identifying and placing a value upon the myriad varieties of C.S.A. and state-issued notes of the South in the mid-1860s.

While the last edition was published in 1976, and values on the notes have changed somewhat, the prices quoted in Criswell will still give the collector an idea of the relative worth of Confederate money.

Perhaps the most popular specialty area of U.S. paper-money collecting is national bank notes. A catalog titled *Standard Catalog of National Bank Notes* was printed in November, 1982. Published by Krause's and authored by the most respected dealers in national currency, John T. Hickman and Dean Oakes, the book is the first comprehensive listing of all known surviving national bank notes. Much of this information has come from Hickman's personal archive of more than 100,000 photocopies of national currency that he has compiled in the course of several decades of specialization in this field.

The catalog is also an attempt to bring some order to the pricing of national bank notes that realistically considers the actual rarity of each type of note issued by some 13,000 banks during the period 1863-1935. Previously, the pricing of national bank notes has usually been done on the basis of a seller gauging the depth of the potential buyer's wallet before setting his price. Using the publisher's data-processing expertise, the new National Bank catalog presents the U.S. government's own records on each note in a format that the average collector can use and understand with ease.

A similar cataloging effort—this one to list, picture, describe, and assign a market value to every known private bank note issued in the U.S. in the early nineteenth century, is well underway at Krause's. Because of the enormity of the project—with more than 30,000 photos already taken—it will not be ready for publication until early in 1984.

This book is expected to present, for the first time, the only reasonably complete list of obsolete U.S. bank

Fig. 5-6. The accepted reference book in the foreign currency field is the *Standard Catalog of World Paper Money*. It gives the hobby the universally used Pick numbers (named after the author).

notes ever compiled. The field of "broken bank notes," as they are sometimes called, remains as the only major uncataloged area in U.S. paper money. Because of the beauty and historical significance of most of these notes, coupled with their relative low cost, this has been an extremely popular collecting specialty for most of the late 1900s.

Authored by James Haxby, publication of this catalog is expected to be the impetus that raises the collecting of obsolete bank notes to the consciousness of every numismatist. It should create a new market that will make current prices on this century-old material seem unbelievable.

In the field of world paper money, another Krause Publications reference is in the forefront: The *Standard Catalog of World Paper Money,* by Albert Pick (Fig. 5-6). An official at one of Germany's largest banks, Pick accumulated over the years as much learning about the entire spectrum of world paper money as it is possible for one man to do.

The result is another telephone-book sized volume that covers the government-issued paper currency of the entire globe for most of the period in which paper currency has been issued. Only a handful of official paper currencies circulated before the seventeenth century.

Heavily illustrated—although most topical collectors would like to see front and back of each note presented photographically—the book offers pricing data that has been extracted from dealers and collectors all over the world. The data is the basis on which paper money prices are set between dealers and collectors from Calcutta to California. In essentially the same format as the world coin catalog, the paper money book gives the collector a short look at the government that issued each note and the economic system of which it is a part. Prices are provided in several states of preservation.

Introductory information presents a history of world paper currency from the mulberry-bark notes of Ming Dynasty China in the 1400s, to the concentration-camp currency of World War II, to the latest modern bank notes produced on high-technology equipment to foil counterfeiters.

The only other world paper-money cataloging effort of note is the on-going project of the International Bank Note Society. This is a cataloging of all the world's paper currency on a nation-by-nation basis. Work is going slowly with the top-collectors in each country providing input. For the collector who would specialize in the paper money of an individual nation, there are few such books available. Most of the English-speaking world has been thus covered. Nevertheless, it is usually in a catalog that also covers the coins of the nation or nations under study.

The rest of the many and diverse numismatic catalogs are too numerous and too highly specialized to present here. You can be virtually assured that almost everything you might want to collect has been the subject of some type of catalog. Naturally, because they have been collected for so long, ancient coins are well documented in the pages of numerous catalogs—old and new. Likewise, there are hundreds of catalogs devoted to the many specialty collecting avenues in the token and medal field.

While the larger book and hobby shops handle the more popular cataloging titles, the best place to find the books you need is at a coin shop. Most dealers handle a fair number of the titles. If they don't have them in stock, they usually know where to get them quickly. For information on any of the Krause Publications titles, you can write directly to the company at 700 E. State St., Iola, WI 54990.

Chapter 6

Price and Grading Guides

LONG EXPERIENCE IN THE COIN-RELATED PUB-lishing field has led me to the conclusion that the average collector wants most to know: How much will I have to pay for this coin I want to buy? And sometimes even more importantly: How much can I sell this coin for? The current popularity of the coin collecting hobby and the fast pace at which most collectors seem to want to do business has given rise in recent years to coin-pricing guides that provide this information on an ever-increasingly faster pace.

For most of the hobby's recent past, at least until the 1960s, an annual update via the traditional July publication of the Red Book was enough to keep most hobbyists current. Today no price guide that involves putting ink on paper can be considered timely enough (Fig. 6-1).

Virtually every coin dealer of any consequence has one of two major Teletype networks connected in his shop. The endless traffic printed out on this machine is a pulse of the coin market. The systems are like an open party line. One coin dealer can offer to buy or sell an item to as many as 500 others on the same system. This ebb and flow of real coin transactions provides the other dealers with a realistic view of the market. They can see what coins are selling and which are not—and at what prices.

If their offers to buy a specific coin at a specific price go unmet hour after hour, they know they must raise their offered price if they are to get any action. They have, in effect, learned the actual market price of that coin at that specific moment.

Because ownership of a Teletype station is an expensive proposition, few collectors can afford it. With the trend toward personal computers in millions of living rooms, it is not going to be long before somebody begins offering a service of coin market information via the home television screen.

About the best most collectors can do for now is to get their coin market information on a weekly basis. Currently, they have two choices: the *Coin Dealer Newsletter* or *Coin Market*. Each provides a complete summary of activity in the most popularly traded areas of the U.S. coin market in essentially the same format.

The Coin Dealer Newsletter is more popularly known in the hobby as the "Gray Sheet." As might be expected, it is printed on gray paper, (8½″×11″). The CDN's standard format is eight pages; it consists of six pages of coin pricing data and two pages of paid advertising. Now in its 20th year, the Gray Sheet is published weekly and mailed to subscribers by first-class mail. A monthly summary provides extra pages of market information that

Fig. 6-1. Annual price guides can no longer keep pace with the current rapidly moving coin market. Books like the Red Book have been supplanted in recent years by more timely editions.

is generally geared to one specific U.S. coinage series.

Most of the first page of the Gray Sheet is a weekly analysis of the coin market. Editor/Publisher Allen Harriman, or occasionally a guest columnist from the professional ranks, provides subscribers with his insights. These might include interpretations of a recent major coin show or numismatic auction, a detailed inspection of the coin dealers' Teletype traffic over the past week, or a guess at what the market faces in future weeks. Generally, this analysis is aimed at the coin dealer rather than the collector or investor.

In "This Week's Market," the Gray Sheet looks at the ups, downs or, status quo of each of the major areas it covers: cents, nickels, dimes, quarters, halves, dollars, proof and mint sets, and commemoratives.

The rest of the nonadvertising content of the Gray Sheet is price charts purporting to reflect the current price structure of those U.S. and world coins most commonly bought and sold. The emphasis is on utility to the professional coin dealer. Prices are quoted in "Bid" and "Ask." Bid is generally regarded as the wholesale price. That is the price one coin dealer will pay *another coin dealer* for a coin he needs to stock or to fill the order of a retail customer. Ask price is the price at which one coin dealer will sell a coin from his stock to *another dealer.*

In reality the quoted prices are merely beginning points for negotiation between the dealers. If a coin is especially choice or in demand, it is not uncommon for it to be sold at levels in excess of the CDN's presented bid and ask figures. Similarly slow-moving coins or series might well be traded at levels under the Gray Sheet quotes. It is not uncommon to hear one coin dealer offer to pay another "5 percent back of bid" for an item. The "back of" means 5 percent lower than the bid price quoted.

To allow dealers to see at a glance any changes in market prices, the Gray Sheet uses a system of plus (+) and minus (–) signs between the bid and ask figures if the price of that coin has changed during the week. Originally intended to serve the professional numismatists only, the Gray Sheet quickly caught on with "vest pocket" dealers (part-timers who work the coin show and shop circuit), high-rolling collectors, and speculators, because it was the information source so many dealers seemed to rely on when buying or selling coins. As such, they reasoned that "inside" knowledge of the wholesale/retail structure of the market could assist them in buying coins at the lowest possible price, and selling them for the maximum available price.

It is not uncommon to see a dealer and a collector sitting across a table at a coin show negotiating over the price of a coin. Each will consult the Gray Sheet to get the last cent out of the deal.

The principal drawback to *The Coin Dealer Newsletter,* for the average coin collector, is that it currently costs $60 a year. Other hobby observers fault the sheet for not listing its contributors, the coin dealers, and market watchers who provide input on which the printed prices are based. These critics charge that it is too easy for prices to be manipulated when the subscriber can't see up front who is providing expertise.

The other principal weekly coin pricing guide is the "Coin Market" section of the weekly newspaper *Numismatic News* (Fig. 6-2). Providing reliable pricing data since its inception in the early 1950s, *Numismatic News* adopted the "Coin Market" formula in the mid-1970s to give its readers—collectors, investors and dealers—a more useful price guide on a weekly basis.

The format chosen was a modification of the Gray Sheet's "Bid-Ask" arrangement; it offered a third column of prices titled "Buy." Unlike the Gray Sheet, the Coin Market spells out very clearly just what each column of prices is intended to reflect: "The COIN MARKET is a wholesale/retail guide intended to accurately reflect the three principal market levels that influence the values of collector and investor coins. BUY—What dealers pay to purchase coins for inventory, or to wholesale to other dealers. BID—what dealers pay for coins, generally

Price Boosts Ahead for Copper Lincolns?

Coins

The Complete Magazine for Coin Collectors

JAN 1982
$1.50

47448

Value Guide
1970-S Small-Date
Cent Proof: $125

Taking Aim:
Satirical Medals
Blast Famous

Find Hidden
Rarities Among
Minting Varieties

Fig. 6-2. For the beginning collector, the coin value guide in the monthly magazine, *Coins*, offers timely price information.

through other dealers on teletype, which will sell immediately. SELL—average price realized for a coin sold at retail."

Coin Market also details the basic manner in which its prices are arrived at: "Valuations are based on monitoring of nationwide teletype dealings, advertised offerings, public auction and coin show sales, and recommendations provided by a consulting panel of selected professional numismatist." And they are named.

The editor of the Coin Market is Bob Wilhite. He is a long-time coin dealer who was hired by *Numismatic News* specifically for the purpose of creating and running the Coin Market section of the paper. Each week, Wilhite lends readers his market expertise in the form of an analysis of current and projected trends and what they mean to the subscriber. Unlike the Gray Sheet, Coin Market's analysis is aimed at the collector and investor rather than the dealer alone. This weekly market summary is intended to give the investor and serious collector insights into the workings that influence up and down price movements, and spell out how he can best profit by that information.

Printed back to back in the newspaper, the Coin Market section is intended to be torn out and used by the collector at coin shows, auctions, etc. Its format consists of the equivalent of four magazine-size pages that can easily be folded to pocket size.

Areas of Coin Market's coverage are diverse, it blankets on a weekly basis the most popularly traded types, series and single coins. A monthly eight-page Expanded Coin Market gives pricing data for virtually every U.S. coin in all collectible grades of preservation.

For the precious metals investor, and because the price of gold and silver bullion is so intricately tied to collectible coin prices, Coin Market offers up-to-date price spreads on U.S. and world gold bullion coins (coins collected for their metal value rather than their worth as collectors items), and U.S. 90-percent and 40-percent silver coins.

There are prices of U.S. proof sets from 1936 to date and U.S. mint sets from 1947-1981. Lengthy listings give the price of Morgan and Peace silver dollars of all dates and mints in the three uncirculated grades that collectors and investors are generally interested in: uncirculated-typical, uncirculated-select, and uncirculated-choice. There are also prices for the Eisenhower and Anthony dollars.

In the popular investment and speculative medium of rolls of brilliant, uncirculated modern (1934 to date) coins, prices are quoted in all denominations. There are also prices on rolls of proof singles from 1968 to date.

The popular U.S. commemorative coin market is covered in the three uncirculated grades along with the XF/AU (extremely fine to about uncirculated) condition in which these coins are sometimes encountered and traded.

Prices are also included for both circulated and uncirculated U.S. coins, scarce and rare date coins in each denomination, sets of modern coins, rolls of older type coins, etc. Proof U.S. coins of the nineteenth century and twentieth century are also detailed.

To give the reader a grasp of the Canadian and world markets, there are sections of the Canadian proof-like coinage sets and a weekly presentation of foreign exchange rates for some 75 commonly encountered world monetary units.

The same system of plus and minus signs used in the CDN is used in Coin Market. An exception is that here they are reserved for significant price changes.

Coin Market and the Gray Sheet contain most of the same coin market data in much the same manner of presentation. Because they are both based on the same basic types of input, the prices they quote are generally quite close to each other and both can be said to accurately reflect the state of the market at the time of publication.

The principal difference between the two seem to be the price. At the same time the Gray Sheet's annual subscription price was $60, the 52-issue annual price of *Numismatic News*, with the weekly Coin Market and the monthly Expanded Coin Market, was $15.

The other weekly coin newspaper, *Coin World*, also provides a page of U.S. coin-price data, but it is nowhere near as comprehensive as the Gray Sheet and Coin Market. It is also not seen by knowledgeable market observers as having the basic impartiality necessary to be accepted by hobbyists.

On a monthly basis, the newsstand magazine *Coins* provides a price-guide section that is geared toward the beginning collector. Coins that are most generally bought and sold at the grass roots hobby level are detailed. Because *Coins* magazine is produced by the same publisher as *Numismatic News*, the pricing information is taken from the same sources and is provided by Coin Market's Editor Bob Wilhite.

A number of other coin pricing sheets arose during the halcyon days of the great gold and silver boom of 1979, but none of them gained any type of following. If they still exist at all, they are very low profile. A recent numismatic price sheet that did catch on to some degree was the *Currency Market Review*. Patterned after the Gray Sheet, the *Currency Market Review* is an eight-page monthly price guide for U.S. paper money dealers, collectors, and investors.

The familiar bid and ask price structure is used for hundreds of popular U.S. currency notes. The CMR is published by Kagin's, a Des Moines, Iowa, firm with many years of professional numismatic experience that includes specializing in U.S. paper money. There are the expected market analysis and guest commentary columns along with the prices of type notes in up to six grades.

Currently priced at $15 a year, including expanded quarterly reviews of the market, the *Currency Market Review* is trying to build the type of niche for itself that the Gray Sheet and Coin Market have in the U.S. coin field. Whether or not there is a pressing need among paper money collectors, dealers, and investors for a monthly buy sell sheet remains to be seen, but at about the same time gold and silver (and collectible coins) were making their run up the price ladder, U.S. paper money was not far behind.

These price guides and sheets can be found in almost any coin shop. They are not usually offered for sale there. Exceptions are *Numismatic News*, and its Coin Market section, and *Coins* magazine. Your friendly neighborhood coin dealer should, however, be willing to give you the names, addresses, and current subscription information.

Another type of coin price guide that many beginning numismatists find to be inexpensive, handy, and relatively accurate are the pocketbook price guides that come out periodically, and usually when the coin market is in an active stage (Fig. 6-3). The House of Collectibles' "Black Books" on U.S. coins and paper money come from a Florida firm that specializes in price guides for all types of collectors. Their annual editions are well thought of in the hobby as good beginners' price guides. They offer a modicum of basic hobby background as well as prices that are as up to date as an annual can be. The Black Books, however, might be difficult for the noncollector or new collector to find. They are primarily sold in coin and hobby shops.

Another type of pocketbook price guide is put out by several of the nation's largest publishers (including Dell). They are generally found in the small book racks at the end of the checkout lines at the grocery store. These books are of very limited use to the collector because they provide almost nothing but minimal price data that is generally too obsolete or incomplete for all but the most novice numismatist.

For this type of book, I recommend a Krause Publication titled *Standard Guide to U.S. Coin and Paper Money Valuations*, authored by myself and co-worker Bob Wilhite. Bob provided the price data, in the course of his

Fig. 6-3. Publication of pocketbook price guides sold on newsstands all over the country help keep the general public or the very casual collector abreast of current coin values.

normal work preparing prices for Coin Market, etc., and I provided the historical and numismatic background, introductions, etc.

The book, now in its 8th edition, is a well-illustrated retail guide. It lists the prices the collector could expect to pay for thousands of U.S. coins and paper money. A feature is the column that lists "Average Buy Price." This is for the collector who wants to sell average circulated specimens to a dealer. It provides a realistic guide to what they will bring.

Priced at $2.25, the intention is to make it as widely available as possible, and to help promote the coin-collecting hobby by giving the newly interested collector the type of price information he can best use in an easy-to-understand format. To make the book as widely available as possible, it is sold at the same newsstands that handle the monthly *Coins* magazine. The book is also sold in book stores, coin shops, and hobby shops.

In all of these same locations, you can find yet one more type of U.S. coin price guide; *Coin Prices* (Fig. 6-4). *Coin Prices*, aside from the annual Red and Blue Books, is probably the best selling price guide on the market. Currently published six times a year, it is a magazine-format price guide of approximately 128 pages that is bought by some 125,000 collectors, dealers and investors.

Next to the Red Book, it is the most complete coin pricing index available to the collector today. In some ways, it is even more comprehensive. During one year, the magazine includes several different types of price information not found in the Red Book. Examples are U.S. large- and small-size paper money, Canadian coins, Mexican coins, U.S. error coins, Confederate and military paper currency, and Fractional Currency.

Coin Prices provides valuations in the full range of collectible conditions for each type or series. It is well illustrated and it includes detail photos that allow the reader to distinguish rare varieties. Besides the coin prices, there are several information-packed articles in each issue that help the reader understand the market. A summary of auction results also provides insight into where coin prices are headed.

The current price of each issue is $1.95. An expanded annual issue, published in February each year, sells for $2.45.

Fig. 6-4. Published every two months, the newsstand magazine *Coin Prices* is widely used by collectors and dealers alike.

You have probably noticed that, throughout this discussion of coin price guides, there has been frequent mention of coin grading. This is because no other single factor affects the price of a coin or piece of paper money as its grade. Each of the three most commonly used systems of grading for United States coins is contained in a different book.

That coin grading books are needed at all is a reflection of the way in which the coin business is conducted today—largely by mail order. When buying a coin face to face, a collector can easily look at it and determine if the condition of the coin fits into his collection and if the price attached is fair in relation. When buying through the mail, he needs a description to go by. Thus has evolved the short-hand system known as grading.

For coin grading to mean anything, both the buyer and seller have to be working with the same set of standards. In other words, when the seller describes his coin as "extremely fine" in condition, the buyer should be able to conjure up in his mind's eye an image of exactly what that coin looks like. A collector who has bought coins from a coin dealer for a long period of time will soon get to know how that dealer grades his material, and how the dealer's grades fit into the collectors interpretations of coin grading. It then becomes easy for them to do business through the mail.

When ordering for the first time from a dealer, however, the collector has no reference point unless the dealer specifies that he grades his coins by one of the commonly accepted methods. That is where the coin-grading books come into play.

In the United States today, there are three major coin-grading systems in use. The most widely accepted is also the newest. It was adopted in 1976 by the American Numismatic Association and embodied in a book titled: *Official A.N.A. Grading Standards for United States Coins.* Collectors and dealers simply call it "ANA Grading". See Fig. 6-5.

If a dealer's ad in *Numismatic News* says, "All coins graded by ANA standards," the potential buyer knows he can look up any coin in the grading guide and be presented with a drawing as well as a detailed word description of the coin in question.

Published in early 1982 in an expanded second edition, the ANA grading guide now includes all types of regular issue and commemorative U.S. coins. The ANA grading guide was the end product of many years struggle to set up one universally acceptable set of grading standards for U.S. coins.

A long-standing official ANA committee chaired by veteran California coin dealer Abe Kosoff and then Red

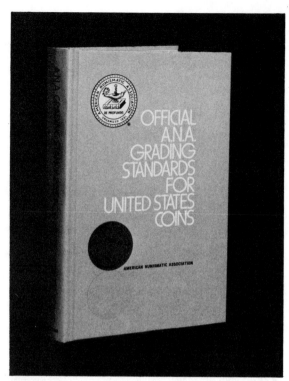

Fig. 6-5. The current standard U.S. coin grading reference is *Official A.N.A. Grading Standards for United States Coins,* from the American Numismatic Association.

Book Editor Ken Bressett compiled, arranged, and edited the grading standards into a handy book that is easily understood by even the beginning collector. Input from hundreds of dealers and collectors was sought in the creation of the official ANA standards. While there was much trepidation in the beginning as to whether they would be acceptable to large numbers of hobbyists, those fears proved unfounded. In just a few short years, the ANA standards became the measure by which the vast majority of coins were bought and sold in the United States.

The ANA standards are based on a modification of a grading system. Devised in the early twentieth century, for grading U.S. large cents. In this system, coins are ranked on a numerical scale that runs from 3 to 70. Three is the lowest ranking an undamaged coin can receive. It indicates an "about good" specimen. This type of coin is worn nearly smooth, but enough design and date details are still legible to determine its type and date of issue.

The 70 rating is reserved for the "perfect" coin. This is perhaps the source of greatest disagreement with the ANA system. Many collectors don't believe that a perfect coin exists. Examination (as is recommended) with a 4-power magnifying glass, will always, these purists contend, turn up some flaw of striking or handling that eliminates a coin from the perfect 70 realm. Indeed, this philosophy seems to have become the generally accepted view and it is very seldom that a legitimate dealer will advertise a coin as a perfect 70. Nevertheless, it does happen occasionally. The buyer should view with justifiable suspicion the dealer who advertises nearly all of his wares as being perfect 70-condition coins.

To reconcile this numerical grading with the adjectival grading that had been the basis of all earlier standards, the ANA has combined its numbers with familiar grade designations in the following manner. Coins at the basal 3 state of preservation are tied to the About Good designation. Good coins rate a 4; Very Good—8; Fine—12; Very Fine—20; Choice Very Fine—30; Extremely Fine—40; Choice Extremely Fine—45; About Uncirculated—50; Choice About Uncirculated—55; Average Uncirculated—MS-60 (for Mint State); Select Uncirculated—MS-63; Choice Uncirculated—MS-65; Gem Uncirculated—MS-67, Perfect Uncirculated—MS-70.

Although the ANA system does not encourage the use of intermediate grades, they are allowed and frequently used. For example, a coin that falls just a hair's breadth from the uncirculated condition is sometimes seen advertised as AU-59. Many observers feel, however, that such hairsplitting is more of an attempt by the seller to jusitfy an unrealistic price for his coin than a true attempt to accurately describe its condition.

To use the ANA grading guide, the collector simply digests the introductory material to the system itself and then turns to the pages covering the type of coin he wants to grade. There he will find further introductory material that will be applicable to that particular type of coin. For instance, the section on Indian-head cents notes: "The copper-nickel cents of 1859, 1862, 1863 and 1864 are often weakly struck and lack sharp details. The 1864 L variety must show the L clearly even for the grade of About Good. Coins with full sharp diamond designs on ribbon are unusual because this feature is often weak even on Uncirculated coins."

The collector compares the coin in his hand to the enlarged line drawings of the coin in each grade of preservation and refers to the written description of that grade. Arrows point to trouble spots on the coin that the reader should be careful to examine closely. There are other helpful tips to assist in assigning the proper grade.

With a little practice, and perhaps with the assistance of an experienced numismatist to check your grading, even the beginning collector can learn, in a relatively short time, to grade coins accurately with the ANA system.

In the second most popular system of U.S. coin grading, coins are also compared to pictures in a book. In such a book, the pictures are enlarged photographs of the coin in each grade. That is how the name came about for the grading system and the book: *Photograde*.

First published in 1970, James F. Ruddy's *Photograde—A Photographic Grading Guide for United States Coins*, was an instant hobby success. In 1972, before the introduction of its own grading system, the American Numismatic Association designated the Photograde system as an official grading guide (Fig. 6-6).

With its 11th printing in 1979, the book had sold some 250,000 copies. In its latest edition, *Photograde* has been cross-indexed with the ANA's official grading guide to allow collectors more familiar with the Photograde system to reconcile that terminology with the ANA standards.

A former photographic engineer and co-founder of Bowers & Ruddy Galleries, one of the world's largest coin dealerships, Jim Ruddy created the Photograde system to be the easiest method then available for grading U.S. coins. He spent years scouring his own stock and those of coin dealers all over the country to find specimens of every United States coin—from the half-cent to the $20 gold piece in each state of preservation—and photographing them in minute detail. In all, more than 1000 sharp, clear black-and-white photos are presented in the book.

To accurately grade his coins using Photograde, the collector merely matches his coin to the picture in the book. A description of each grade's principal characteristics accompanies the illustrations.

The third principal grading system for U.S. coins was the easiest attempt to create a universally acceptable, easy-to-understand standard by which U.S. coins could be described. It was produced, beginning in 1958, by Martin Brown and John Dunn. Popularly known as "Brown and Dunn," the system is embodied in the various editions of the book titled: *A Guide to the Grading of United States Coins*.

Produced by Whitman Coin Products Division of Western Publishing Co., the publishers of the Red Book and the Blue Book, it is not surprising that the Brown and Dunn system was used as the source of grading information in those popular annual price guides. As such, the Brown and Dunn system was once quite popular. It has

faded almost into obsolescence today. No new edition of the Brown and Dunn book has been published for many years.

A portion of the Brown and Dunn system lives on today, however, in the ANA grading guide. This is in the form of the line drawings, used in the ANA book, that were the same or modified from the B&D system. Because the rights to those drawings were owned by Whitman, it was an easy matter for the ANA to get permission for their use in their own grading book, which was published by Whitman.

Some veteran dealers still advertise that they grade their merchandise by Brown and Dunn standards. Today's numismatists do owe the pioneering pair a debt of gratitude for their work in creating the first widely used grading system out of the hodgepodge of individual systems that had been the norm prior to 1958.

Whatever, indeed, if any, grading guide you choose to use for your own collecting pursuits, it will only be as good as you make it. Remember that a grading guide is only a guide; it is not an absolute standard. No matter

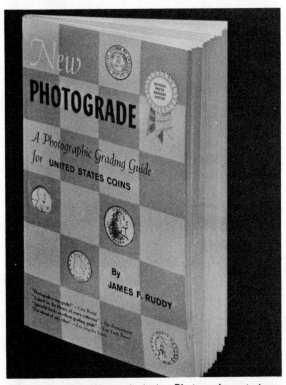

Fig. 6-6. Developed by a coin dealer, *Photograde* went a long way toward teaching the average coin collector to grade coins accurately.

what a seller advertisers in the form of grading, the buyer is the final judge. If that coin, in your judgment, does not measure up to the standard you follow, it is your right to return it for a refund or replacement.

You might have noticed that I have said nothing about U.S. paper money or world coin grading standards or guides. That's because there are none! The field of world coins is so diverse that it is impossible for a single grading guide to cover all types of coins: from the rough cob-cut and hammer-struck coins of the Spanish Empire to the modern proof issues struck at the world's most modern mints. In attempting to grade world coins, most collectors extrapolate American coin standards to the foreign coins. While this is not precise or universally acceptable, it does seem to be effective. At least it will be until the world coin market becomes as exceedingly condition conscious as the market is in U.S. coins.

The situation in U.S. paper money is currently in flux. The American Numismatic Association currently has a committee studying the feasibility of creating official grading standards for currency notes. Collectors, dealers, and investors are sharply divided on the subject. Those with some experience in the paper-money field generally believe "official" grading standards to be unnecessary. The feeling is that the problem of accurately grading a piece of paper are not as complex as those associated with a piece of stamped metal.

Many new paper money collectors—and some veterans who do not want to see overgrading become a problem as U.S. currency collecting grows in popularity—are all for setting up standards now, before there is too much confusion.

It is my opinion that we will eventually see the ANA adopt a standard system for grading paper money. Perhaps the experience already gained in setting up a coin grading system will stand them in good stead and eliminate the problems and doubts that dogged the ANA coin-grading system in its formative years.

Numismatic Periodicals

I N THIS CHAPTER I PROVIDE A CRITICAL REVIEW of each of the major commercial numismatic publications. You will notice that I am biased toward those published by Krause Publications. Let's take a look at the several weekly and monthly coin collectors' newspapers and magazines that are published for informative purposes. These are not value guides (primarily) or investment advisories. Each of these publications should be available for your inspection or purchase at any coin shop. Most of them can be found at the larger newsstands around the country. In addition, all are currently available by mail subscription.

There are currently three commercial weekly newspapers published in the United States that are devoted to the coin-collecting hobby. One of them, *Numismatic News*, deals strictly with United States coins. A second, *World Coin News*, as its name implies, covers the broad spectrum of foreign coins (and paper money). The third, *Coin World*, opens its pages to all numismatic topics (U.S. and foreign).

Because it covers all numismatic topics, *Coin World* is the largest of the three weekly coin papers (in terms of subscription base as well as in number of pages). It is also the most expensive at $18 a year, or $1 a copy when bought over-the-counter at a coin shop.

Coin World was the hobby's first weekly newspaper. It started life in 1960 as an offshoot of the Amos Press organization in Sidney, Ohio. The 52-times-a-year frequency coincided with a boom in the coin-collecting hobby at that time and made the paper an immediate success. While its circulation was once in the 125,000 range, it currently sells about 90,000 copies per issue. This reflected the early 1980s slump in the coin market.

The paper's biggest advantage is its size. It is always well over 100 pages of news, features, and advertising pertaining to all aspects of numismatics. That wide scope is seen by CW's fans as its main selling point. In *Coin World*, between the front and back pages, is a handy weekly summary of just about everything that went on in the coin hobby in a week's time. To its critics, that is also the paper's biggest fault. Few numismatists collect everything: U.S. coins, world paper money, wooden nickels, foreign military decorations, etc. They charge that because it tries to cover the entire spectrum on numismatics, there is too much in every issue that is of no interest to them.

Because *Coin World* does not appeal to a specialized audience within the numismatic fraternity, it has come to be associated with the beginner or casual collector who does not yet have a specialty within his own numismatic interests. After a coin collector focuses his attention to a more limited sphere of hobby interest, he usually graduates from *Coin World* to one of the more specialized papers.

A more serious problem more collectors see with *Coin World* is the paper's reluctance to recognize the principal hobby issues and to take a firm stand on them. Critics—including the paper's own former staff members—charge that the editorial policy of that publication is to sit on the fence and not risk displeasing the powers that be: the U.S. Mint, the American Numismatic Association, or the segment of coin dealers who are of dubious reputation. The paper's detractors say this is done at the expense of the average collector.

Another reason *Coin World* is the largest weekly coin paper in number of pages is that it contains more advertising than the others. Coin collectors—indeed, collectors of all kinds—buy their papers and magazines as much for the ads as for the news and features. They want to buy, sell, and trade. Advertising is not detrimental to a coin paper. Bad advertisers are detrimental to a coin paper.

It is well known in professional hobby circles that *Coin World* has such a large number of advertisers because the paper is not extremely particular about who it allows to advertise. Most numismatic periodicals screen their advertisers very carefully to ensure that the persons who use their pages to transact business with the subscribers are going to transact their business in an honorable manner.

While each publication's advertising policy differs, all should place the welfare of the reader above the consideration of advertising revenue. *Coin World's* critics charge that the paper is lax in doing so. Many coin dealers who are not allowed to advertise in any of the other commercial hobby publications are still allowed to peddle their sometimes suspect wares in *Coin World's* pages. A number of these advertisers are well-known overgraders. The coins they advertise as "uncirculated" at a bargain price are not uncirculated at all. The buyer will discover this when he attempts to sell the coins at a later date.

Most overgraders will cheerfully refund a customer's money if he returns a coin, as overgraded, during the usual seven-day examination period. But most overgraders count on the fact that the unsophisticated reader will not know that the coins he bought are overgraded and so will not complain in the required week.

So widespread is this practice that overgraded coins that could be passed off on the inexperienced collector as a higher grade have been seen advertised on the FACTS

dealer-to-dealer Teletype network as "Coin World Unc." The implication is that they will pass muster under that paper's advertising policies.

This is not to impugn the honesty or business methods of every *Coin World* advertiser. The majority of them are legitimate coin dealers delivering a fair coin for a fair price. Nevertheless, on the basis of my observations for some 18 years that I have been familiar with *Coin World*, I would advise caution in dealing with any advertiser who is not allowed to do business in the pages of any coin paper except *Coin World*.

No such caution is generally necessary when dealing with the advertisers in *Numismatic News*. The advertising policies of that weekly paper are so stringent that an average of $40,000 in ad revenue is rejected each month because the publisher feels the persons seeking to buy that ad space are not of sufficient character to be entitled to reach the NN readership.

That policy was initiated in 1952 when the first issue of *Numismatic News* was published in Iola, Wisconsin; as a part-time enterprise by Chet Krause. The paper grew from a monthly to a bi-weekly, and then went weekly in the early 1960s when *Coin World* emerged as competition.

Numismatic News was the first commercial coin publication to adopt the tabloid newspaper format. As the least expensive way to put ink on paper and into the hands of subscribers, that format was adopted for the *News*. The paper originated as a vehicle to put one coin collector in touch with another across the nation or around the world. That original purpose survives in an unofficial Krause Publications' motto that holds that all of the firm's periodicals are "Published by collectors, for collectors."

As it grew from a strictly classified advertising medium to the hobby's only newspaper, NN initially tried the same approach that *Coin World* copied when it came along eight years later—covering the whole world of numismatics. The realization that, in today's complex numismatic hobby scene, no single publication can properly serve every collector led Krause Publications to begin spinning off new periodicals. In 1974, *World Coin News* took non-North American news, features, and advertising under its own banner. In 1979, paper-money coverage was divorced from *Numismatic News* with Krause's acquisition of the monthly *Bank Note Reporter*.

Today, *Numismatic News* stands as a weekly newspaper dedicated to the interests of the collector of U.S. coins. Its current circulation of about 50,000 is shown by demographic surveys to be made up of relatively advanced numismatists who are seeking solid reliable hobby news reporting, entertaining and educational features, accurate price information via the paper's "Coin Market" section, and trustworthy advertising.

Because the paper insists on the absolute integrity of its advertisers, there are fewer of them in each issue of *Numismatic News*. The number of pages is generally around 64. *News'* fans say that a tight editorial content is an asset because they are spared the puffery and space filler content.

The paper has had a role in virtually every major piece of legislation affecting coin collectors in the past 20 years. Through a no-nonsense editorial stance, as well as by staff testimony on Capital Hill and even participation in special Congressionally and presidentially appointed committees, *Numismatic News* has been lauded as taking the side of the collector in such things as restoration of mint marks to U.S. coins in 1968, the form of the Bicentennial commemorative coinage and medals programs of the 1970s, and the fight for an appropriate plan for 1984 Olympic commemorative coinage.

The *News* also boasts the fastest publication schedule in the business. News and advertising that arrives in the office as late as Wednesday is in reader's hands as early as that Saturday. *Coin World* requires at least six more days to do the same job. Many collectors who subscribe to both papers note that NN gets them the news first in the majority of cases.

World Coin News is another weekly coin paper. It is also the smallest and most highly specialized of the three papers. It appeals to the collector who takes his pleasure soley in the coins, paper money, tokens, medals, and related areas issued outside the United States (Fig. 7-1). With some 12,000 subscribers in the United States and abroad, WCN is the only publication of its kind. The nearest competition is the "International Section" published each week in *Coin World* since that paper merged the old *World Coins* magazine into its pages in the mid-1970s.

The basis for founding *World Coin News*, in 1974, was the realization that most numismatists collect either U.S. coins or world coins. Few people collect both. It was felt that, by devoting a weekly paper entirely to the world collectors, they would be better served. Advertisers would benefit by not paying to have large numbers of uninterested collectors skipping over their ads.

The idea has been a success. The paper is given much of the credit for the recent increase in interest in foreign numismatics, both at home and abroad, in the past five years. WCN is the most valuable source collectors have for information on new issues of collectible numismatic items from all over the world, and for access to coin dealers whose stock is geared to the world market. The

paper also serves as a periodic update between volumes of the Standard Catalogs of world coins and world paper money. Significant price changes in any area of world numismatics can be featured on as fast as a weekly basis. There is no need to wait for the next edition of the catalog to be released.

As is the case with *Numismatic News*, the publisher's strict policy regarding quality of advertisers ensures the readers that they can deal with WCN advertisers in confidence.

Each of the three weekly coin papers is sold by subscription or at coin shops. They are not the type of publication you are going to find at the magazine rack in your local grocery store. Fortunately, there are two magazines to satisfy that market: *COINage* and *Coins*. Both selling about the same number of newsstand and subscription copies each month—in the 125,000 range—these magazines are, at least on the surface, very similar.

Each has about 128 pages per issue. *Coins* is generally a little larger than *COINage*. Sometimes *Coin* goes as high as 152 or more pages. Each costs about the same—about $1.95 to $2.25.

Fig. 7-1. The only weekly periodical for the world coin and paper money collectible is the highly regarded *World Coin News*.

Both magazines have colorful, glossy covers, depicting coins and other numismatic items to let you know at a glance that they are coin magazines, and to induce you to pick them up. Inside, each is filled with feature-length articles, regular columns, news digests, and more full-color photos. Many of the same authors and photographers sell their material to both magazines.

Both magazines are reaching for the casual or beginning collector who probably does not yet receive one of the weekly coin papers, but has enough of an interest to occasionally buy a magazine at the newsstand or drugstore.

As is the case with *Numismatic News* and *Coin World*, the biggest difference between *Coins* magazine and *COINage* is the advertising policy. *Coins* is strict and *COINage* is not; it's that simple. Knowledgeable observers will tell you that after an advertiser is kicked out of the Krause Publications, he is likely to appear in *Coin World*. In the unlikely event he is banned from their pages, he might well turn up in *COINage*.

I hope all of this hasn't scared too many new collectors off the idea of buying coins by mail. I just feel that the collector—especially the beginning collector—should be given the benefit of others' experiences.

Besides this pair of monthly newsstand coin magazines, there is one more commercial monthly numismatic periodical: the newsmagazine *Bank Note Reporter*. BNR was started in 1973 by Col. Grover C. Criswell, Jr., a well-known Confederate paper money dealer. It passed into the hands of the Sheheen family, noted collectors of South Carolina paper money, before being purchased by Krause in 1979. It is the only commercial publication dedicated solely to paper money and related collectibles such as antique stock certificates, checks, and scrip.

While the emphasis is primarily on U.S. paper money, there is also coverage of world paper-money topics. BNR provides in-depth news coverage of interest to the rag picker, as well as feature-length articles and advertising specially aimed at paper collectors. Because

virtually every serious collector of U.S. paper money is a subscriber to the $11-a-year monthly paper, many paper money dealers have given up mailing out a price list to their customers. Instead they advertise their stock in the pages of BNR. This makes the paper very popular with the collectors because it is like being on many dealers' mailing lists at no extra charge.

BNR also features a monthly price guide section that covers regular-issue U.S. paper money on a revolving basis. There are also specialty price guides that cover such diverse fields as Military Payment Certificates, Confederate paper money, Fractional Currency, Hawaiian paper money, Canadian paper money, and others.

One other commercial numismatic periodical of note is *Canadian Coin News*, a biweekly tabloid newspaper that is Canada's only commercial coin paper. Canadian coins and currency are a collecting specialty of many American numismatists. Now in its twentieth year of publication, with a circulation of nearly 30,000 (at $13.50 annually), CCN is devoted principally to Canadian coins, currency, and tokens. There is a smattering of world-oriented coverage, mostly of British Common-wealth nations. The paper avoids the U.S. scene.

There is a strong news and feature content about all phases of Canadian numismatics. A solid advertising package should give even the most sophisticated Canadian collector enough good material to choose from. This paper is not generally available at most coin shops. Here is the address interested readers can write to for further information: Canadian Coin News, P.O. Box 12,000, Bracebridge, Ontario POB 1CO Canada.

That pretty much exhausts the list of available commercial numismatic publications in this part of the world. To be sure, there are dozens more being published all over other parts of the world. There are hundreds of club and dealer-issued periodicals that range from a few editorial or market remarks on a dealer's fixed price list to the prestigious monthly magazine of the American Numismatic Association, *The Numismatist*.

Chapter 8
Acquiring Coins

AFTER VERSING YOURSELF ON THE LORE OF-numismatics via the many books, catalogs, and papers available, you will be ready to go about expanding your collection in an intelligent manner. Besides such frowned-upon practices as making your own coins or stealing them, there are only two ways I know of to obtain coins— you have to find them of buy them.

Let's cover the former method first; it's less expensive. The best way to acquire coins is to have somebody give them to you. Indeed, that is the way most coin collectors get their start. A relative or friend gives them interesting coins or a little envelope full of coins that were saved from days gone by or acquired on a trip to a foreign country. The curiosity this type of thing inspires is the usual inspiration for starting in this great hobby of ours.

If you're a beginning coin collector who has not yet been the beneficiary of a hand out from your relatives or friends, you might try a little subtle hinting. You could show them your collection the next time they visit the house. Once you've tapped out the family sources for freebie coins, you're on your own. But that doesn't mean you have to buy every last coin you will ever add to your collection. There are still several free, or nearly free, methods of acquiring collectible coins that don't involve paying a premium for them.

The first, most widely used, and most potentially rewarding (when you hit the jackpot) is searching your own pocket change for collectible specimens. You can also search rolls and even bags of coins. I have filled a book with stories about people finding rare and valuable coins in their pocket change. Even today, when you hear so many people bemoan that "all the good coins have been picked out of circulation," you don't have to believe it. My boss is an expert on the subject of coin finds. At the office, we hear regularly about silver coins and better-date coins being found by the sharp-eyed collector who watches his pocket change.

I often find at least $1 face value in 90 percent silver (pre-1965) coins in my own pocket change over the course of any given year. I squirrel it all away in the corner of my desk drawer and then I cash it in at the local coin dealer and buy something nice for my collection. The $10 and $12 profit I realize from the deal each year enables me to buy a nice token or medal, or an interesting piece of world or U.S. obsolete paper money.

Certainly the days when you could build a full set of Jefferson nickels, Lincoln cents, or anything besides clad coinage from your pocket change are gone, but the fun isn't. Go ahead and try to complete a collection of clad quarters or half-dollars from your change. You won't be amassing anything that will have great value in the future, but it does give you a reason to look at every coin handed to you in change. That's a good habit to foster.

If you like searching through circulating coins for premium-value finds, you can expand your search to rolls or bags of coins obtained from the bank. Unless you're looking for error coins, you won't want to search through new coins. Don't waste your time trying to obtain mint-fresh coins.

Unfortunately in today's chronically cent-short world of commerce, it is almost impossible in most parts of the country to get your bank to let you have a $50 bag of cents. If you have connections at a bank, you might be able to swing the deal. If you are going to get a bag of cents, be sure that your car is parked at the door; the darn things weigh 35 pounds. You are more likely to be limited to acquiring a roll or a few rolls of coins at a time. You can search them and then turn them in for others.

It is my experience that, unless you live in a city where you can turn in the rolls at a different bank than that from which you obtained them, you will probably soon begin looking over the same coins time after time. One way to avoid this is to mark each roll you have searched with your initials or other identifying mark.

I have given up looking through rolls and bags. I'd rather spend my time at other pursuits that are more lucrative (such as writing coin books). If you are like most collectors, you will also soon tire of searching quantities of coins. The returns just aren't great enough to justify the time and effort spent. The really collectible or valuable coins simply do not stay in circulation long enough.

There is another way to search for good coins, but it requires an initial capital outlay that can run into a couple of hundred dollars. I'm referring to getting a good metal detector and hunting for numismatic treasure. Treasure can be anything from common date current coinage found on the beach to old and even rare coins found in such places as abandoned church yards. For the inventive coin-shooter (as persons who use metal detectors to find coins are called), the money paid for the metal detector is quickly recovered in coins that are found. There are many books and magazines available on the purchase and use of a metal detector. Many larger coin stores sell a line of metal detectors. There is usually somebody on hand who can show you the basics of using a detector. Perhaps they will be willing to tell you of a couple of places to start your search.

City dwellers can take detectors to the parks after rock concerts and pick up many coins. Be sure to get a good enough quality detector so that you can weed out the false signals of pop tops and gum wrappers. If your city has its parking meters in grass or sand, you'll find lots of dropped coins right around their bases.

If you live in the country, in a small town, or have a car to take you out of the urban setting, you can do even better. The key is to be imaginative. Think about where people handle or handled coins. Some were bound to be dropped and lost. Old churches really are good spots. This is especially true if the church building is gone. In the days of wooden floors, lots of coins headed for the collection plate got dropped and rolled between the cracks of the board floor and into the dirt below.

One coin-shooter I know says his favorite hunting spot is around old houses. He reasons that a lot of coins fell out of pockets over the years. He cautions that you don't want to dig too deep.

Coin-shooting is good outdoors exercise that sooner or later pays off for the dilligent treasure hunter. And it is especially pleasurable to be able to point out a prized coin in your collection and tell the viewer: I found it myself; it didn't cost me a dime.

Another method for finding coins is also a treasure hunt of sorts. It's called *cherry picking*. Cherry picking involves buying a valuable coin for the price of a common piece. And thereby some questions of ethics arise. My philosophy is that if I am offered a coin or note, that I know to be rare or valuable, by a fellow collector or a noncollector, I will treat that person as fairly as I would want to be treated. If that person offers me the item with his price attached, and I know it to be a bargain, I feel justified in paying that asking price. I also feel it is not right to gloat or make fun of the seller. If I have made a great deal, I don't rub the seller's nose in it. It is my opinion that a person should know the value of any item he is trying to sell. If he misses the mark by a wide margin, it is his loss.

If a person with an item to sell offers it to me and asks me to make an offer, I try to be as fair as I can. If it is an item I want for my collection, and I have the money to pay for it, I will offer that person fair market value for it. If it is an item I know I can make a couple of bucks on by reselling it, I offer something closer to a wholesale price.

I guess it just boils down to following the rule. I know that I couldn't look at a coin or note in my collection and enjoy it if I knew I had ripped it off from some little old lady who had trusted me to be fair with her in naming my price.

The best cherry picking is from a coin dealer's stock. That way you don't have to feel bad if you get a bargain. A coin dealer should be knowledgeable enough to avoid pricing his merchandise at giveaway levels. Yet, there are few, if any, coin dealers who can claim such universal

Fig. 8-1. Searching through a dealer's "junk box" can be very rewarding for the knowledgeable collector who might cherry pick some valuable coins outside the area of the particular dealer's expertise.

expertise as to know all things about all coins. In other words, if you're going to become good at cherry picking, you've got to hit the dealers in their individual weak spots.

All too many coin dealers in this country have only passing knowledge of world coins. If they happen to buy a large estate or a collection that contains a handful or a cigar box full of foreign coins, they are likely to pay gold or silver bullion price for any precious metal coins in the lot and then throw the rest into their junk box on the shop counter for a quarter each (Fig. 8-1). Maybe they intended to look those coins over "some day" when they had time to sit down with the *Standard Catalog of World Coins,* but too often they never get around to that.

If you are on your toes and can spot a rare date or type of coin in these junk boxes, you'll build a fine collection at a modest price. Perhaps you will find valuable coins that you can sell to a foreign specialist for coins you want for your own collection.

When you travel to a coin show or visit a coin shop—if you don't see a junk box on the counter or table—ask the dealer. I don't know of any coin dealer who doesn't have some type of box or coffee can full of coins, medals, tokens and other "junk" that he can't identify. As long as you don't boast about your finds, few dealers will object to having you browse through these assortments.

The great gold and silver boom of 1979-80 was a real paradise for cherry pickers. Most retail coin shops were so busy buying silver coins by weight and trying to keep ahead of the fast-rising prices that they had no time to sort through the coins for rare dates, mint marks, or varieties. One fellow in our office, who is well known and implicitly trusted by most of the coin dealers in this part of the state, spent his weekends during that period searching through the paint cans full of silver coins that had been sold for bullion. He picked out those coins that had significant retail value above silver price and split the profits with the dealer.

Another Wisconsin dealer, after locking his doors following a particularly busy day, was idly fingering the stacks of silver dollars he had purchased (for $17 each) when he discovered a rare 1895 Morgan dollar. These had been originally issued as a proof-only collectors item by the Philadelphia Mint (and have no mint mark). Even though it had been circulated, he later sold the coin at auction for nearly $6,000.

The good cherry picker will always be discreet. If you have found a $100-coin in the 10-cent box at one dealer's table at a coin show—and take it across the room and sell it, bragging after you get your money where you bought it—the word will soon get around among the dealers and you are likely to be refused permission to cherry pick.

An amusing story of this is told about James Ruddy, author of the *Photograde* grading guide. It seems that Ruddy was nearing the end of his search for specimens that exemplified each state of preservation for each type of U.S. coin. Needing only an "about good" dime of the Seated Liberty series to complete his photo files, he was idly flipping through the junk box of a fellow coin dealer at a coin show. He spotted a Seated Liberty dime in the perfect stage of wear to illustrate an about good specimen. When he asked the dealer the price on the coin, the owner became suspicious. Why, he wanted to know, was the president of one of the world's largest coin dealerships interested in buying this coin? The dealer examined the piece from every angle with his jeweler's loupe and looked it up in every reference book he had at his table before he would accept Ruddy's explanation and a couple of dollars for the coin.

Chapter 9

Buying from a Dealer

T HE MOST COMMON WAY FOR COLLECTORS AND investors to acquire their coins today is to buy them from a coin dealer. The hobby has grown to the level of sophistication that there has developed a well-established dealer class who make their living selling coins. For better or worse, the days when collectors traded coins with each other or bought their specimens directly from the mint are, for the most part, past.

A life-long collection, built carefully and according to a master plan, will, for many collectors, represent the investment of hundreds, thousands, even tens or hundreds of thousands of dollars. Unfortunately for many of these collectors and investors, there are too many persons out there who go by the name of "coin dealer" who will try to separate you from your money by less than honest methods.

There are no federal, state, or (to my knowledge) local laws that regulate or license coin dealers. The collector or investor who has been stuck with a bad coin may wish to heaven there were such regulations to protect him. It is a fact of the free enterprise system that anybody with a handful of coins, a three-piece suit, and the price of a month's storefront rent or the table fee at a coin show can call himself a coin dealer.

Fortunately, there are ways for you to avoid the pitfalls of letting a crook get his hands into your wallet. The best way is to take the advice of a knowledgeable numismatist whom you trust. If you take my advice, you should be able to pick your coin dealers in relative safety without paying for your education through a lot of bad deals beforehand.

When assessing a coin dealer, the numismatist is faced with a wide variety of factors that must be weighed in determining whether or not that coin merchant will get some or all of your hobby business. First, there is the very basic element of what type of business does this dealer operate. Is he a wholesale-only specialist? Does he have a retail coin shop? Does he travel the country on the show circuit? Is it a mail-order firm? Each of these specialties has its own strengths and weaknesses.

Most coin collectors do business with dealers of several types. They are likely to have a couple of coin shops in their immediate area that they like to frequent. They probably go to several coin shows a year. They usually order from advertisements in the coin papers they receive and they might even bid in the major auctions that come along regularly.

If they have done their homework, collectors can find honest, reliable dealers in each of these businesses and conduct their hobby transactions in confidence. But no matter what type of business a coin dealer is engaged in, there are certain desirable traits the collector should look for before spending the first dollar.

How good is that dealer's name among your fellow collectors, among his professional colleagues, and in the numismatic press? More than any vault full of coins, the legitimate coin dealer values his good name above all else. If the coins are lost, stolen or sold, they probably can be replaced by money alone. Once a coin dealer's reputation has been lost, his good name can never be fully restored. There is a phrase often heard in the hobby/industry and especially around the advertising department of coin periodicals. It goes "once a crook, always a crook." From my years of experience, I agree with that phrase. A person either has the integrity to deal honestly with his fellow numismatists from day one or he does not.

Luckily, there are some very reliable guideposts to help you make your decisions on choosing a dealer and assessing his reputation. First figure out how the dealer came to your attention. Did you meet him at your local coin club meeting, see his table at a show, see his ads in the coin papers, find him listed in the telephone book, or receive his price list in the mail?

It has become a trend around the nation for coin dealers to take a very active role in the government of coin clubs. This is true of the American Numismatic Association; a majority of the Board of Governors are active coin dealers. It is also true for local coin clubs in most towns. The sad fact is that the 1970s were a hard time for most coin clubs and, in many cases, the dealers in the area had to step in to keep the club in operation. They have a personal and professional interest in maintaining a healthy coin club in their locale because it can mean new and continued business for them.

The dealer who is there just for his business interests is probably not somebody you want to buy your coins from. If your club has a dealer who never opens his mouth during the meeting, except to move for adjournment so he can open his attache case for the buying/selling or auction session, you can reasonably assume he is there for monetary purposes alone. You might also observe whether this dealer volunteers for committee work when the club's annual show comes around or if he is just interested in making sure he gets a good table at that show.

Most collectors don't mind the aftermeeting business session at all. Many go to the club meetings especially for that purpose. If there is a dealer there who comes on too strong and pushes his stock book under your nose, you will want to avoid him as a business contact.

The more astute dealer will conduct his business quietly at a meeting. He'll show you what he has in your collecting interests or will offer to bring some items for your inspection at the next meeting. Most good coin dealers realize that club-meeting night is not the time to try to make their entire month's overhead and they will not go into a hard sell pitch.

The club meeting is a good "neutral" ground on which to meet the dealers in your area. You are not on opposite sides of a shop counter or bourse table, and the situation is more relaxed and informal. You are also afforded the opportunity to watch that dealer in action to see where his priorities lie.

Just as there are many types of coin dealers to be found at your local club meeting, there are also a number of them you will encounter at a coin show. As a general rule of thumb, it can be said that the dealers you will find on any particular coin show bourse floor are only as good as the show itself. If you are attending the American Numismatic Association's annual convention, you can be assured that the dealers set up there have at least the modicum of respectability necessary to maintain membership in good standing in that organization.

At your hometown club's coin show, however, the situation could be quite different. While some clubs make an honest effort to screen the dealers who are allowed to have tables at their show, other clubs are only interested in selling as many tables as possible. Such clubs will give space to virtually anyone who can come up with the table rent.

You can often tell much about a bourse dealer by looking at his table. While most larger coin shows provide dealers with display cases, many of the more experienced dealers have their own. Others bring fancy table cloths, powerful lights to help you see what you are buying, well-organized stock books, etc.

Look out for the dealer whose table consists of a handful of 2 × 2s laying on the bare bottom of a display case. He might not even bother to turn on the table lamps the show host might have provided. His scribbled signs strewn around the table will advertise great bargains, but the coins you buy there are not likely to be bargains.

No matter how new a dealer is to the game, or how seldom he sets up at a coin show, if he hasn't taken the time and made the effort to present a table that speaks well of his image, you should walk quickly by—with one hand on your wallet.

The ads in the numismatic publications are probably the first place you will encounter most of the dealers with whom you will do business. No reputable dealer wants to be seen consorting with the known crooks in the hobby. This extends to the advertising pages as well. It is also in the printed advertisements for coin dealers that you will find what are perhaps your most significant indicators to a particular coin dealer's trustworthiness. They take the shape of three logos that might be found in the ad (either singly or in combination).

The logos are those of membership in the American Numismatic Association and the Professional Numismatists Guild, and that indicating receipt of the Krause Publications' Customer Service Award. Each of these logos has a special significance and even a different "weight" to be considered in making the decision as to whether to do business with the dealer displaying them. Because a dealer's ad does not display any or all of these awards does not mean he is a questionable character. It should be cause for further investigation on your part before you spend the first dollar on his merchandise.

The easiest logo for a dealer to get is that of the American Numismatic Association. Any of the more than 30,000 members of that national coin-collectors body is entitled to use the logo in their advertising. What the presence of the ANA logo in a dealer's ad means to you is that, if you have a legitimate complaint against that dealer, he is required to give you satisfaction or he can lose his ANA membership. Because ANA membership is a prerequisite to ever holding a table at any of the organization's large (and, usually very profitable for the dealer) coin shows, most reputable dealers value their ANA membership very highly. The association has specific grievance procedures that are followed if you raise a complaint against one of its members. Staff members will investigate your claim, validate it, mediate the dispute, and, if necessary, recommend suspension or ejection from the group if it is felt a dealer has not acted in good faith.

If a dealer displays the logo of the Professional Numismatists Guild in his ad, you are assured that you are dealing with one of the nation's elite coin dealers. As is the case with the ANA, the use of the PNG logo is strictly limited to members only. Not just any coin dealer can become a member.

Among the PNG's membership requirements are provisions that the applicant must have been a full-time coin dealer—actually making a living in the business—for the past five years or more, and that he have numismatic assets in excess of $25,000 (though that figure could soon change upward). Additionally, the character and reputation of each applicant is carefully passed upon by the full membership in that the group offers each of its member dealers the opportunity to vote for or against all applicants. The extremely effective dealer grapevine insures that no shady operators will penetrate the ranks of the PNG.

Also like the ANA, the PNG offers a mediation service between dealers and their customers. If all efforts to negotiate a settlement in a dispute are in vain, remember that it is a precondition to PNG membership that all of its members submit to binding arbitration. This takes the form of a three-man panel of judges. One judge is chosen by the dealer in question, one judge is chosen by the customer, and one impartial judge is chosen by the Guild's executive secretary. These three persons hear the facts of the matter, review any evidence, and issue a binding decision. The PNG logo is an effective gauge of a dealer's reputation. You can generally deal in confidence with the member who displays it.

The third indicator of a dealer's reliability is the Krause Publications' Customer Service Award. For more than 10 years, Krause has been presenting this award to coin dealers who meet the highest standards of responsibility within the hobby. To the average collector, the CSA is an indication that the dealer who displays it has no unsettled complaints in the files of the KP coin periodicals. Moreover, the dealer must not have received three justified complaints of any nature during the past year.

This last aspect is important because some of the hobby's worst offenders at cheating the collector are also the quickest to settle a complaint. They make their dishonest dollar on the large percentage of unknowledgeable collectors who can't tell they have been had until it is too late or who are too lazy to complain and just chalk their losses up to educational tuition.

The KP customer service department watches carefully for patterns of this type of activity. An advertiser will be thrown out for such conduct just as quickly as if that advertiser had refused to settle a legitimate complaint.

Don't be immediately turned off by a dealer who does not display the Customer Service Award in his ad. But you might consider asking around to get a handle on his reputation.

Telephone book listings are another source for finding coin dealers. This method is especially useful if you are new to the area. You can tell a lot about a business by its ad in the phone directory. You can save yourself the gas and time of a trip by checking the ads to see dealers maintain regular shop hours or if an appointment is required to view special merchandise. By placing an introductory phone call, you can also judge a dealer by how your initial inquiry is treated. If he is too busy to give you the time of day or to invite you to stop by, he might also be too busy to give you the kind of personalized attention the coin buyer has a right to expect.

Another way in which a coin dealer might come to your attention is by sending you a brochure or a coin price list. If the material is sent to you unsolicited, it is not even worth the reading time. No reputable coin dealer can honestly expect to send out a list to persons with whom he has never done business or who have never expressed an interest in doing business with him and expect that mailing to pay off in new business and large orders.

Every mail-order dealer I know considers his mailing list his most valuable asset. A good mailing list is built up very slowly and at a considerable cost to the dealer. His list contains those customers with whom he has done business and who he knows trust him and his coins. Many, many coin dealers run ads in the coin papers more to gain new persons for their mailing list than to actually sell the coins being offered. The material in the ad is generally only a sampling of any dealer's stock. Most figure that if you like what he sells enough to place an order from his ad, you will likely become a good customer.

Because these lists are so important to a dealer, they are kept very secret. Few reputable coin dealers will loan or sell their customer mailing list to a competitor. Nevertheless, every coin collector receives some volume of unsolicited numismatic "junk" mail. I really can't tell you where all of these questionable outfits get your name as a coin collector, but once you are so categorized on the huge mail-order computer banks, you are fair game for every con man with a dime for the photocopier, 20 cents for a stamp, and an overgraded coin to sell.

In past months, it has become very popular for mail-order firms doing business under a number of fancy and official sounding names to deluge your mailbox, your daily paper, and even the *TV Guide* with impressive-looking ads offering you great coin bargains. After you strip away all the colorful printing, bold headlines, semiofficial name, numismatic buzz words, and get down to the bottom line of the coin being offered and the price asked, it is a sucker bet.

These firms are hoping to trade on the popularity of certain coin series (currently the Morgan and Peace silver dollars) and public interest in numismatic investment in order to make a profit. Generally, the coins they offer are priced at two to three times what the same item could be bought for from a respectable dealer. And that's assuming you will receive a properly graded and unaltered coin. That is assuming a lot when you do business by mail with a firm you never heard of before.

I can't stress too strongly the warning not to do business with coin dealers who send you unsolicited offers to buy or sell. They attempt to prey on the beginning collector or, especially, the noncollector. Many collectors protect themselves from such vultures by coding their name or address so that they always know the source of their mail. For example, in my personal numismatic transactions, I use a post office box address. All of my other hobby activities—association memberships, work-related contacts, etc.—are conducted through my office address. Anytime I receive a fixed price list or "special offer" either at the office or at home, I know my name has been obtained from somewhere outside or, at best, on the fringe of the hobby.

I don't know how it happened, but somehow I got my name on a list of persons who are evidently taken to be big time investors in precious metals; I did own two Krugerrands once. They have my office address, but they also have my name as "Bobo Lemke." I'll bet I get two different solicitations a week under that name. My "name" and address is bought and sold by gold and silver dealers of all manners of legitimacy. So far, I have managed to live without their "once in a lifetime" opportunities. Now if I could just live down the name that so many people at the office find so funny . . .

Chapter 10

Coin Dealers and Auctions

THE COIN BUSINESS IS CARRIED ON AT DIFFER-ent levels of sophistication. Not all levels are right for every collector even as a collector matures in the hobby.

The retail coin shop is probably the type of dealer most commonly encountered by the beginning coin collector. Such a shop might be located in a one-room storefront, an expensive complex, or a shopping mall. The one thing they all have in common is that they rely on the walk-in traffic to make or break their business (Fig. 10-1).

Many coin dealers do not operate strictly as one type of business. They cross over to take advantage of every opportunity to make an honest dollar. For instance, the guy who owns the neighborhood coin shop might leave the counter in charge of his employees on the weekends and travel to a coin show across the state or across the country. He might also solicit mail-order business through ads in the trade papers.

Surprisingly, many coin shops do not keep regular hours or business days. For many owners, the shop is a sideline that is open evenings and weekends. The best thing about the local coin shop is that it is handy. If you need some 2-×-2 coin holders, a copy of this week's *Numismatic News*, a recent proof set, etc., it is right there. You don't have to wait for the Sunday coin show or

send away by mail order. Chances are that the dealer who runs the shop is a member of the same coin club you are and over the course of time, he might become a trusted colleague in your hobby activities.

Because most retail coin dealers attempt to service walk-in clientele, their stock is necessarily geared to the fast turnover of items in order to make a profit. Most shops will have on hand a solid stock of U.S. coins in prices ranges from a dime to several hundred dollars. The dealer will try to keep on top of what is popular in the market, keep a good supply of the "hot" coins or series, and know what his customers will want.

Because no coin dealer can afford to stock everything, do not be surprised if your neighborhood coin shop is lean in areas like paper money, world coins, or medals and tokens. As a general rule, the shop dealer will handle only familiar material. That's good for the buyer because you can learn to rely on the dealer's expertise in specialized areas.

Just because the local coin shop does not stock the multithousand dollar rarities or the more esoteric items that you might want, it does not mean you have to go elsewhere for them. Nearly every coin shop of size and consequence is part of one or more of the dealers' Teletype circuits. It is not at all unusual to see a message go

Fig. 10-1. At the upper level of retail coin establishments are plush galleries such as New England Rare Coin Company's Boston facility. Customers peruse their purchases in private viewing rooms.

across the system that reads something like, "Customer in shop looking for MS-60 1895 Liberty nickel. Who can supply at bid?" Within minutes, the dealer is likely to have obtained the needed coin and will have it in his customer's hand in just a few days. Those dealers who are not on a Teletype circuit generally know who they can call on for most types of numismatic merchandise and will gladly make a few calls to locate a coin for a serious customer.

One of the biggest advantages of having a coin shop in your town is the easy access to supplies such as coin papers, catalogs and books, albums, storage devices. Because of the high cost of postage, few mail-order dealers attempt to serve the retail customer with these items. And often when the collector wants them, he wants them now.

Surprisingly, many coin collectors do not subscribe to coin papers. Instead they prefer to pick up their copy each week at the coin shop. While this is more expensive than having a subscription, some collectors feel it is better not to have anyone—not even the mailman—know that they are coin collectors.

The trade papers realize there is a market for over-the-counter shop sales and they make quantities of their papers available to shop owners at discount prices. Most shop owners, besides making a couple of dimes on each copy sold, like the arrangement because it brings regular customers into the shop at least once a week. Customers generally don't go home with just the paper under their arm.

Even if there is no retail coin shop in your town or neighborhood, there is probably some type of more general hobby shop that includes coins and numismatic supplies as part of its stock in trade. While it is most common to find such shops dealing principally in coins and stamps, many have other hobby lines like electric trains, models, baseball cards, and fantasy games. Most of these shop owners realize that the collecting urge is seldom limited to one area and that many coin collectors also have related hobby pursuits.

The dealer often realizes that some towns are just not big enough to support a one-hobby retail outlet. He must add other popular product lines to stay in business.

The biggest drawback to this type of shop is that the dealer is seldom a coin specialist and his stock is likely to be somewhat limited. If you pursue numismatics seriously, you might soon discover that you know more about the coin hobby than a shop owner who has half a dozen other hobbies to keep abreast of.

While his stock of coin books and supplies might be nearly as good as the retail coin shop, his stock of coins is likely to be quite elementary and geared more toward the beginning collector. As you mature in the hobby, it is likely you will soon outgrow shopping for your coins in the hobby shop and you will look for a coin specialist.

While it is not quite so common today as it once was, many large department stores maintain a coin department. I'm not referring to about a rack of Whitman coin albums and some plastic coin tubes. I mean a real coin department (usually) with a full-time, knowledgeable coin dealer in attendance. It has been my experience, however, that these coin departments are not really for the serious collector.

In my youth, one of the only places a person could buy old coins, in the town where I lived, was at the coin counter of a local men's wear store. I went in there every week to buy a copy of *Numismatic News*, look over the shop's selection of coins, and make a purchase. I was pleased with my purchases because I was buying old Barber dimes, quarters and halves, Liberty nickels, and three-cent pieces. To me the prices seemed good. It was only after I had gained some years of hobby experience, that I realized the coins I had been sold were really not very desirable at all. They generally had some type of excessive wear or damage. While that doesn't make any difference to a 10-year-old child buying a coin that was minted the same year his father was born, it does make a difference when that child becomes a serious numismatist and realizes that his coins are of too low a grade to be considered collectible.

As the years went by and I continued to visit department-store coin counters all over the country, I saw that many such coin departments still specialized in low grade or damaged older coins (as well as recent proof sets, etc.).

I have since learned that most such coin departments are not really trying to serve the collector. They are there to lure the impulse buyer. A small box of two-cent pieces for $4 apiece is not likely to entice the avid coin collector when he examines them and finds them either worn nearly smooth or holed for jewelry wear. Such old coins in a denomination most of the general public is not aware ever existed, might induce the noncollector to buy.

Because most department-store coin counters obtain their merchandise from central buyers for their chains, and these buyers generally trade with the same limited number of wholesale coin dealers, I guess it is not unusual to find that most of them carry the same type of merchandise. There certainly might be exceptions to this general picture of the department-store coin counter. When you shop at one for the first time and the clerk can't show you anything that isn't low grade and/or damaged, you will probably decide not to shop there again.

Even if you find coins you are interested in at the department-store coin counter, it is unlikely that you will be able to make your best deal there. While nearly all dealers set up at coin shows, and even many shop dealers are willing to negotiate a bit on the price of a coin, the department store employee is limited by not being the owner of the coin. He can't come down on the price that has been set by management.

Another rather unusual place where you are likely to encounter coins for sale is the local flea market. Whether this is a flea market set up Sunday morning at the local high school or drive-in movie theater or a big weekend flea market with hundreds of spaces, you will almost always find some coins for sale. You will also almost always find that the coins for sale are common, low grade and overpriced. The flea market coin dealer is not looking to do business with the knowledgeable coin collector. He is more interested in attracting the noncollector who has heard that coins are a good investment, and might be attracted to the less desirable material on display. Because such a person knows little about actual coin values, he will often pay the vendor's inflated asking price.

Still, the really sharp coin collector does not neglect flea market vendors' stock. Without tipping your hand, you can ask a few questions to determine just how much the seller really knows about coins. Perhaps you will get lucky and cherry pick a scarce variety from among his stock.

A word of warning is also necessary if you find good coins inexpensively priced at a flea market. They may be counterfeit, altered, or stolen. Certain flea markets around the country have the reputation as "thieves' markets." One well-known large flea market in southern

Wisconsin is located about an hour's drive from Chicago. It is a commonly heard phrase that everything stolen in Chicago on Saturday night can be found for sale at that flea market on Sunday morning. Unless you want to risk getting stuck with a bad coin or a "hot" coin, watch out carefully for "bargains" at the flea market. It is unlikely that, if you are ripped off, you will ever again see your money or the guy who sold you the coin.

In my estimation, the best place to buy coins is at a coin show. Every coin show in the country is more of a marketplace than a real show or exhibition. The real reason people go to the show is to spend time on the bourse floor (*bourse* is derived from the French word for purse). While they might also take in the exhibits or educational forum while they are there, the vast majority of the time spent at a coin show is spent buying and selling (Fig. 10-2).

Unless you live in Alaska or the more sparsely populated areas of our Western states, there is probably a coin show within a comfortable distance's drive at least

once a month. Many collectors in the Midwest and especially in the East, can find a good coin show virtually every weekend.

A coin show can be as small as a couple of dozen tables set up in the basement of the VFW Hall and sponsored by your local coin club, to the huge American Numismatic Association's annual convention that has more than 300 dealers set up most years. The attraction of a coin show is the many different coin dealers all set up in the same room and ready to buy and sell. Besides many of the local coin shop operators, you are likely to find dealers from all over the state at a good show. And even some from other parts of the country.

My job spoils me in regards to coin shows. I travel to large and small shows around the nation all year long, attending at least one a month. I have been able to form some idea of what makes a show good for the average collector. Besides the show host exercising some discretion as to who is allowed to hold a table, the biggest asset a show can have is the variety of types of dealers present.

Fig. 10-2. A lot of buying and selling activity takes place in a short time on a coin show bourse floor. Both dealer and collector have the opportunity to transact more business when brought together on a convention floor.

Most established coin clubs, or commercial coin shows (those put on strictly for profit by a professional promoter) are in the enviable position of having sold every available space in their show facility. Most have long waiting lists of dealers who would like to rent space. Therefore, most shows are able to be a bit choosy about whom they grant table space to.

As a member of the board of governors of the Wisconsin state coin group—Numismatists of Wisconsin—and the Central States Numismatic Society, the 13-state regional group which holds the nation's second largest annual coin show, I have sat in at decision-making time when it is determined who will get a table and who will not. Quite often, the deciding factor is what type of merchandise that dealer specializes in. An applicant who deals in ancient coins or world paper money is more likely to get the nod from the bourse selection committee than another dealer who sells U.S. coins. Most show sponsors realize that a wide variety of material on the floor will draw in many more collectors than would be the case if virtually every dealer there were trying to sell the same silver dollars, BU cents, and type coins.

When you go to a coin show of decent size—say 75 tables or more—you can be assured that you will find somebody there who sells what you are in the market to buy.

With so many dealers in one spot, the buyer is in the advantageous position of being able to shop around a bit. It is quite probable that, unless you are looking for a particularly rare or unusual item, more than one dealer will be able to fill your needs. You can then shop for the best price. Don't be in a hurry to buy the first coin you see that is on your want list. The dealer at the next table might have a similar specimen for a lower price. If you find two dealers with the same coin that you need at about the same price, you might be able to get one of them to come down a bit. Nearly every bourse dealer is willing to knock something off his original asking price unless the coin is so popular that he knows he can sell later for the full price.

Because the pace is quick at a coin show, with many dealers trying to generate a week's worth of revenue from a day or two of business, there is not usually time for the dealer to chat with you and expound on the state of the hobby. If you know what you are looking for and in what price range, you should have no trouble spending all of your hobby budget at a coin show. The wide variety of dealers present means you will find coins for whatever level of sophistication to which you have advanced in the hobby. There will be common date Indian cents in a junk box at 50-cents each to great rarities priced in the tens of thousands of dollars (Fig. 10-3). The show is also your

Fig. 10-3. Stacks of stock books means hours of enjoyment for collectors searching the coin show floor for specialty items.

opportunity to look over the merchandise of dealers who are new to you, who have come to the show from a distance, and whose coins will be a change of pace from the stock your local dealer has been carrying for as long as you've been going into his shop.

Another way to do business with coin dealers from a long distance away is by mail order. When you choose your dealer with care, and follow a few simple mail-safety rules, you can learn to buy coins through the mail in complete confidence. Every issue of the coin periodical that you receive will become like your personal coin show. Hundreds of dealers will be offering material for your consideration.

The first decision to make in considering mail-order buying is what publication you will work from. I can recommend any of the Krause Publications line because, in the unlikely event that a disreputable dealer gets an ad in their pages, the publisher is always willing to go to bat for you to get satisfaction if you are victimized. The same is not true of all other numismatic publishers.

The best advice when dealing with a mail-order advertiser is to test him. At Krause Publications, we test nearly every advertiser, at some time or another, by sending in a blind order. Our advertising staff has a list of friends and relatives around the nation that we use to test the advertisers. We send a friend in another state (after all, any dealer probably would be smart enough not to send overgraded coins to Iola, Wisconsin) a list of coins to order from the ad of the dealer we are testing, along with the proper money for the coins, postage etc. The friend orders the coins by paying with his own check and having them sent to his own address. When the coins arrive, our friends do not even open them; they just forward the coins to us to be evaluated to see if they are as good as advertised.

If the coins are not what was claimed, we might ship them back to the friend, with instructions to return them to the dealer, telling him they are overgraded and asking for a refund or replacement. In this way, we can see if a dealer is genuinely interested in treating our readers fairly. If the dealer makes prompt adjustment, he might still not be off the hook. Some crooked dealers will always give a refund when asked, but they make a huge profit on those who don't ask. If we have found a dealer has sent substandard merchandise on a test order, he is likely to receive several more test orders. If they show a pattern that indicates an intention to defraud, that dealer will not be permitted to advertise in the paper. Krause Publications spend thousands of dollars a year on such test orders so that readers can buy with confidence from advertisers.

That still doesn't mean that the collector can go ahead and sink his life's savings into coins by mail without doing his own evaluation. My advice, when you find a dealer's ad in the paper that appeals to you, is to send your own test order. Even if the dealer has ten coins you want to buy, order only one or two. When those coins arrive, you can determine whether or not they meet your personal grading standards and whether they were delivered on a fast-enough basis to suit you.

Slow delivery is perhaps the biggest cause of complaints about mail-order dealers. Too many collectors think their coins should be in the mailbox the day after they send their check. Many do not realize that the dealer will also be testing *them* if it is a first order. No coin dealer I know will send out coins to a mail-order buyer he has never previously dealt with until the check clears. This usually takes 10 days or two weeks. This problem can be avoided by sending a postal money order, cashier's check, or other type of guaranteed payment. Some dealers even take credit cards.

Dealers do not drop everything else when they get your order and rush right out to the post office to ship your coins off to you. There is much recordkeeping to take care of first. The coin must be taken off inventory, packaged, invoiced, and taken to the post office—where it is registered or insured. All of which takes time. Perhaps the dealer has closed his business for the weekend to attend a coin show and left no one behind to process orders. It may even be that it was simply a good week and the dealer is swamped with orders.

While it might seem an inordinately long amount of time, most complaints of late or nondelivery are not acted upon until four to six weeks has elapsed from the time of order. If there is a special reason an order is going to be delayed, we encourage the advertiser to drop the customer a note of explanation.

As a coin collector, you should also be aware that you have certain rights when you order from a mail-order dealer—at least in the Krause Publications. Part of the advertising agreement which each dealer must adhere to as a condition of placing his ads is an explicitly spelled-out return policy. One aspect of that policy says that the buyer has the right to return coins within three days of receipt if the coins have not been removed from the dealer's holder (this is to prevent a buyer from ripping off the dealer by switching coins in the holder and then claiming the dealer sent an overgraded specimen).

The policy also spells out the buyer's right to return a coin at any time if it is discovered that the coin is counterfeit or altered, (again assuming it has not been removed from the original packaging).

Just as the smart dealer always sends out his material to you by registered or insured mail, you must always take care to use one of these when returning coins. That way you can prove the coins were mailed, prove that the dealer received them, or, if they are lost or stolen along the way, reimbursement can be made.

As might be expected, the biggest advantage of shopping for coins by mail is the convenience of being able to do it from your own home. You are also free to "shop" the many different ads at your own pace and compare prices. There will often be photos of better material included so that you can see what you're buying.

Do yourself and every other coin collector a favor when you deal by mail and hold the advertiser to his claims. If he advertises a MS-65 coin and delivers only an MS-60 specimen, send it back and demand a refund or a replacement. Too many collectors are lazy about this or

just don't want to make a fuss. It's your money that has been lost. Even if the dealer is otherwise honest, he may soon realize that he can be careless in his grading if his customers rarely take the time to complain.

Being located in a small central Wisconsin town of 1000 people, I have come to depend rather heavily on mail-order buying for many of my collecting and investing needs. By following all of the preceding rules, I have rarely had a problem.

One of the most sophisticated—and for most collectors, intimidating—ways to buy coins is through auction (Fig. 10-4). Because of the high costs of acquiring material for auctions, cataloging it, presenting it to bidders, and conducting the auction the coins found in large auctions are generally rare or high priced. For such coins, however, the auction is generally felt to be the best way to determine the actual value of a coin. When they be-

Fig. 10-4. Usually conducted in sumptuous hotel suites, the rare coin auction is the top echelon of numismatic dealing. The late George Bennett, famed numismatic auctioneer, recognizes a bid during a session of Bowers and Ruddy Galleries' auction of the Garrett Collection.

come available, such great American rarieties as the 1804 silver dollar and the 1913 Liberty nickel are almost always offered at public auction. The coin market moves so far and so fast that few numismatists can predict the true value of one of these extremely rare and popular coins on any given day.

Only by offering it up to competitive bidding can the seller of a first-rate rarity be assured of getting top dollar. When the finest known example of the rare Colonial American Brasher doubloon gold piece came onto the market in 1980, no one could say with any degree of certainty how much it would sell for. Some knowledgeable observers said $300,000 was about the limit. Others said $1 million was more likely the mark. The coin sold for $700,000 after extremely spirited bidding.

The coin's owner was sure he had obtained the last dollar out of the coin. If he had listened only to those who said the value was in the $300,000 area, he would have sold the coin for too little. He was virtually deluged with prospective purchasers at that price. If the owner had held out for the $1 million that others said the piece would bring, he would still be the coin's owner today.

Similarly, the coin auction affords the collector the chance to buy coins at *his* price. Mind you, I said the chance. It might be that all a collector is willing to pay for a particular coin is not enough. Others might believe the coin is worth more money. In the example of the Brasher doubloon, the buyer at the $700,000 level was assured that he paid the right price for the coin. If it had been offered at a fixed price on the $300,000 recommendation, it is likely the coin would have been sold before he had the chance to bid. If priced firmly at $1 million, the collector would have felt it overpriced and out of his grasp. When bidding competitively, he was able to buy the coin at his price of $700,000. He knew that there was at least one other bidder to whom the coin was worth very nearly that amount. Knowing that somebody else wanted something you bought and was willing to pay nearly as much for it as you were helps assure the buyer that he has made a wise deal.

The mechanics of buying coins at auction are quite simple for the beginning collector, provided he has the money to spend on the material. Because of the costs involved in running a major auction, most lots are arranged so as to have a minimum value of $100, $250, or even more.

Many large coin shows have an auction as part of their activities. Generally, several coin auction houses bid themselves for the right to conduct the auction. In the case of the American Numismatic Association's annual convention, the bidding among auctioneers is fierce, and the ANA has exacted fees in excess of $50,000 for the right to hold an auction. If the auctioneer is willing to pay a $50,000 fee on top of his other auction costs, you can imagine how profitable the auction can be for the auctioneer.

Generally, the auctioneer offers a combination of his own stock (virtually every major numismatic auction house is also a coin dealership, as well) plus consignments from other dealers and collectors. The auctioneer makes his money by charging a fee to the consignor (generally around 15 to 20 percent) and—becoming increasingly common in the United States in the past couple of years—to the buyer who might be asked to pay a 5 or 10 percent "buyer's fee" on each lot purchased.

The coins to be sold are gathered together, graded, grouped in lots, arranged in bidding order, sometimes photographed, and then a catalog is issued. The auction catalog lists and describes each coin in the sale, often with photos, and sometimes even full-color photos of the coins to be sold. At a better auction, no expense is spared in preparing the catalog because an attractive catalog will result in increased bidding and higher prices (Fig. 10-5).

The catalogs are sent to the auctioneer's regular customers and to new customers who have requested it. Usually, collectors who have not been active bidders are asked to pay $5 or $10 for the auction catalog. In this way, the dealer can weed out the curiosity seeker who only wants a copy of the expensive auction catalog, but has no intention of buying anything. Regular bidders will usually be kept on the auctioneer's mailing list for free because they are valued customers.

The auction catalogs are often valuable reference books for the collector. They are usually saved along with the printed prices realized. Most auctioneers offer the prices for $1 or $2 after the sale has been concluded (Fig. 10-6).

After perusing the auction catalog, the collector who wants to bid on any of the coins has two options; he can bid on the floor of the auction, either in person or through a representative, or he can submit a mail bid.

If the auction is being held at a convenient site or at a coin show which the collector is attending, most prefer to be there in person. That way they can alter their bidding strategy right up until the time the auctioneer's hammer knocks down the lot for the final time. When bidding by mail, your options end with your specified bid.

When attending a coin auction in person, you will be registered and given a bidder number. If you have previously done business with the auctioneer and established your credit, you will be able to pick up your lots and be invoiced for them at the close of the sale. If you do not

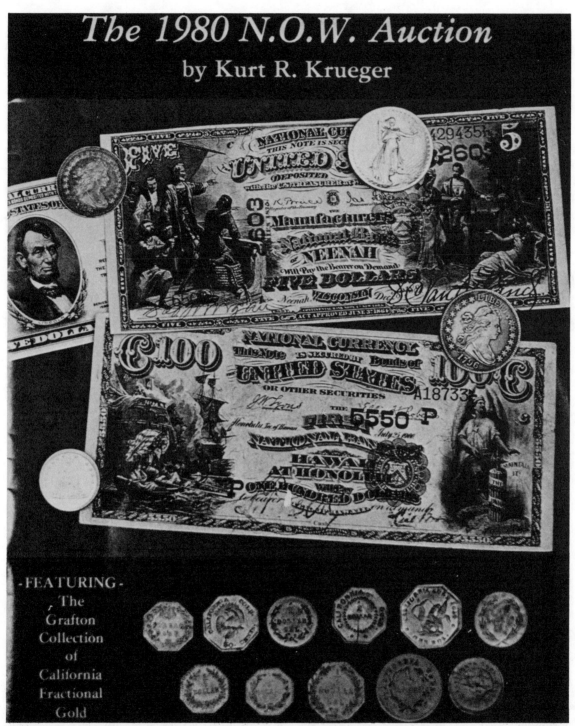

The 1980 N.O.W. Auction
by Kurt R. Krueger

-FEATURING-
The Grafton Collection of California Fractional Gold

Fig. 10-5. The preparation of an expensive and attractive auction catalog helps the auctioneer get top dollar for his consignors' coins—and for his own commission. The catalogs make useful reference works for the collector.

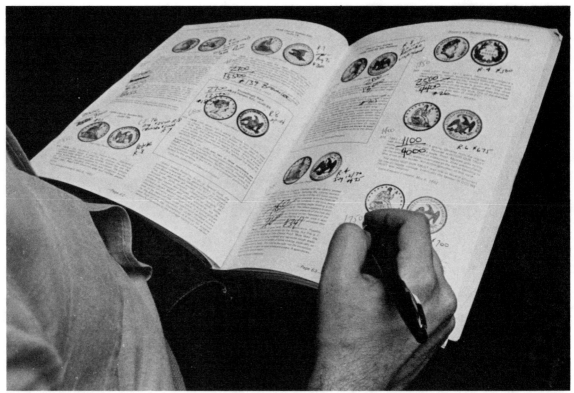

Fig. 10-6. Numismatic auctions are fast and furious. The potential bidder has to be careful or he will miss the coins he is interested in. This person is filling in the sale catalog with prices realized in order to help guide him in future buying decisions

have suitable credit references, you will be expected to pay cash for your material when it is picked up.

Coin auctions proceed at a relatively rapid pace. It is imperative for the in-person bidder to pay attention or he could miss the lot he was interested in or bid on the wrong lot.

There is little or no ear-pulling or winking to signify bids at a coin auction. Most bidders simply hold up their bidder card with their number on it when they want to bid. In that way, the auctioneer can see the number of the eventual buyer and relay it to the bookkeeper sitting at the table in front of the room.

By being there in person, you can make that last price adjustment to your bid if you really want to buy the coin. You will usually have the advantage of seeing the coin in person. Floor bids are considered final. If you are winning bidder you are expected to pay for the lot at the bid price, plus any applicable bidder's charge.

Bidding by mail, you have some of the same protection against overgraded or otherwise misrepresented coins that you would when buying retail by mail order.

This applies particularly to return privilege. If there is ample time before the auction, and if you are a regular customer, many auctioneers will send lots from the sale out to you for your prior inspection. They usually ask that you return the lots within a day or two so that other interested parties can have the same advantage. You are usually expected to pay the charges both ways.

Whether you have seen the coin or only a photo and description in the catalog, you then figure out the highest amount you want to pay for the coin you want. Make sure to include any buyer's charge the auctioneer will impose. You then submit this in writing to the auctioneer (usually) on a special bid sheet provided with the sale catalog. New bidders are expected to furnish appropriate trade and bank references or submit a deposit of 25 percent of their total bids. If you are a successful bidder, your deposit will be used as partial payment of your lots. If you are not the winning bidder, your deposit is returned. The deposit is a form of insurance for the auctioneer that you will actually honor your bids and pay for the material.

Nearly every coin auctioneer today has a policy of

reducing your mail bid, if possible, to secure the lot. It works this way. Say there is a coin in the sale that you want and you have decided that you want to pay a maximum of $200 for it. You make that your mail bid. That bid, along with all other mail bids on that coin, is entered in a bid book prior to the opening of the auction. To determine an opening price at the auction, the auctioneer will usually begin the bidding at a figure 5 or 10 percent over the *second* highest bid. Those attending the auction are then free to place bids.

For example, let's say that the coin on which you bid $200 received a second highest bid of $150. The auctioneer then opened the bidding to the floor at $160, received an opening bid, and—for the sake of argument—another bid of $170. A representative of the auction company, acting on your behalf, would then place a $180 bid for you. If the two floor bidders dropped out, the coin is yours for $180—$20 less than your maximum—and it all would have taken about 10 seconds.

Don't allow yourself to be carried away by this benefit. What if you had decided you really wanted that coin and you put in a $1,000 mail bid. Perhaps another collector felt the same way and put in a $500 bid. Your $200-coin would then cost you about $550.

In the same way, don't get carried away when bidding in person. "Auction fever" is a very real malady and the "cure" can be costly to your pocketbook. Always know exactly how much you want to spend on a coin and never let yourself get carried away by competitiveness or the spirit of the moment. The auctioneer's gavel can be an awful jolt back to reality when you realize you have just paid much more for a coin than you really wanted to spend. By keeping your head, you can make auctions work for the good of your collection. As you advance in the hobby, you will find that more and more of the better material you seek is most often available only at auction.

Chapter 11

Buying from Other Collectors

IN THE EARLY DAYS OF NUMISMATICS, VIRTUALLY all transactions were between collectors. The first coin dealers were actually just collectors who found more success in the business end of the hobby than their peers. Today, very little buying and selling of coins goes on among collectors—although it can be beneficial for both parties—given the wholesale/retail structure of coin pricing. It would seem that the principal reason there is not many monetary transactions among collectors is that the average numismatist's limited circle of coin-collecting friends usually does not have the coins he needs for sale at the time he needs them.

To get back to the financial benefits, it works something like this—at least in theory. If I have a 1952 proof set I want to dispose of, and you happen to need a 1952 proof set, it is likely we can do business. Retail price on this five-coin set is about $200 and the wholesale price is around $160. If I were to walk into the local coin shop and offer him my proof set, the dealer would probably pay me $160 for it. If you walk into the store 10 minutes later and ask to buy such a set, you will pay $200. If it somehow comes to our attentions that you need the proof set I have to sell, we are both likely to do better in the deal, and the local dealer will miss out on a $40 profit.

While I know that full retail value of my set is $200, I am also aware that the most I can expect from a dealer is $160. Therefore, if you want what I have to sell, I am going to make you an attractive offer—say $175. Because I have the coins you want at a price lower than you are likely to find them for elsewhere, you will probably make the deal. I make an extra $15 and you save $25. That's the benefit of collector-to-collector transactions.

The drawback is that unless you had happened to come along needing a 1952 proof set, I might have had to hold those coins for a considerable period while I looked around for a fellow collector to buy them. Conversely, if you had not found out I had the set to sell, you could have spent a lot of time searching for the coins among your other collecting friends without success. That's precisely why there are professional coin dealers in this hobby and that's how they earn their profits.

The biggest single factor that mitigates against buying your coins from other collectors is that there is no economical way to bring buyer and seller together. While the *Numismatic News* started out as just such a medium, it is now rare to see an advertisement from one collector looking to sell his coins to another collector. Similarly, *Coin World* used to have a very healthy trade section where collectors could do business, but that has degenerated over the years to a series of ads that all seem to have been placed by someone looking to make an unusually good deal at the expense of another collector.

There have been some attempts in recent years to begin new coin "shopper" papers, geared to the individual collectors, but they have all (to my knowledge) failed because of limited circulation and the high cost of distributing such a publication. Another problem was that with no experience or limited experience in numismatic publishing, few of these papers had the expertise to recognize the rip-off artists or to settle complaints that arose against their advertisers.

Just as dealing with a new coin dealer through the mail requires caution, so does dealing with a fellow collector. It is even harder to establish suitable references for another collector than for a dealer who is likely to belong to one or more reputable trade organizations.

Your best bet in trying to buy coins from other collectors is to keep your sights set fairly locally. Join one or more of the coin clubs in your area and get to know the members. You will soon see that most of them have at least some aspirations of being coin dealers, if only of the "vest pocket" variety. Nearly everybody who comes to the Tuesday-evening, coin-club meeting brings a little stock book of coins for sale. You have the benefit of knowing who you are doing business with and being able to personally examine the coins you might want to purchase.

You will also be free to haggle a bit about the price. Because the wholesale/retail price of most U.S. coins and related numismatic items is easily available through the "Coin Market" or the Blue Book, you will have a starting figure on which to base your offer. Even if there are also several full-time dealers at the meeting, you will be at an advantage because you can afford to pay more for a coin for your own collection than they can afford to pay for it to keep in stock.

Chapter 12

Selling Your Coins

IT IS REALLY NEVER TOO SOON TO LEARN THE basics of disposing of your material for the best possible price. You will probably find, as you progress in numismatics, that you have surplus coins that you no longer want in your collection because your interests have changed, you have obtained higher-quality specimens, or you have been lucky and made some good finds.

The most common way to sell your coins is to let them go to a full-time dealer. While you will not realize full retail value for your coins, you usually will have the advantages of being able to make a quick, clean sale. Many new numismatists do not understand why they cannot sell their coins for retail value when disposing of them to a dealer. After all, they paid full retail when they bought them. The reason is that the coin dealer is in the business of buying and selling coins to make a profit.

If the current "coin market" selling price on a particular coin is $100, he cannot afford to buy that same coin for $100 because when he turns it over to another customer he will only be able to ask $100 for it. More likely, he will only be able to offer you $60 to $80 for the coin. Much depends on how popular the particular piece is in the current market and how long he anticipates he will have to hold it in stock before making a sale.

It is only in extremely unusual circumstances that you will be able to get a dealer to pay retail price for a coin he buys from you. It can happen. For instance, if a dealer has good reason to believe that a certain coin or series of coins is going to begin a sharp and steep upward price movement in the very near future, he might well be willing to gamble on his instincts and experience and begin buying those coins at retail price with the expectation that he will be able to sell them in a few days or a few weeks for a price well in excess of the currently quoted retail valuation.

When selling your coins to a dealer, rather than buying from one, you don't have to be as careful about his reputation. After all, you are only looking to get the best price for your coins that you can. Nevertheless, it has been my experience that the same reputable dealers from whom you buy your coins are also generally the best market for them when the time comes to sell. For one thing, they know that the coins you are selling are of good quality and that you have not tampered with them. The dealer from whom you buy also has a stake in making you happy when you sell so that you remain a good customer.

If for no other reason, you might consider offering the coins you want to the dealer from whom they were purchased as a test of his ethics. You'd be surprised at how many collectors do business for years with a coin dealer, who they think is entirely reputable, only to find out his true colors when the time comes to sell.

It usually happens like this: You buy a nice collection of high grade MS-65 U.S. commemorative half-dollars over the course of many years from a particular dealer, always paying full retail for them. Then when the time comes to sell your coins, you offer them to the same dealer. Rather than advancing an offer to you of current wholesale prices for your coins, he tells you that these coins aren't MS-65 quality at all. He says that they are only MS-60 and, as such, he has little use for them at your price. Even if the dealer is told that these very same coins were purchased from him as MS-65s, the dishonest dealer will try to weasel out of it by saying that grading standards have changed or that he cannot use your coins. This is an expensive lesson for the collector to learn. It is a lesson that can be avoided by carefully choosing from among the dealers.

You can sometimes get a clue to this type of dealer's true identity by looking at his ads in the coin papers. If a dealer consistently offers to buy only MS-60 quality coins, at MS-60 prices, but consistently is selling only MS-65 quality coins at MS-65 prices, you can see that something is wrong. He is obviously trying to pass off the MS-60 coins he buys as MS-65 specimens. That is to the detriment of every collector who buys the reputed MS-65s.

If you have found a legitimate coin dealer to buy from, you will usually be offered a fair price for the same coins when you want to sell them because it is merchandise he knows he can sell again.

Getting the best price for the coins you sell comes down to finding the dealer who has the best resale market. If you have commemorative half-dollars for sale, you would logically offer them to a dealer or dealers specializing in the commemorative series. Their regular customers will snap up the coins he has bought from you and the dealer knows he will not have to hold the coins for a long time or pay a great deal of money to advertise them.

If you can make a deal at your local coin shop, you will save the expense of having to mail your coins to an out-of-town dealer, or maybe even several of them, for their inspections and offers. One fellow in our office has found that the Main Street coin shop in a nearby town is the very best outlet for his current-year proof and mint sets. Because that coin shop has a good volume of demand for these sets from walk-in trade, the owner is always willing to pay 50 cents or $1 more per set than the mail-order buyers in the coin papers. If you have a small quantity of "junk" silver U.S. coins that you have found in circulation, or with your metal detector, or some common date material that is the average coin shop's stock in trade, it is a good place to start looking for an offer when the time comes to sell.

Many retail shops offer a *bid board* to offer coins to fellow collectors who patronize the shop. Bid boards are usually run on a weekly basis. They consist of a large board hung prominently in the shop with coins for sale that are securely fastened. There is usually an index card nearby on which registered bidders write their bids for the coin and their bidder number.

At a specified time, the highest bid written for each coin is announced and the winner buys the coin. Things can get quite exciting around the bid board as the last minute approaches and collectors try to get that last, highest bid in to buy the coin they want. The shop owner generally collects a 10 to 20 percent commission for running the board.

If the dealer doesn't have a bid board, he might agree to take your coins on consignment. In this way, he doesn't have his own money tied up in the coins while he waits for a buyer. The dealer will often accept your coins on consignment at a figure that you give him. You tell him you want a certain price for your coin and he adds a markup for his profit. When the coin sells, you get your money.

With bid boards and consigning coins to a dealer, you should have a firm, written understanding of who is responsible for your coins if they are stolen or lost. Generally, the dealer accepts this responsibility because he is likely to have some types of insurance or he considers it part of the overhead for which he is taking a commission on the sale of your coins.

Even if the type of coin you have to sell is not what the local dealer normally stocks, you can ask him if he will run a Teletype message for the piece. In this case, a dealer might send out a message like the following to the several hundred other dealers on the circuit: "Have a customer with a full, uncirculated Indian cent set. Who can use at bid? Answer direct." In this way, if you hang around the shop for a half-hour or so, the dealer might receive an offer to buy your coins. He will then figure out what kind of profit he needs on the deal, subtract it from the other dealer's bid, and present it to you. In this way, he is not tied up with your coins in his inventory with little likelihood of selling them quickly. And he will have made a nice profit on the transaction by acting as the middleman.

You can see from these examples that it pays to have a good relationship with your local coin shop dealers. There are many ways they can help you when the time comes to sell.

You are far less likely to have good luck selling your coins to a department store coin counter or to a more general hobby shop. They almost always buy their coins for stock in prepackaged deals set up by their store's management or by hobby supply houses. They have little, if any, expertise in buying coins, and might not even have the authority to make any kind of offer for your material.

Whatever you do when selling your coins, don't be lured into one of the fly-by-night, motel-based buying outfits that regularly come to most towns. You have surely seen their ads; Generally, they are full-page extravaganzas in the local newspaper offering what they claim to be "top dollar" for your coins, gold, and jewelry. You can get some hint of what type of business they really operate by looking at the fine print in the ad. They generally offer to buy everything from coins and stamps to guns, collector plates and even dental plates—if the price is right (and that means low). While most of these motel-based buyers make a good show of advertising their prices, the prices they advertise are woefully low in comparison to true market value—and wholesale at that.

Such operations generally are looking to buy your coins at about 20 to 25 percent of their retail value. They can then turn around and sell them to a reputable dealer for a fair wholesale price and still double their money. Obviously, they know they will not be doing much buying from informed collectors. Rather, they are generally hoping to attract the noncollectors among the general public. Such noncollectors will have no real idea of what their coins are worth and they are likely to be pleased with the offer made.

Their "prey" is the proverbial little old lady in tennis shoes who might be selling her lifetime accumulation of souvenir and keepsake coins without any idea of their worth. It is not uncommon for some of these transient buyers to use scare tactics to obtain a person's coins. One favorite ploy, when a seller comes in with some gold coins, is to tell them that it is illegal for U.S. citizens to own gold; but they will be glad to save the seller the risk of arrest by giving them face value—or even less—for the gold pieces.

You wouldn't have to get away with that one too often to retire comfortably. These days a common $20 gold piece sells for $450 or more. While it was illegal for Americans to own nonnumismatic gold coins from 1933-1974, there are absolutely no such restrictions on private gold ownership by U.S. citizens today—in any form.

Because motel-based buyers are not very demanding about proof of ownership, it is easy to speculate that they might also be willing buyers of stolen coins (if the price is right).

One last word of advice, if you are a little old lady in tennis shoes, or even a coin thief—don't take a check from a buyer who sets up in a motel room for the weekend. A much better place to sell your coins is at the coin show. There you have the same advantage of a lot of dealers under one roof. Here you can take your for-sale material around to different dealers and get their offers. By shopping around a bit, you should be able to get the best available price for your piece on that particular day.

Don't be afraid to shop around for your price. If you offer a coin to a dealer, get his price and then say you want to ask around a bit more. You might encounter a testy dealer who will say something like: That's a take it or leave it price; if you don't sell now the deal is off. Words like that are a clue that it's best for you to "leave" the price. If a dealer offers you a fair price for your coin, he knows you are unlikely to do better elsewhere on the floor. If he has low-balled you, trying to "steal" your piece for a bargain bid, he might well be afraid that you'll find any number of more reasonable buyers from among his colleagues. Always remember, whether buying or selling, that no legitimate coin dealer objects to fair competition. Those that do express such objection usually have something to hide.

The key to successful selling at a coin show is to know your potential buyer. Examine the various dealers on the floor and see what type of merchandise they offer for sale. If it looks like they specialize in the type of material you have to sell, they might well be a willing buyer. A coin dealer who has a reputation among his customers and fellow dealers as a knowledgeable specialist in a particular area will often have a hard time keeping that material in stock and is usually on the lookout for it.

When selling at a coin show, you might be offered cash for your coins or a dealer's check. In almost all cases, it is safe to take a dealer's check at a show. Generally, he has been checked out by the show sponsors and is well known among the other dealers at the show. There is little risk of taking a bad check in such circumstances.

Another potential outlet for the coins you want to dispose of is the mail-order dealer. Looking through the pages of any coin paper, you will find dozens of ads from dealers offering to buy coins. The best dealers to sell to are those from whom you have bought in the past; look up their ads first. Many of the buy ads will advertise for specific coins such as uncirculated silver dollars or early proof sets. If you have the coins these dealers are looking to buy, you will very likely get your best price there. Other ads just state they are interested in buying all types of coins and numismatic material. I suggest responding to this type of ad only if there are none looking more closely for what you have. The all purpose buyer might be trying too hard to get a bargain price.

Some mail-order buyers will ask you to ship your coins with an invoice and your asking price. Others will ask you to ship your coins for their offer. Still others want you to write first with a list of what you want to sell. In all cases, follow the dealer's instructions or you might just be wasting your time and postage.

If you are setting the asking price on your coins, be realistic but also be fair to yourself. There is nothing wrong with asking the current wholesale value for your material. You probably shouldn't try to get much more than that unless you know the dealer has a specific need for exactly what you are trying to sell.

Usually, when selling your coins by mail, you are responsible for the postage and insurance. Always insure or register your coins when sending them to a dealer for an offer. The dealer is responsible for returning them the same way if no deal is struck. If the buyer has asked you to put a price on your material, he might do one of several things. First, if you are lucky, he will accept your deal and fire off a check to you for the full amount. He might decide he wants only part of your coins, send you a check for those, and return the rest. Or he might respond to your offer with a counteroffer. For this reason, it is always a good idea to include your phone number when sending coins off for sale.

The cost of postage and the time involved in selling coins by mail sometimes deters collectors from going this route. If you live in an area with no coin shops or access to coin shows, selling by mail might be your best alternative.

Remember that some papers and magazines are not as strict as others. Not all publications have been cleared of buyers who are trying to conduct their purchases in a less than legitimate manner.

Another outlet for your material, provided it is of sufficient rarity and dollar value, is to go the auction route. Generally, you should consider this only if your coins are valued in excess of $100 or more apiece and if the total consignment of material is valued at $1,000 or more. Because of the high cost of record keeping involving consignors, most auction houses do not want to accept small consignments.

If the coins you want to sell are of this high caliber, your next step is to get brochures from each of the major auction houses. Each of the coin auctioneers that conduct regular sales have impressive brochures printed up telling you why you should choose them to sell your coins. I think I can help you narrow the choice down a bit.

Virtually all of the top half dozen or so auction firms appeal to the same clientele. They schedule their auctions in conjunction with a reputable coin show or to stand on their own. Each prepares essentially the same type of eye-appealing sale catalog so you can probably get right to the bottom line—which is where you want to be in the first place.

How much commission is the auction firm going to charge you? The actual bid price you will receive for your coins is dependent far more on the condition of the coin market on the day of the auction than on any skill the auction house musters in terms of cataloging your coins. If you deal with any of the top firms—each of which advertise regularly in the pages of the trade papers—your actual dollar return is more dependent on how much the auctioneer skims off the top. Depending on the value of your coins, you will find commissions ranging from under 5 percent to 20 percent or more. Nearly all of the auctioneers prominently spell out their commission schedule in their brochures.

A related consideration is an advance on the sale. If you are in need of some fast cash, most of the auction houses will offer you a cash advance against the proceeds of your coins' eventual sale. This is always a negotiable item. If it is a consideration in the sale of your coins, you should definitely shop around for the most liberal advance.

You will probably also be interested in a relatively fast sale of your coins. Always inquire of the auctioneer when their next upcoming big sale is scheduled. If they have no definite plans for an auction in the coming months, you might want to look for a firm that is actively seeking consignments for its next event.

Another factor of no small import and no small controversy is the practice of protecting your material. While no coin auctioneer likes to talk about this practice to anybody but his consignors, it is an established part of the American numismatic auction scene that consignors often buy back their own material if the legitimate bids do not reach a certain agreed upon price. In this way, the seller can be protected against a market abberation, causing him to lose money on his coins, or against a conspiracy by others to obtain his coins at a low price by collusion.

While you might agree that such practices as secret buy backs are unfair to honest potential purchasers, as a consignor you have an undisputed right to receive a figure for your coins that is at least fair. You should be ready to pay for that "insurance." When considering consigning your coins, make a point to discuss with the auctioneer his policy on bidding back your own material. Some houses will charge you a greatly reduced commission on material that doesn't sell and which you are forced to buy back through a bid of your own. Usually a bid is placed on the "book" so that the other bidders on the floor don't know who actually bought the item.

Some auctioneers will even let you buy back your material at no charge if you are a consignor of significant importance. One or two firms do not allow buy backs. If you want to protect your material, you are asked to set a reasonable minimum bid on it. The minimum bid is then publicly displayed in the auction catalog. This is the fairest way for potential buyers who can see that a particular item will not be sold for less than the specified figure.

Still other auctioneers will allow you to buy back your material only at the full commission rate.

When selling your coins at auction, you should also be aware that it could be 30 to 60 days, or even longer, after the sale before you receive final settlement for your coins. Because large numbers of coins sold at auction go to coin dealers who are invoiced for their lots and given 30 days to pay, and because there might be some disputes over payments with mail bidders who refuse to honor their bids, the auction houses are generally not willing to settle in advance of the time they receive their full payment for the lots.

There are special elements that come into play when you decide to make a final sale of your entire collection. The following advice should be heeded whether or not you intend to keep your coins until the day you die. Your survivors should know how to properly dispose of your collection to maximize the dollar return.

Many of the same considerations of selling single coins are involved when selling an entire collection. The cardinal rule is that unless you have the time and knowledge to carefully break up the collection and sell it in pieces to different dealers for top dollar, you should always sell it intact. In other words, don't let the first dealer to whom you offer the collection cherry pick the best material and leave you with less desirable coins that cannot be easily sold for a good price.

One of the best places to sell your collection is to one of the dealers who helped you build it. If you are talking about a sizeable collection or a lifelong effort, it is very likely that the sheer dollar value of the holding will limit the number of qualified buyers.

If your collection is someday in this category, you might do well to sell by auction, but only if the auctioneer is willing to take the entire collection. He can offer the better coins or sets as individual lots and group the less-valuable material together into lots of suitable size to meet his cataloging needs.

If you don't want to invest the time in an auction or don't want the publicity, there are a number of large dealers who make a specialty of buying entire collections and then parting them out to other dealers, investment clients, or collectors. Many of these dealers advertise in the coin papers, and might indicate: We travel to buy large collections. After assuring yourself of the dealer's reputation, your first step is to call or write the dealer and give him an idea of what you have to sell and an estimate of its total value.

If the dealer feels you are serious about selling, he might well travel across the country to meet with you, view the coins, and make an offer. If you can strike a good deal, this is a safe, fast and quiet way to dispose of your collection. Be sure to sell it all and not just the fast-moving items.

If it is your intention to keep your coins until death, be fair to your family and leave specific instructions for the disposal of your collection. Have your lawyer write your instructions into your will. Name a trusted friend or dealer to act as advisor for the sale. You could even name the specific dealer or auction house to which the coins should be offered, along with an idea of current value. Naturally, this requires you to keep your will updated, but it insures that your heirs will reap the greatest possible benefit from your coins.

Another method of disposal is to give your coins away, as a tax write-off, to a qualified charity or numismatic organization.

Depending on your tax bracket at the time of donation and the value which a qualified appraiser places on your gift, you can reap significant tax advantages. If you consider the capital gains taxes which you might be liable to at the time you sell your collection, assuming that it has increased greatly in value over the years, you might well find it almost as advantageous to make a gift of your collection as to sell it outright. If you find yourself in such a situation, you should seek the aid of a qualified tax accountant or attorney in insuring that you reap maximum return on your donation.

A great number of numismatists who make gifts of their collections to such educational groups as the American Numismatic Association or the American Numismatic Society, or who donate their collections to a city or university library, do so more to keep their life's work intact rather than see a collection that took so long to assemble disposed of piecemeal.

You should be aware that your numismatic endeavors might cause you to incur some tax liability even though you conduct your affairs strictly as a hobbyist. This principally occurs in the area of capital gains (or capital losses) on coins you buy and sell through the years. Consult a tax advisor.

Whether you decide to report the (sometimes significant) profits from the sale of coins is your own business. Many collectors do not. A large percentage of the coin business is conducted on a cash basis; no receipts are asked for or given. This makes it impossible for the government to get its cut of your profits, but that is a strong appeal for a great number of collector/investors who see the underground nature of some of their numismatic transactions as a fringe benefit that most of the more traditional investments mediums do not offer.

Chapter 13

U.S. Coins

T HE GENERAL TERM AMERICAN COLONIAL COIN-age covers a wide range of coins, pseudocoins, and tokens issued in America and abroad in the period roughly from 1616 to 1820. Their single common denominator is that they were all used—or at least intended to be used—as money in the American Colonies in the days prior to, and immediately following, the American Revolution.

The lack of an exchange medium was one of the early Colonists many problems. To increase their dependence on the mother countries and to insure that the balance of trade remained favorable to the folks in Europe, virtually every Colonial power at the time forbade the Colonists from producing their own coinage.

In the face of chronic coin shortages that often threatened to strangle commerce, the Colonies almost universally ignored these orders and either gave active cooperation to, or at least turned a blind eye toward, the many private coining ventures. At least until the late 1780s, when independence had been achieved and the Colonies were close to forming a federal constitution, all of the "Colonial" coins were privately issued.

The incentive for private enterprise to undertake the production of coinage was simple. By keeping their cost of metal content and production below the "face"

value of the coin, and then selling or spending the coin substitutes at par value, they made a small profit on each coin struck. As long as the coins were close in intrinsic value to their stated value, the coin-starved Colonists were eager to accept them.

It should be noted, however, that in a vast majority of the cases this was copper coinage. The public was much more demanding about full intrinsic value for a gold or silver coin in the days when even a small silver coin represented a day's wages for the average man.

The first coins struck for the American Colonies were actually not for the mainland colonies that came to be part of the United States. Nevertheless, they are actively collected as part of the series. These were the Sommer Islands "hog money" of 1616, circulated in Bermuda in denominations from 2d (d is the British abbreviation for "cent" from the Roman coin, denarius. It is still used today in America for sizing nails, as in 10d) to shilling (12d, the British monetary system was based on 12 pence to the shilling and 20 shillings to the pound). The coins pictured a sailing ship on one side and a wild boar, native to Bermuda at the time, on the other. Very rare and popular, the prices range from about $1,500 for a well worn good-condition piece to more than $10,000 for a high-grade circulated coin.

Fig. 13-1. This Pine Tree shilling of seventeenth century Massachusetts was once carried as a "witch piece." The flat areas across the coin show where it was straightened after having been bent to ward off spells in the days of the infamous Salem witch hunts.

As is the case with virtually all American Colonial coins, the beginning collector should be aware that these coins have been extensively counterfeited and reproduced from the time they originally circulated right up to today. A collector contemplating the purchase of any American Colonial coin should insist on authentication papers for the item.

The first coinage in the mainland Colonies (other than the Spanish colonies in Mexico, which had coinage from the Mexico City Mint as early as 1535), was in Massachusetts, in 1652, when struck silver planchets replaced waupum beads as legal tender in the Massachusetts Bay Colony. The first coins were simply round silver discs with the initials NE and a Roman numeral denomination stamped in the corner. Finding that these were too easily counterfeited, the coiner soon replaced them with coinage depicting willow, oak, and pine trees.

The collector will soon discover that many of these Massachusetts coins are found bent in the middle or bent and later straightened. This represents an interesting souvenir of the famous days of Salem witchcraft (Fig. 13-1). A bent silver coin, carried in the pocket or worn around the neck, was believed to protect the owner from a witch's spell.

Maryland and New Jersey both had semiofficial coinage struck in England for use here. The New Jersey pieces are unusual in that they have two depictions of St. Patrick, front and back.

Another class of imported coinage in the Colonies were tokens struck under Royal Patent for such colonies as Virginia, or designed to pass current in all of the British colonies. These tokens, usually in denominations of halfpence and one penny, had portraits of the King (George I, George II or George III) on the obverse and differing designs on reverse. One popular type features a rose on the reverse and the legend "Rosa Americana Utile Dulci" which translates to America Rose—Useful and Pleasant (Fig. 13-2).

Among the more scarce Colonial coinages were the tokens struck in America or in England, at the order of specific merchants, for use in trade. Two of the most popular examples are the Elephant tokens circulated in the Carolinas and New England, and the Granby coppers

Fig. 13-2. The Rosa America half-penny is an example of private coinage struck under British monarchial authority to be circulated in the American Colonies, circa 1722.

of Connecticut. The Elephant tokens date to 1694 and they carry legends on the back such as "God Preserve Carolina and the Lords Proprietors." This legend was a holdover from similar tokens struck in London 30 years earlier during a time of plague.

The Granby coppers, named for the town where Dr. Joseph Higley had his copper mine that supplied the metal for these coins, were sized to correspond to the British threepence. They carried designs such as a deer, broadaxe and hammers, and legends like: "I Am Good Cooper—Value Me As You Please." The several different obverse and reverse designs make the series challenging to collectors—as do price tags that start about $5,000.

Besides the British colonial coins, American collectors generally consider several series of coins struck in France (for their colonies of the New World) to be collectible as part of the American Colonial coinage. These copper and silver pieces were produced between 1670 and 1770. They circulated from Newfoundland to Louisiana and in the French West Indies.

While the Colonial Period can be accurately said to have ended with the achievement of independence, collectors generally include state-authorized coinage issues of 1776-1788. Among the coins struck under authority of the sovereign states in the days before there was a true United States coinage, were issues from New Hampshire, as early as 1776, Massachusetts, Connecticut (the most prolific), New York, New Jersey, and Vermont.

Although many of these early state coins can be purchased for $25-$100 in nice collectible condition, others range much higher in price. An example is the famous Brasher doubloons struck by George Washington's New York City neighbor, Ephraim Brasher, as a trial coinage. While the doubloons had a value of about $16 when they were minted in 1787, they have sold in the last couple of years at prices well in excess of the

Fig. 13-4. A popular series collected alongside colonial coins are the many Washington copper medals struck in cent size to circulate as monetary tokens. These pieces represented the first president's popularity at the time and their collectibility today is undiminished.

$500,000 mark. They represent the most valuable American coinage issue (Fig. 13-3).

Circulating right along with the states coinage, and for several decades after, were privately issued tokens from all over the new United States. The most interesting of these are the lengthy series of coppers picturing George Washington, dating from roughly 1783-1795 (Fig. 13-4). Many of the portraits were faithful renderings of the nation's first president. The series quickly became popular with the American public, and it remains so today.

EARLY FEDERAL COINAGE

Traditionally collected as part of the American Colonial coinage, but more accurately classed as pattern or trial coins for proposed Federal issues, was a series of copper and silver pieces in several basic types. Only the Nova Constellatio coppers are available at prices under $100 in collectible grade. Only the popular and oft-reproduced Continental dollar can be bought in decent condition for under about a thousand dollars.

The Continental dollar was significant in that it was the first silver dollar proposed for America. Never struck in quantities more than minimally required to test dies and provide samples for legislators, the 1776 date on the coin has made it popular with collectors ever since (Fig. 13-5). The Continental dollar is also the most frequently reproduced of the Colonial coin series. It was replicated

Fig. 13-3. The king of American Colonial coins is this Brasher doubloon. The gold piece was struck by George Washington's New York City neighbor in 1787. It recently sold for more than $500,000.

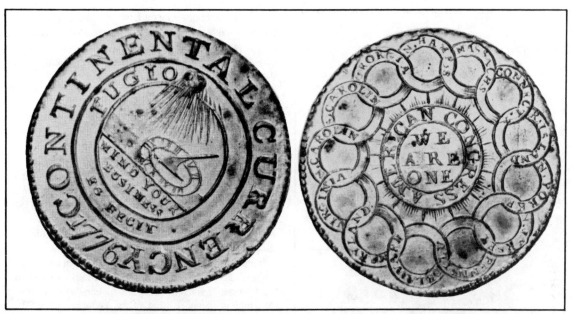

Fig. 13-5. The 1776 Continental dollar was America's first silver dollar coin even though it was never officially adopted. It is also the most often reproduced early American coin.

in quantity as early as 1876 during the U.S. Centennial Exposition in Philadelphia. Naturally, the Bicentennial celebration of 1976 was cause for even further reproduction of the piece. Modern replicas can usually be detected by the grainy, soft image that is the result of having been made of a casting of an original coin.

The least expensive of the early Federal coinage is the Nova Constellatio copper series. The name means New Constellation and refers to the stars representing each of the states that appear as part of the coin's design (as on early American flags). Bearing dates of 1783 and 1785, the coins also carry the initials U.S., an all-seeing eye as a symbol of the favor of deity upon the new nation, and the Latin words for liberty and justice. It is thought that these coins were produced in England and imported for use in the United States, as a private venture, by Gouverneur Morris who was assistant financier of the federal government under the Articles of Confederation.

Several types of proposed copper coinage were presented in the 1780s. There were patterns for a silver coinage using the Nova Constellatio design, denominations for Morris' proposed decimal coinage system of 100 copper units to a silver "Bit," and other silver pieces of a "Quint," 5 bits and "Mark," 10 bits.

AMERICAN TERRITORIAL COINAGE

Analogous in many ways to the American Colonial coin-

age, but separated by most of the American continent and half a century, were the diverse coins and ingots that make up what is collected today under the banner of "territorial and pioneer gold pieces." As the name suggests, these pieces date to the pioneer days and generally eminated from the American West. It should be noted that some of the material collected under this banner is actually from the goldfield areas of North Carolina and Georgia (dating to 1830).

These private issue gold pieces are lineal descendents of the famous Brasher doubloon of the earlier period. Such terms as "pioneer" and "territorial" gold refer to coins struck outside of the U.S. Mint. Naturally, no territory—or state for that matter—had the authority to strike coinage. These terms simply help catalog the wide array of coins of different dates, designs, sizes, gold purity, shapes and intrinsic value that circulated or were intended to circulate as emergency coinage in isolated areas of the country in the days before branch mints were established to officially coin the gold discoveries. Such private gold pieces were minted and circulated by bankers, assayers, and individuals (Fig. 13-6).

For the average collector, these rare gold relics are more a matter of historical interest than serious contemplation for ownership. Most sell for prices beginning at $1,000 and many are never sold at prices beneath five figures. Nevertheless, they are an interesting part of the

Fig. 13-6. During the California Gold Rush, everybody from private mining firms and bankers to the U.S. Assay Office in San Francisco produced unofficial gold coins.

Denominations ranged from tiny fractional coins of 25 cents and 50 cents to huge octagonal gold "slugs" with a face value of $50. Collectors should be aware of the existence of many fake California fractional gold pieces struck in brass and perhaps gold plated. The easiest way to avoid these souvenirs is to remember that genuine California fractional gold coins, of the 1850s all have the denomination "CENTS, DOLLAR," or abbreviations of them on the reverse. The modern replicas do not (Fig. 13-7).

The pioneer gold pieces generally followed the accepted U.S. coinage designs of the era. They bear on obverse a portrait of Miss Liberty and on the reverse they usually depicted an eagle. The legends and inscriptions on the coins generally name the actual issuer of the coin and the territory of issue. The most popular of the territorial gold pieces depart from these established design themes using such devices as a cowboy on horseback with lariat (Baldwin & Co., San Francisco, 1850), a beaver on a log (Oregon Exchange Co., 1849), lions and bee hives (Mormon issues of Salt Lake City, 1860) and even Pike's Peak (Clark, Gruber & Co., Colorado) (Fig. 13-8).

The most popular denominations and sizes of the pioneer gold pieces corresponded to regularly issued

Fig. 13-7. To provide "small change" during the Gold Rush years when coined money was short, private minters produced tiny gold coins in denominations of 25-cents through $1. Genuine California fractional gold pieces (top) features a stated denomination in cents or dollars. Most modern reproductions carry a fractional value, but no stated denomination.

nation's coinage history. Just as in the case of the colonial series, pioneer gold coinage has been heavily reproduced. Usually it is in brass or another base metal rather than gold. The collector who buys such a piece without authentication by experts is taking a very big risk.

The producers of private gold coins followed the gold strikes in this country from Georgia and North Carolina in 1830-1832, to California in 1849, and even into Alaska and the Yukon at the turn of the century. Because the use of gold dust or nuggets as currency was subject to many frauds and much inconvenience, miners were willing to pay minters a commission to strike their ore and dust into coins of uniform size and with a stated value thereon. The coins were almost uniformly struck of short-weight gold in comparison to the 90 percent pure gold content of U.S. Mint-produced gold pieces of the era. But they were all that was available at the time and were readily acceptable.

Fig. 13-8. Territorial gold pieces were minted all over the American West: from Colorado (top), Utah (center), to California (bottom).

U.S. gold coins: $2.50, $5, $10 and $20. A radical departure from that are the stamped ingots of early California. They have such "face" values as $9.43 and $14.25 (Fig. 13-9).

Prices in excess of $250,000 have been realized from the sale of these coins in the collector's market. This reflects their extreme rarity. Most of the pioneer gold coins were remelted when the U.S. Mints at Charlotte, N.C., Dahlonega, Ga., and, especially, San Francisco, began operations. The crude and intrinsically less valuable private issue gold pieces could not compete with the government coins. As the government mints became established, the privately issued coins were welcomed right along with raw gold dust and newly mined nuggets to be converted into shiny new U.S. coins. In most cases, the goverment took a smaller percentage for its assaying and minting costs than had their predecessors. The days of private-issue gold pieces were over.

PATTERNS OF 1792

The first serious consideration of a coinage issue for the United States was undertaken by the House of Representatives in 1792. Congress authorized the preparation of sample coinage in denominations of cent, half disme (pronounced "dime") and disme.

It was proposed that the portrait of George Washington be placed on these coins, as it had on numerous circulating tokens of the previous decade, but Washington himself is said to have expressed the opinion that the use of the President's portrait on coinage was a monarchical practice too closely linked with England, which placed the picture of the King on all coins (Fig. 13-10).

The legislators favored a design "emblematic of Liberty," in the form of a female figure. Two different type of cents were proposed. One was a novel approach to the problem of the large size of the cent in that day. Because people demanded near full intrinsic value in their coins, the copper cent was quite large; it was the size of the current U.S. half-dollar. Consequently, they were heavy and they tended to cause excessive wear on pockets and purses. The proposed alternative called for a smaller diameter copper piece to have an inner center plug of silver that brought the face value of the whole to one cent.

Because problems were forseen with such things as the silver center falling out or being replaced with a base metal plug by the unscrupulous, the idea was abandoned. The figure of Liberty used on the silver center cent is closer to the originally adopted design than the more attractive portrait on the larger 1792 coin.

The 1792 pattern half disme and disme were produced in both silver and copper versions. It is said in coin-collecting circles that George Washington donated his personal tea service to provide the metal to strike these pattern coins. It is also said that the portrait of

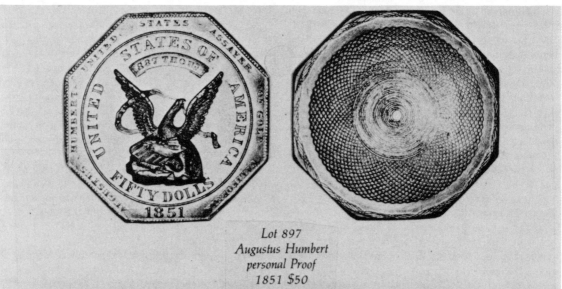

Lot 897
Augustus Humbert
personal Proof
1851 $50

Fig. 13-9. Besides denominations like those of official U.S. coins, the pioneer gold series includes such unusual specimens as the gold ingots of odd value, such as $14.25, and the big gold $50 "slugs."

Fig. 13-10. It is said George Washington took an active hand in the production of the country's first official coinage and the 1792 patterns that preceeded it. The back of the 1971 U.S. Assay Commission medal depicts a scene of Washington supervising the first striking on a hand press.

current, or with coin collectors. Although they are extremely scarce in terms of surviving specimens from already small mintages, they do not command prices as high as their one-cent counterparts.

From the troubles encountered with the cent design, it is evident that it was the first denomination produced (the half-cent coming later). The first 1793 cent is a

Fig. 13-11. It is said that Martha Washington was the model for the 1792 pattern disme and half disme (pronounced dime).

Liberty on the half disme is actually modeled after Martha Washington (Fig. 13-11). Both of these denominations used the design of an eagle on the reverse.

In addition to these somewhat official pattern coinages, there exists a pattern, in copper and white metal versions, for a 1792 quarter-dollar. A female portrait of Liberty on obverse and an eagle on reverse are used. Because of the disimilarity of its design to the other coins in the 1792 group, it is unknown whether the piece was being seriously considered or was merely a timely private proposal. All of the 1792 patterns are extremely rare and valuable.

18TH CENTURY COPPER COINS

Following the experimental pattern coinage of 1792, the government of the United States, with its newly established mint at Philadelphia, began to strike copper coins the following year. Most collectors mark 1793 as the year for the actual beginning of United States coinage. Only half-cents and cents were produced in 1793. While there was but a single design of 1793 half-cent, there were three major types of one-cent coins produced that premiere year.

The half-cent has never been a popular coin, either with the general public in the days when they were

The half-cent series of 1794-1797 is characterized by a number of design varieties that collectors find interesting. On some 1795 half cents, the edge of the coin is found plain. On others, there is the incuse (punch in) lettering "Two Hundred For a Dollar."

In 1796, the large cent (as they are called by collectors to differentiate them from the now-current size adopted in 1856) appeared with a new portrait of Liberty. This time Liberty was portrayed without the Liberty Cap, but with a bit of clothing. This design is known as the draped bust type. This time there really is a ribbon in Liberty's hair, with a bow in the back. Dozens of major and minor varieities of draped bust cents were produced from 1796 until the design was changed in 1807.

The half-cent did not adopt the draped bust design until 1800. Because there was so little demand for the half cent among the public, and so few struck, the master dies did not need replacement and the basic design continued with only a new date stamped into the die in 1796-1797. This was a common practice in earlier days at the mint. Another reason the draped bust figure of Liberty was not

singularly unattractive coin. It depicts a hawk-nosed figure of Liberty with straggly hair blowing out behind, as if in a high wind. The American public did not find that portrait nearly as objectionable, however, as the reverse design. On the back of the coin, the union of the 13 former Colonies was symbolized by a chain of 13 links. Americans, having recent memories of their throwing off the chains of colonial repression, felt the symbol was inappropriate (Fig. 13-12). A change was quickly made to a wreath with 13 berries representing the Colonies (Fig. 13-13). The third type came about later when the wild-haired portrait of Liberty was replaced with a more serene-looking figure that included, as part of the design, a Liberty Cap perched on a pole. This was a symbol of freedom contemporarily seen in Revolutionary France and dating back to ancient Rome. On worn specimens of the Liberty Cap cent and half-cent, the cap looks more like a large hair ribbon bow on the back of Liberty's head.

For the 1793 half-cent, the same basic design was used—except the Liberty faced left. The next year, the half-cent Liberty did an about-face. Thereafter the design of the half cent followed that of the cent fairly closely (Fig. 13-14).

Fig. 13-13. The wreath on reverse replaced the chain in the first year of minting. The homely flying-haired Liberty was replaced later in the year. The plant above the date is strawberry leaves.

Fig. 13-14. A more attractive Miss Liberty, with the Liberty Cap and pole symbolizing the nation's new independence, was adopted for the nation's smallest denomination coin, the half cent, in 1794.

adopted on the half cent until 1800 is that no half cents at all were struck in the years 1798-1799.

18TH CENTURY SILVER COINS

The coinage of silver did not begin until the year after the mint had begun to turn out copper coins. In that year, only three denominations of silver coins were produced, half-dime (five cents), half-dollar, and dollar. All are very rare today (Fig. 13-15).

The basic design of the United States' first silver coinage incorporated a flowing-hair figure of Liberty on obverse with an eagle surrounded by a wreath (with 13 berries) on reverse. Because of the furor over the unattractive Liberty on the first cents, a different portrait was used on the silver pieces. It is an altogether more ap-

Fig. 13-15. The tiny silver half-dime shared its basic design with the other U.S. silver coins of the 1790s.

Fig. 13-16. Flowing-hair Liberty and a rather scrawny-looking eagle were the first design for America's silver coinage, as typified by this 1795 silver dollar.

pealing picture (Fig. 13-16). There was considerable criticism of the eagle on the back. It is a scrawny, malnurished looking thing that hardly befits the status of the bird as the national emblem.

By 1796, the dime and quarter had been added to the denominations in production, and all the silver coins had adopted the draped bust portrait of Liberty. Two years later, in 1798, a much more appropriate eagle design was adopted for the back of the silver coins in all denominations. In this view, a majestic spread-winged bald eagle was shown with an American shield on his breast, a bundle of 13 arrows in his right talon, and an olive branch in the left talon. In the eagle's beak, a ribbon bears the motto "E Pluribus Unum"—One From Many—in reference to the Union (Fig. 13-17).

New states were added to the country and, in 1797, the mint tried for a while to add a star to the obverse of the coinage designs for each new state. By the time we hit 16 states and stars, the design became unwieldy and the idea was abandoned (the designs reverted to 13 stars). This has created collectible varieties of the 1797 half-dime, dime and dollar. Only one type of half-dollar, 15 stars, was struck in 1797. No quarters at all were produced, after the initial 1796 offering, until 1804.

American silver coinage of the period suffered frequent setbacks because of its high integrity, Struck of nearly .900 fine silver, the coins carried nearly their full face value in intrinsic metal. In times of national or international stress, when the value of silver rose, large numbers of these coins were taken out of the United States and sent to Europe to be melted down for their bullion. This placed a great strain on the mint to keep up with coinage demands and caused the cessation of minting of certain denominations of gold and silver coins at several points in the country's early history.

Fig. 13-17. The rising price of copper forced a change to a smaller 1-cent coin in 1857. Copper was alloyed with nickel to keep the intrinsic value close to 1 cent.

18TH CENTURY GOLD COINS

Coinage of gold in the name of the United States of America was authorized by the first coinage act of 1792, but it was not until 1795 that the nation had sufficient gold on hand to commence production of the coins. In 1795, $5 and $10 coins were struck. The official names for the U.S. gold coins are based on the "eagle," the $10 coin. A $5 coin is called the half eagle, the $20 piece a double eagle, etc.

The authorizing legislation specified that the first gold coins contain 91.67 pure gold. This subjected them to quick export and melting. Very few are in collectors hands today.

Like the early silver coins, the gold pieces of the 1790s shared a basic common design. The portrait of Liberty on the gold coins showed her wearing the Liberty Cap. The backs of those first gold coins showed another rather anemic eagle, perched on an olive branch, with a wreath in its beak. By the time the first $2.50 (quarter-eagle) gold coins were struck in 1796, the "Heraldic" eagle was adopted. Later it was added to the silver coinage.

Fig. 13-18. Like the silver coinage, gold coins of eighteenth century America bore no statement of value. Those who used them were expected to recognize them by size and weight. This is a $10 Eagle.

The 1796 $2.50 gold coin has two major types. The rarer of the two has no stars on the obverse design. The other type incorporates the familiar 13 stars. Produced in 1796-1798, minting of the $2.50 gold coin was then halted until 1802 to prevent the export of all U.S. gold to Europe. The $5 gold piece was struck continuously from 1795 through the turn of the century. The Eagle $10 coin was also produced each year.

There are many varieties among the early U.S. gold coinage caused by changes in the number of stars, style of eagle, overdates and differences in the sizes of numerals in the dates. It is interesting to note that U.S. gold pieces, before 1807, do not carry any indication of denomination. In those days the relative sizes of the coins were deemed sufficient to avoid confusion. Such coins were seldomly encountered by the average man. While the early silver half-dime through quarter-dollar coins also followed this practice, the half-dollar and silver dollar were marked on their edges with a statement of value.

19TH CENTURY COPPER COINS

The mid-nineteenth century saw the greatest change in the history of the United States one-cent coin. By 1857, the rising cost of copper and associated minting costs had rendered the old, large (29mm) cent cost inefficient and it was replaced with a new, smaller (19mm) cent of copper-nickel composition (Fig. 13-19). The inclusion of nickel in the alloy was designed to keep the intrinsic value of the coin near its face value. There was, however, a great deal of change in the large cents between 1800 and the dawn of the small cent.

The half-cent continued to be struck off and on from 1800 through 1857. From 1800 through 1808, the draped bust design of the large cent was used. In 1809, following the pattern set by the cent a year earlier, Liberty again

Fig. 13-19. The draped bust obverse and Heralic Eagle reverse were mated in 1798 to produce what collectors regard as the most attractive eighteenth century silver coinage design. Denomination on the early silver dollars was inscribed on the edge of the coin.

did an about-face. She appeared, once again facing left, in a new pose. Known today as the classic head type, the new design featured Liberty without drapery at the shoulder and with a different style hair ribbon.

In 1816, the large cent began using another new portrait of Liberty that was not too much different from the classic head. The hair ribbon had been replaced with a coronet. In 1835, the coronet stayed on, but the face and hairstyle were changed on the cent. This was the coronet head portrait the half cent finally picked up in 1840 and continued to use until the demise of the denomination in 1857 with the change to the small cent (Fig. 13-20).

The specialist in early American coppers will find hundreds of varieties and design variations to keep him challenged. Other collectors prefer to go the established-date set route (there being no branch mints striking the copper coins at the time).

The nineteenth century ushered in the small cent, but in a slightly different dimension than we know it today. The first small cents—in the Flying-Eagle design of 1856-1858 and the early Indian-Head cents from 1859-1864—were struck of copper/nickel composition. The actual mix of metals is 88 percent copper and 12 percent nickel. To keep the intrinsic value of this new content near one cent, the first small cents were quite thick (nearly twice as thick as today's cent).

While the 1856 Flying-Eagle cent is actively collected as part of that short-lived design, it is actually a pattern coin that was struck in an edition of only 1000 pieces for distribution as samples to influential legislators and lobbyists. The coin was struck for circulation only in 1857 and 1858 before being replaced by the popular Indian-Head cent.

A representation of an Indian girl as Liberty was adopted for the cent in 1859. On the back was a laurel wreath surrounding the denomination (Fig. 13-21). The next year, a different reverse design was adopted using an oak wreath and American shield—a more pleasing design. The Indian cent continued to use the copper/nickel composition until mid-1864 when the change to bronze was made. Bronze is an alloy of 95 percent copper and 5 percent tin and zinc. It adopted to make a lighter and thinner cent that was less expensive to produce. The earlier copper/nickel cents are sometimes referred to by collectors as "white cents" because the color of the metal is much lighter than the bronze cents in use since 1864.

Still found occasionally in circulation as late as the 1960s, Indian cents are a great collector favorite. There are enough rare coins in the series to make it challenging, yet none so rare as to make the set prohibitively expensive for the more advanced collector.

Fig. 13-20. By the 1850s, the half-cent was a nearly useless coin; it was abandoned in 1857.

The nineteenth century saw one other significant development in copper coins; that was the striking of a two-cent piece in the years 1864-1873. Struck in bronze of the same alloy as the then-current cent, the two-cent coin was just a little larger in size than the five-cent nickel in use today (Fig. 13-22).

Featuring a shield, arrows, and foliage on obverse and a wreath on reverse, surrounding the denomination, the two-cent piece also featured a major design innovation: the inclusion of a religious motto. Inspired by public fears caused by the Civil War, the new denomination carried as part of its obverse design a ribbon with the motto "In God We Trust." That was first use of this now standard motto on our coinage.

Fig. 13-21. The Indian-head cent is a popular collector favorite today. It was produced for 50 years.

19TH CENTURY NICKEL COINS

The 1800s saw the first use of nickel in American coinage. It was first used as a minor part of the one-cent composition and later in other denominations. A hard, durable metal is ideal for coinage and alloying with copper because it gives the softer brown metal strength to stand up to circulation.

It will surprise most beginning collectors to learn that the "nickel" isn't really a nickel coin. The country's first "nickel" was actually a three-cent piece. As used in American coins, the composition we call nickel is actually 75 percent copper and 25 percent nickel. The minority metal gives the finished coins their familiar white color.

The first three-cent nickels were produced in 1865. They were designed to replace a silver version of that denomination that had been in use since 1851 (Fig. 13-23). Strangely enough, because of lobbying from the powerful silver interests in the West, both types of three-cent coin were produced in the years 1865-1873 (before the nickel version won out).

Almost exactly the size of our current dime, the three-cent nickel bore a design of Liberty facing left on the obverse. The reverse showed a laurel wreath surrounding the Roman numeral III as denomination.

Evidently there was not much demand for three-cent coins. After a first year production of more than 11 million coins, the mint never produced more than 5 million

Fig. 13-22. The 2-cent bronze coin was an experiment of the 1860s-1870s that found little public support.

three-cent nickels in any given year. The mint often produced under a million a year.

Collectors like the series today because of its unusual denomination and because, except for a couple of years when proof coins only were struck for the benefit of nineteenth century numismatists, there are no really scarce issues.

A year after the first three-cent nickel appeared, the five-cent nickel coin made its debut. It also circulated alongside a silver coin of the same denomination until 1873. Using the same 75-percent copper and 25-percent nickel composition, the shield nickel is so named because its design borrowed the theme of an American shield for the obverse. The reverse features a large number 5

surrounded by 13 stars appearing to emanate beams of light. This so-called "rays between stars" reverse design was used for only two years: 1866 and 1867. In mid-1867, the rays were removed from the back design, leaving a cleaner look (Fig. 13-24).

The shield nickel continued in production until mid-1883 when the famous Liberty nickel was introduced. This coin takes its name from the figure of Miss Liberty on the front. And takes its fame from the ultrarare 1913 Liberty nickel.

As was often the case with new coinage designs in the nineteenth century, the Liberty nickel had a flaw that required change during the first year of production. The original 1883 design has on the back the Roman numeral

Fig. 13-23. The first U.S. nickel coin had only three cents of face value. The three-cent nickel was current from 1865-1889.

Fig. 13-24. The shield nickel was introduced in 1866. It was a 75-percent copper and 25-percent nickel coin designed to replace the then-current silver half-dime.

Fig. 13-25. Popular with collectors today, largely because of the rare 1913 version, the Liberty (sometimes called "V" nickel") nickel was officially struck for circulation from 1883-1912.

V surrounded by a wreath. Because this design did not specify the word "Cents," sharp operators began to gold plate the new coin and pass it off as a new $5 gold piece.

With so many different coins in circulation in that era, and so many design changes, the public was easily fooled by the gilded nickels that soon acquired the nickname "racketeer nickels." Even today, traces of gold plating can be found on some examples of the 1883 nickel. More often, though, when the coin is found gold-plated today, it is a modern plating job and the coin is being sold as a souvenir. It is not illegal to plate a coin in such a manner. It only becomes a criminal offense when a person tries to pass the coin as a $5 piece, creating fraud. The mint took quick steps to prevent such fraud by adding the word "Cents" beneath the wreath later in 1883 (Fig. 13-25). The nickel five-cent coin continued to be struck in relatively large quantities through the end of the nineteenth century.

19TH CENTURY SILVER COINS

The century 1800-1899 saw some significant developments in the United States silver coinage. The high quality of the coins continued to cause them to be exported for melting in times of crises. For large parts of the century (1804-1840 and 1874-1878), no silver dollars were struck at all.

Perhaps the most interesting numismatics development in the century was the production of a trio of unusual silver coins; the three-cent piece, the 20-cent piece and the Trade dollar.

The silver three-cent coin was designed to play a definite role in the monetary system when it was authorized in 1851 (Fig. 13-26). At that time, the copper cent and half-cent were not actually legal tender coins (indeed, the cent remains officially legal tender in only limited amounts today). That meant they circulated on good faith alone. Neither the banks nor the U.S. government could be forced to redeem them for gold or silver.

At the same time, three cents represented a fair amount of purchasing power in those preinflationary days. The three-cent silver, or *trime* as it was sometimes called, was struck of the same 90-percent silver and 10-percent copper as the other U.S. silver coins of the day. A very thin, very tiny (14mm, only about ½" in diameter) coin, it was not especially popular among the citizenry because it was easily lost. While some 35 million of the coins were struck in 1851-1853, the rest of the coin's 22-year mintage history witnessed only about 6.5 million additonal specimens produced. Many of them were proof coins for collectors rather than for circulation.

The design of the trime featured a six-pointed star on obverse with a shield within. On reverse, the Roman numeral III was placed within a large C, (for Cents).

The silver half-dime continued to be minted through 1873. At that time, coinage authority for all silver U.S. coins expired (Fig. 13-27). While most of the other denominations were renewed, the silver five-cent coin bowed out permanently to the nickel version. While the half-dime began the nineteenth century with the draped bust design, it changed to the capped bust design in 1829. This portrait showed Liberty, facing left, wearing a Liberty Cap along with a rather silly expression. A new, more natural-looking eagle was added to the reverse.

In mid-1837, a new design was introduced for the then-current half-dime. A seated Liberty design showed the female personification of the American ideal, in full figure, seated on a draped rock (or something), cradling an American shield, and holding a Liberty Cap aloft on a poll.

The seated Liberty design was carried over from a group of pattern silver dollars begun in 1836 by Christian Gobrecht. In the next few years, the design was adopted by all the silver coins of half-dime and higher denomination.

With the change to the seated Liberty obverse, the eagle was dropped from the reverse of the half-dime and

Fig. 13-26. Called the "trime," the tiny silver three-cent coin has never been especially popular with the general public or collectors, even with its unusual denomination.

Fig. 13-27. Before production stopped in 1873, the silver half-dime had the seated Liberty design.

replaced with a simple statement of denomination surrounded by a laurel wreath. In 1860, the wreath was changed to a conglomeration that included wheat, corn, tobacco, and other produce.

As in the half-dime series, in which no coins were produced from 1806-1828, the early nineteenth century saw spotty production of 10-cent coins. The last draped bust dimes were produced in 1807 and in 1809 the capped bust portrait was adopted. No dimes of that design were produced in the years 1810, 1812-1813, 1815-1819 or 1826. Thereafter, dime production became more regular. The seated Liberty dime used essentially the same basic design as the half-dime of the era.

With the minting of the seated Liberty dime, the production of silver coins at branch mints became more common. A few silver three-cent coins and half-dimes were produced at New Orleans (the "O" Mint, as it is designated on the mint mark). Dimes were minted at Philadelphia, San Francisco, New Orleans, and Carson City. This was reflective of the greater utility and popularity of the 10-cent coin.

It was beginning in the 10-cent denomination that the last U.S. silver coin design of the nineteenth century was adopted. The Barber type was named after the designer of the rather masculine figure of Liberty facing right that was placed on the dime, quarter, and half-dollar beginning in 1892.

The 20-cent piece was a silver coinage phenomenon of the nineteenth century. So similar in size and design to the seated Liberty quarter with which it was contemporary, the coin fell into immediate public disfavor. It is also said the piece was unpopular in certain influential temperance circles because it was conveniently the exact price of a shot of whiskey about the time it was minted.

A short-lived coin, produced only in 1875-1878, the 20-cent piece managed to include three mints in its short production life: Philadelphia, San Francisco and Carson City. The coin was really produced in quantity only the first year, 1875, when some 1.3 million were struck at the three mints. In 1876, only 15,900 were produced at Philadelphia and 10,000 at Carson City. Surprisingly, the 1876-CC 20-cent piece is one of the greatest rarities in American coinage. Almost all of the 10,000 pieces struck were melted down. An about uncirculated specimen sold for $85,000 in 1980 (Fig. 13-28). The final two years of 20-cent piece production, 1877-1878, saw the coin produced only in proof versions for collectors.

Following a single year of silver quarter production (1796), mintage of that now-standard denomination began with regularity with the draped bust design in 1804. It lasted until 1807 when production of the denomination was again halted until 1815 and the advent of the capped bust design. Design changes to keep the coin compatible with the other U.S. silver followed into the seated Liberty and Barber eras.

As was the case with the quarters, there was a lull in 50-cent piece production at the turn of the nineteenth century. No coins were produced in that denomination from 1798-1800. When coinage began again in 1800, it was in the draped bust series with the heraldic eagle reverse design. This denomination was the most regularly produced in the early 1800s. It continued uninterrupted, except for the year 1816, through the capped bust, seated Liberty and Barber eras. Mintages were quite low from 1879-1890 (Fig. 13-29).

Silver dollar coinage in the 1800s is one of the most interesting periods in American numismatics. This is the era of the famed 1804 dollar. Most beginning collectors are surprised to learn that no silver dollars were actually struck in 1804. The few examples known were produced much later, in the period 1834-1860, to be used in presentation sets to foreign potentates in an era when silver-dollar coinage had been regularly suspended.

Fig. 13-28. One of the rarest regular-issue United States coins is the 1876-CC, 20-cent piece. Because of its similarity in size and design to the quarter, it was unpopular in commerce. Most of the Carson City-minted 1876 20-cent pieces were melted before reaching circulation.

Fig. 13-29. A portrait of Liberty facing left, wearing a Liberty cap, was adopted for most denominations of U.S. silver and gold coinage in the early nineteenth century. The banner with motto was dropped from the half-dollar reverse in 1836.

The draped bust dollars of the nineteenth century were produced for regular issue only through 1803. Silver-dollar minting was suspended until the late 1830s (when the Gobrecht patterns were started). While some of these first seated Liberty design coins were indeed pattern issues, numismatic researcher and author R.W. Julian showed, in an exclusive series of articles in *Coins* magazine in the late 1970s, that the Gobrecht dollars of 1836 and 1839 were actually issued for circulation. The back of the Gobrecht dollars shows a majestic eagle in flight in a starry sky (Fig. 13-30A). Several other types of Gobrecht dollars were struck as patterns. This included types with the eagle flying through a starless sky.

When regular silver-dollar production resumed in 1840, the seated Liberty figure was retained, but the flying eagle was dropped in favor of a ground-bound version holding the familiar shield, arrows, and olive branch. Coinage of silver dollars of the seated Liberty type expired in 1873 with the issuing authority.

Silver-dollar coinage took a four-year hiatus, until 1878, when the cartwheel reemerged in the currently popular George Morgan design. This is known to collectors as the Morgan dollar (Fig. 13-30B).

Fig. 13-30B. Perhaps the most popular coins with investors and speculators today is the Morgan silver dollar. It was minted between 1878-1904 and again in 1921.

Largely to satisfy the powerful Western mining interests, mintage of silver dollars was enormous in the Morgan-design era. This was true even though the public could not absorb them all into circulation. Millions and millions of the coins were stockpiled into government vaults to be melted during World War I. Others were later released to the general public, first at face value in 1964 and then at special collectors sales in the 1970s (Figs. 13-31 and 13-32).

Another type of nineteenth century U.S. silver coinage is the Trade dollar (Fig. 13-33). The United States Trade dollar was not intended for domestic use. It contained a slightly higher silver content than the standard

Fig. 13-30A. Christian Gobrecht's silver dollar design of 1836-1839 was not produced in great numbers, but the seated Liberty figure was subsequently adopted for all denominations of U.S. silver coinage from half-dime through dollar.

Fig. 13-31. Millions of unused silver dollars—mostly from the Carson City Mint—were stockpiled in government vaults for nearly a century before being sold to collectors. Each of these bags contains 1000 1882-CC cartwheels.

silver dollar. The Trade dollar was intended to circulate internationally, and particularly in the Orient. The Chinese trade was lucrative in the 1870s, but so highly traditional that the U.S. could not get its fair share because the then-standard silver dollar of 412½ grains silver was too light by international standards. This was particularly so when compared to the Spanish dollar, or *real*, that was the accepted exchange medium at that time in the East.

Legislation authorizing the production of a silver Trade dollar of 420 grains silver content was passed in 1873; the first coins were minted that year. Production for export continued until 1878. The coin then became a collectors-only proof issue until it died off in 1885.

Carrying the same basic design of the seated Liberty dollar, the Trade coin differed in that Liberty is seated facing left, as if to the Orient, extending in her hand the olive branch of peace, and seated upon such American trade goods as a bale of cotton and grain. The eagle on the back shared the reverse with the spelled-out legend of fineness "420 Grains 900 Fine."

Interestingly, until 1876, the coins were legal tender in the United States only to the amount of $5. This was true even though they actually contained more silver than the then-current dollar coin. When the price of silver declined in 1876, Congress repealed the legal tender nature of the coin altogether for domestic use. In 1887, another law was passed allowing the Treasury to redeem unmutilated specimens at face value.

Because of their circulation in the Orient, many Trade dollars are found in collector channels today bearing punched-in Chinese characters. These are known to collectors as *chop marks*. They are actually something akin to a "seal of approval" for the coin. Stamped there by well-known merchants in the Orient, the marks signify that they had personally examined the coin and found it to be acceptable for commerce. Despite this colorful history, chop marked Trade dollars are not particularly popular with collectors today. They will usually command a lower price than a coin in the same grade that has not been so "certified."

19TH CENTURY GOLD COINS

Just as silver coins in the 1800s included some unusual denominations, so did the U.S. gold-coinage series. Most noticeable are a $3 coin that saw extensive circulation and

Fig. 13-32. In a series of sales, the government raised millions of dollars selling its silver dollar hoard to collectors in a complicated mail-order scheme.

a $4 coin that very nearly became part of our regular coinage system.

The nineteenth century opened with only three current gold coins: the $2.50, $5 and $10. The quarter-eagle began 1802 with a continuation of the capped bust type of 1796-1798. In 1808, a one-year type of $2.50 gold piece was created with a capped bust portrait of Liberty facing left. After only 2710 coins of the type were produced that year, minting of the denomination was suspended until 1821 and the introduction of a slightly modified design. This design featured a portrait that stopped at the neck. Therefore, it required no drapery (Fig. 13-34A).

In 1834, the figure of Liberty was again redesigned to replace the cap with a hair ribbon emblazoned with the

Fig. 13-33. Minted for use outside of our borders, the Trade dollar is often found today with "chop marks" applied by Chinese merchants.

word Liberty. It was for this type of coin that the branch mints began production in 1838, Charlotte, and 1839, Dahlonega and New Orleans (Fig. 13-34B).

Yet another new Liberty portrait design was adopted in 1840; a coronet replaced the hair ribbon. This $2.50 gold type remained current for more than 60 years (until 1907).

One of the country's most interesting official gold coins is part of the Liberty coronet quarter-eagle series. In 1848, some 230 ounces of gold, from the newly discovered California gold fields, were rushed to the Philadelphia Mint to be coined into a special $2.50 form. The coins were like all other 1848 $2.50s in design with the exception that the abbreviation "CAL." was punched into the reverse of the 1389 pieces produced from this gold. Something of an unofficial commemorative coin, this variety represented only 3½ percent of the gold $2.50's struck that year. Today they are a great collector favorite commanding prices from 10 to 15 times those of the normal quarter-eagles of 1848.

Fig. 13-34A. A modification of the capped Liberty portrait of the previous century was carried over into the gold coins of the 1800s.

The $2.50 was not the lowest denomination U.S. gold piece produced in the nineteenth century. In 1849, authorization was given to produce a $1 gold piece. Only 13mm in diameter (about ½") when first produced, the size was enlarged to 15mm in diameter in 1854. It was made thinner so as not to affect the gold content or alloy mixture.

Fig. 13-34B. By 1838, the government had followed up gold strikes in the Southeast with the production of new mints. This $2.50 gold coin bears the "O" mint mark of the New Orleans mint.

The first type of $1 gold coin features a portrait of Liberty on obverse. There is a wreath and statement of denomination on reverse. An Indian-head design was placed on the coin in 1854 and a different Indian-head portrait premiered in 1856. The second one was slightly larger than the first so as to better fill up the obverse field (Fig. 13-35).

93

Fig. 13-35. The tiny gold dollar was very unpopular because it was easily lost. That was no small matter in the days when it represented a day's pay for the average man.

Because of its tiny size, it was easy to lose. The coin was unpopular and no great numbers of them were ever produced. The highest minting was in 1853 when just over 4 million pieces were struck. The denomination was allowed to expire in 1889.

An interesting coin in the $1 gold-piece series is the 1861-D version. The D mint mark in those days stood for Dahlonega, Georgia, not Denver, Colorado. The 1861-D is unusual in that it was not struck by authority of the government of the United States, but rather under order of the Confederate States of America. The Confederacy had seized the Georgia Mint at the outbreak of the Civil War. Because no records were kept, it is unknown how many of these "Confederate gold pieces" were struck, but they are rare in collector channels today and are priced from $4,500.

In 1853, the government authorized the production of a $3 gold coin. It is generally believed today that the denomination was created to simplify the purchase of postage stamps. At the time, the stamps were three cents each. It was not well received and it was circulated only on a very limited basis when production began in 1854 (Fig. 13-36).

Very close in size to the $2.50 coin, the $3 coin had a diameter of 20.5mm (slightly larger than today's cent). The coin carried one design through its entire 35-year life span. On obverse was a portrait of Liberty in the guise of an Indian girl. While the portrait bore a resemblance to the Indian-head cent that would follow in a few years, the headdress was different. Collectors today believe the girl who modeled for both coins was Sarah Longacre, daughter of U.S. Mint Chief Engraver James B. Longacre, who designed both pieces. Reverse features the denomination and the date at center surrounded by a wreath made up of corn, tobacco, wheat, and cotton.

Beginning collectors should be aware that the $3 gold piece is one of the most frequently encountered counterfeits in the hobby. When buying a coin of this denomination—especially in consideration that prices for collectible specimens begin in the $500 range—it always pays to have the coin authenticated by an expert.

Another gold coinage experiment of the late 1800s was a $4 gold piece called a "Stella" after the design on the back (Fig. 13-37). On reverse of the proposed coin was a large five-pointed star with the words "One/Stella/400/Cents" inside. Obverse had a portrait of Liberty, facing left, in two basic designs. One design had long, flowing tresses and the other had her hair wrapped in a coil at the top of the head. Though a total of 450 of these coins was produced in 1879-1880, it was not intended for circulation. The pieces produced were merely patterns, struck in proof condition, for distribution to members of Congress who would be expected to vote on the proposed coinage. The denomination was never adopted, but some of the pattern proofs actually did get out into circulation.

Fig. 13-36. Sharing the basic design of the gold $1, the short-lived $3 gold piece (1854-1889) has been heavily counterfeited in recent years.

Fig. 13-37. Actually only a pattern for a proposed coinage, the $4 gold "Stella" is a popular and very expensive coin.

Occasionally a circulated Stella will be offered in the numismatic market.

The most interesting facet of eighteenth century $5 gold coinage is that it was struck at six different mints over the 100-year span: Philadelphia, Charlotte, Dahlonega, New Orleans, San Francisco, and Carson City. Additionally, in 1907, the denomination was struck at the Denver Mint. That makes the $5 gold piece the only U.S. coin produced at all seven Mints.

Ten-dollar, gold-piece production followed a normal sequence of production throughout the nineteenth century. Minting of each new design type was about on schedule with the rest of the coinage (Fig. 13-38).

The mid-1800s saw the introduction of the highest denomination U.S. gold coin ever produced for general circulation—the double eagle or $20 coin. Now when the coin was introduced in 1849, $20 was a great deal of money, equivalent to about $500 today, so it is quite surprising to beginning collectors to find that so many coins of this large denomination were produced. It is not so surprising if you understand that, until very late in the nineteenth century, paper money was not widely used or

Fig. 13-38. In 1838, the $10 gold piece pioneered the Coronet Liberty design for U.S. gold coinage.

Fig. 13-39. The big, heavy $20 "double eagle" was created in the days before paper money was widely accepted. It saw little use in everyday business, but it is popular with collectors and investors.

even trusted by the general public. Checks were financial instruments generally used only between banks. All high finance in the 1800s was carried on by gold coins in large denominations. The average man on the street might never have had his hands on a double eagle.

A magnificent, large (only slightly smaller than a silver dollar) and heavy (about the weight of three half-dollars) coin, the double eagle carried a left-facing portrait of Liberty wearing a coronet on obverse. Reverse showed a majestic eagle and shield design with an array of stars overhead and a pattern of rays, as of sunlight (Fig. 13-39).

While the United States briefly flirted with the idea of producing a $50 gold piece, to be called the "union," in the latter half of the nineteenth century, the project never got beyond the pattern stage. Most of them were struck in copper so as not to tie up too much government gold in trial coinage. A single specimen of the $50 gold pattern is known. It is in the coin cabinet of the Smithsonian Institution.

20TH CENTURY COPPER COINS

For virtually all of the twentieth century, we have had but a single copper coin—the familiar Lincoln cent. While the Indian cent was current in production at the turn of the century, and was the type of cent first produced at San Francisco in 1908, in early 1909 it gave way to Victor David Brenner's design for a one-cent coin to mark the 100th anniversary of the birth of Abraham Lincoln. A public outcry against the prominent display of the initials of the designer on the back of the coin, under the twin wheat ears, caused the mint to remove them early in the coinage run that first year. This created the rare and popular 1909-S V.D.B. cent known to every serious collector (Fig. 13-40).

Fig. 13-40. One of the best-known collector coins is the 1909-S V.D.B. cent. That is the first year for the wheat back design.

With the exception of 1943, when the mint had to abandon the bronze content of the cent in favor of zinc-coated steel while the copper was being used on World War II battlefields, the cent remained remarkably unchanged for a full half-century. In 1959, the wheat back cent received a new reverse design in honor of the 150th anniversary of Lincoln's birth. This was the Lincoln Memorial cent design by Frank Gasparro (Fig. 13-41).

It is quite uncommon today to see wheat-back cents in your pocket change. Many people, mostly nonnumismatists, pick them out of their circulating change and set them aside. They believe that they will be worth additional money some day. Surprisingly, they may be right. At one time in 1981, a well-known Eastern coin dealer

Fig. 13-41. The memorial reverse design was adopted in 1959 for the 150th anniversary of Lincoln's birth.

was widely advertising to pay 1½ cents apiece for "wheaties." Representing a nice 50-percent profit over the "initial investment," this offer created quite a stir in the coin market. Unless you lived in that dealer's home town, however, it would not have been very profitable to take up his offer. The cost of shipping the coins would have been equal to or greater than the one-half cent apiece profit.

Early 1982 saw another significant development in the history of the American one-cent coin. The bronze alloy of 95 percent copper and 5 percent zinc was abandoned in favor of a new composition of 99.2 percent zinc coated with .8 percent copper. In an attempt to avoid public hoarding of the old copper cents in the belief they would soon be worth more than face value, the mint continued to strike both types of cents in 1982 (the 95 percent copper and the .8 percent copper). The new copper-coated zinc cents are identical to the pre-1982 version in design and size. The only way to differentiate the two, without cutting them in half to see if a white zinc core is exposed, is by weight. The new composition is some 18 percent lighter in weight than the old bronze alloy.

The continued rising price for copper and the con-

tinued high demand for cent coins were cited by the mint as the reason for the change in cent alloy. Collectors who might be tempted to begin hoarding the old bronze version should be aware that the costs of transporting and melting the cents would make that process impractical even if the price of copper rises to such a degree that the metal in the old cent is worth more than face value. You'd be better off to convert your cents in to dollars and spend them on collectible coins.

20TH CENTURY NICKEL COINS

It was in the early twentieth century that the most famous American nickel was produced; the 1913 Liberty nickel carried on a design started in 1883. New collectors might not realize that the five existing 1913 Liberty nickels were not authorized coinage. Regular production of that design halted in 1912 with the production of the new Buffalo nickel in 1913. It is believed that an individual mint employee made the pieces from dies that had been earlier prepared, and sold all five coins to a single collector. It is known that all five were once in the hands of eccentric collector E.H.R. Green. They have since been dispersed to a number of public and private holdings. The last known public sale of one of these rarities, in 1978, was for a reported $200,000 (Fig. 13-42).

The final year of regular Liberty nickel production, 1912, was the first year for branch mint striking of the denomination. The Denver and San Francisco facilities joined the mint at Philadelphia in producing the five-cent coins.

For 1913, the Indian/Buffalo nickel debuted in two different reverse design varieties. One shows the great bison standing on a mound and the other shows the great bison on a flat surface, described in collecting circles as a "plain." See Fig. 13-43. The "plain" variety, also known as Variety 2, was the type adopted for the rest of the coinage series—which lasted through 1938.

The Buffalo nickel series also includes one of the better-known, popular and more valuable modern U.S. coins. This is the so-called "3-legged buffalo" nickel of 1937-D. A defect in the coining die obliterated the right front leg of the buffalo on part of the Denver coinage that year. This created a collectible variety that is worth about 50 times the value of the normal 1937-D nickel (Fig. 13-44). Collectors who encounter a supposed 3-legged buffalo should inspect the coin carefully for signs that the leg has been artificially amputated. Knowledgeable authenticators can point to several key die characteristics on the genuine variety that fakes will not exhibit.

The Jefferson nickel, which continues to circulate today, began its circulation life in 1938. Like the cent,

Fig. 13-42. Struck without authorization and smuggled out of the mint, the 1913 Liberty nickel is one of the most highly sought-after American coins. In recent years, specimens have brought more than $200,000 when sold. Only five are known.

World War II caused a change in the composition of the coin so that the copper could be used to make shell casings. Replacing the normal 75-percent copper and 25-percent nickel alloy on Oct. 8, 1942, was a nickel composed of 56 percent copper, 35 percent silver, and 9 percent manganese. To differentiate these "war nickels" from earlier production, the mint mark was enlarged and moved from the right of the building on the reverse to the top. For the first time, a "P" mint mark was used to identify the coins of the Philadelphia facility (Fig. 13-45).

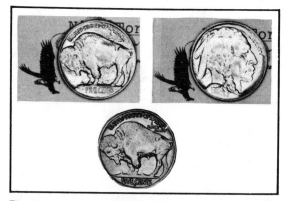

Fig. 13-43. The "real" 1913 nickel was the Indian/Buffalo type. The earliest 1913 coins show the bison standing on a "mound." Later that year the reverse design was slightly modified to show the buffalo standing on a "plain."

Fig. 13-44. A die defect resulted in the loss of a leg on the buffalo on some 1937-D nickels. This created a popular and valuable variety.

98

Fig. 13-45. The use of silver in the nickel coinage of 1942-1945 was marked with the addition of a large mint mark above Monticello on the reverse.

While collectors sometimes encounter 1944 nickels without the mint mark, they are counterfeits produced, in the early 1960s, by an obvious noncollector.

20TH CENTURY SILVER COINS

In comparison to the nineteenth century, the 1900s have been a century of (so far) relatively few design changes in the U.S. coinage. The dime, for instance, has been known in only three types in more than 80 years. The Barber design, which opened the century in 1900, was replaced by the "Mercury" dime in 1916. Then came the Roosevelt dime of 1946 to date.

Though it is popularly known as the Mercury dime, Adolph A. Weinman's design for the 10-cent coin, introduced in 1916, is actually that of a female personification of Liberty, wearing another version of the Liberty Cap, this time adorned with wings to represent, in the artist's words "freedom of thought." See Fig. 13-46. One notable variety in the Mercury dime series is another war-time creation that resulted from the modification of 1941-dated dies for use in 1942. The final numeral of the date was repunched in the old dies to save for the war effort the metal that would have been used in new dies. In re-

Fig. 13-46. While popularly known as the Mercury dime, the figure on obverse of the 1916-1945 dime is actually Liberty wearing a winged cap, symbolic of freedom of thought.

punching the date, however, traces of the "1" remained. The relatively small number of coins struck with those dies are considerably more valuable today than their normally dated counterparts.

The Roosevelt dime was begun in 1946 as a tribute to the late president who had brought the country through a major depression and to the brink of victory in the second world war (Fig. 13-47). It was the smallest denomination coin affected in 1965 by the removal of silver from circulating U.S. coinage. In that year, a composition known as *cupronickel* was adopted for the dime and quarter. Cupronickel coinage features two outer layers of 75 percent copper and 25 percent nickel bonded to an inner core of pure copper. Collectors usually use the term *clad* to differentiate the post-1965 coinage from the silver-bearing version of earlier years. The new coins are a copper core "clad" in outer layers of cupronickel (Fig. 13-48).

Following Gresham's law that states, "Bad money always drives good money out of circulation," the nonprecious metal-clad coinage soon replaced the 90 percent silver U.S. coins in circulation almost totally several years before the price of silver had risen to a degree significant enough to warrant the melting of U.S. silver coins for their bullion content.

So complete has been the conversion to clad coinage, and so valuable has silver become, that collectors today do well to find a single silver dime or quarter in circulation in a year's time.

Like the dime, the quarter has seen three major design types in this century—well, three and a half, considering the Bicentennial quarter 1975-1976. The century opened with the Barber quarter. This coin ceased production in 1916 when a general redesign of America's silver coinage produced the standing Liberty design.

Created at a time when much of the rest of the world was at war, the standing Liberty quarter is a masterpiece of symbolism. The full figure of Liberty was shown in a doorway between two low walls, as if guarding the nation from aggression. In her right hand is an olive branch that symbolizes the national preference for peace. In her left hand is a shield indicative of the country's readiness to defend itself. The shield is undraped to enhance that message. Liberty herself was depicted as partially undraped. Designer Hermon A. MacNeil portrayed her with her right breast naked. This proved too much nudity for the times. The design was modified in midproduction, the following year, to cover the breast with a shirt of chain mail. The back of the coin was also modified for 1917; a trio of stars was added beneath the flying eagle (Fig. 13-49).

Fig. 13-47. Introduced in 1946, the Roosevelt dime continues in production today.

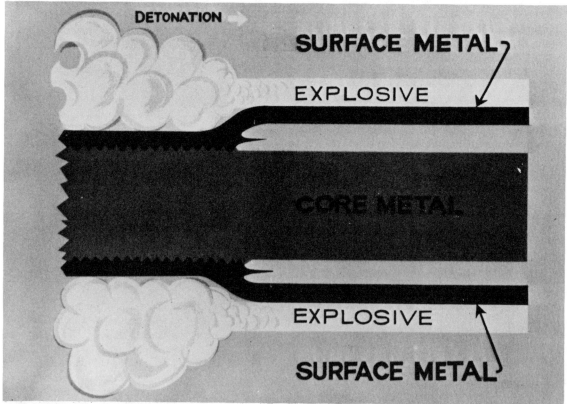

DETONATION

SURFACE METAL

EXPLOSIVE

CORE METAL

EXPLOSIVE

SURFACE METAL

Fig. 13-48. This U.S. Mint drawing shows the process by which cupronickel clad coinage metal is produced for our current dime through dollar coins.

Fig. 13-49. When Liberty's bare breast aroused public resentment in the initial standing Liberty quarter design, a modification was ordered. In 1917, a mail shirt was put on Liberty and a trio of stars was added beneath the eagle.

The standing-Liberty quarter remained current through 1930. No quarters at all were minted in 1931. In 1932, a new type was introduced—the Washington quarter (Fig. 13-50). Originally intended as a one-year only commemorative coin to mark the 200th anniversary of the birth of George Washington, the design has remained for the past 50 years (though none were produced in 1933).

A modification of the Washington design came, in 1975, when the country introduced a trio of bicentennial commemorative coins (quarter, half-dollar and dollar denomination). Like the others, the obverse of the Washington quarter was little changed. The dual dates 1776-1976 were placed where the normal date would have appeared. The back was completely changed. The familiar eagle design gave way to that of a colonial drummer and eternal flame of Liberty. The reverse design, by Jack Ahr, was chosen in a national design competition.

The bicentennial quarter was struck in regular cupronickle-clad composition for circulation, but was also produced in a special 40-percent silver-clad proof and uncirculated edition for collector sets (Fig. 13-51). Some

![Washington quarter obverse and reverse]

Fig. 13-50. Initially intended only as a one-year commemorative coin, the Washington quarter has been minted since 1932, the 200th anniversary of his birth.

misconception on the part of the public that *all* bicentennial coins were struck in 40-percent silver might account for the fact that these commemoratives are not encountered in circulation today as often as might be expected even though they were produced in enormous quantities over two years.

The Barber half-dollar was in production when the twentieth century began. It remained in production for 16 years. The final edition of that design was minted in 1915 (the Barber dime and quarter were struck through 1916 (Fig. 13-52). For 1916, the half-dollar was issued in the new guise of the walking Liberty design. This is considered by many to be one of the country's most beautiful coinage designs (Fig. 13-53). Hard times and the production of silver dollars caused half dollar minting to be suspended in the years 1922, 1924-1926 and 1930-1932. The final walking Liberty half dollars were minted in 1947.

For 1948, the Benjamin Franklin half-dollar was introduced. This was in the same general era that saw the introduction of the Roosevelt dime. Both coinage substitutions were made in an effort to replace the figure of Liberty on our coinage with portraits of famous Americans (Fig. 13-54). A relatively short-lived coin, production of the Franklin half-dollar was halted in 1963 when Congress rushed through legislation to change the design of the half to commemorate the recently assassinated President John F. Kennedy.

An interesting series for collectors, the Kennedy half-dollars began in 1964 as 90-percent silver coins. The debasement of U.S. coinage in 1965 created an interesting metallic composition for the Kennedy halves of 1965-1969 struck for circulation. In those years, the half-dollar was struck with a 40-percent silver content. This is generally known to collectors today as "silver-clad," or simply "40%." Silver-clad features an outer

101

Fig. 13-51. The only bicentennial coins struck in 40-percent silver content were the special proof and uncirculated editions sold in government-issued three-coin sets.

layer of 80 percent silver and 20 percent copper bonded to an inner core of 21 percent silver and 79 percent copper. Because 40 percent of the coin's 11.5 gram weight is pure silver, the coin has some significant bullion value over face value. The .14792 ounce of silver in each 1965-1970

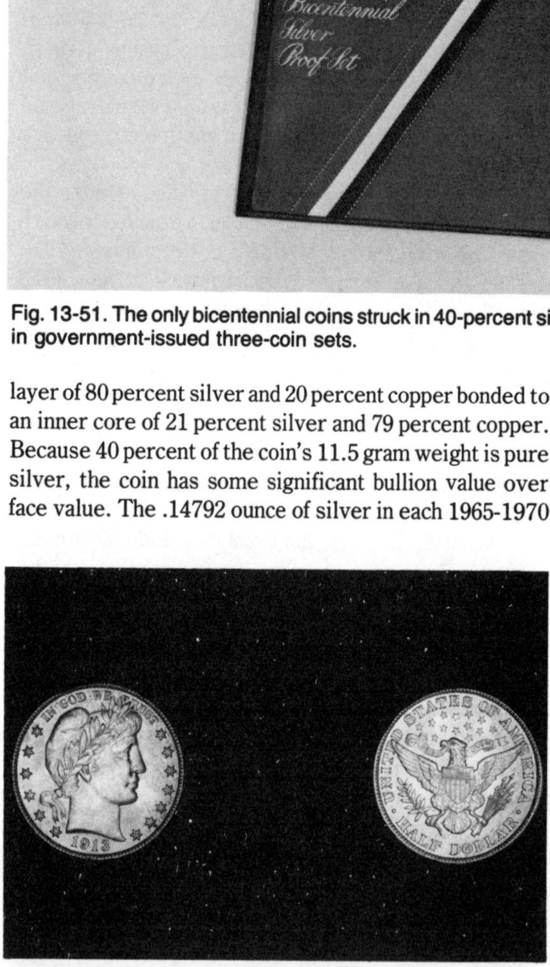

Fig. 13-52. The Barber-designed dime, quarter and half-dollar remained current from 1892-1916. No Barber halves were produced in the last year.

half dollar is worth about $1.50 when silver sells for $10 an ounce.

For 1970, in the face of rapidly rising silver prices, it was determined to cease production of silver-bearing 50-cent coins. Only a few pieces were struck for inclusion in collector-only sets: the 1970-D for that's year mint sets, and 1970-S for that year's proof sets. Because no 1970-dated half-dollars were produced for general circulation, the value of the collectors' editions is significant. The Denver-minted uncirculated version is the more valuable (Fig. 13-55).

Beginning in 1971, the Kennedy half-dollar joined the other dime, quarter, and new Eisenhower dollar in the use of the cupronickel-clad alloy. For 1975 and 1976, the Kennedy half-dollar received the dual date commemorating the bicentennial and a new reverse design, by Seth Huntington, picturing Independence Hall in Philadelphia. This design was produced in 40-percent silver uncirculated and proof versions for inclusion in collectors' edition sets.

Kennedy half-dollars were produced in 1982 in a special collectors-only edition for the approximately four million proof sets struck that year. Early in 1982, it was

Fig. 13-53. The beautiful walking Liberty half-dollar was introduced in 1916 as part of a revamping of most U.S. coin designs.

Fig. 13-54. The Franklin half-dollar was a short-lived coin (1948-1963). In deference to his opposition to the eagle as national bird, the statutory representation of the eagle on this coin was relegated to a minor position.

decided to suspend minting of the 50-cent piece for normal circulation. Public demand for the coin was almost nil. It appears that current supplies of the denomination will last commercial business channels for some time to come.

The first silver dollars of the 1900s were of the Morgan type. They were produced from 1900-1904; then government supplies of silver bullion were exhausted. With silver once again available after World War I, resumption of the Morgan silver dollar minting started in 1921. Later that year, an entirely new design of silver dollar, a commemorative to honor the newly won world peace, was created. It has come to be known to collectors as the peace dollar (Fig. 13-56). The word peace is prominently displayed on the bottom of reverse of the coin. Also shown is an eagle, perched on a rocky crag, with the olive branch of peace in his talon. The eagle is staring into the rising sun, always a symbol of new hope. On obverse, a portrait of Liberty is shown wearing a rayed tiara.

Just over a million peace dollars, dated 1921, were produced in December of that year and released to circulation the following year. It was soon discovered that the relatively high relief of the coin's design did not allow them to be stacked. The images on the coin were flattened somewhat for 1922 and subsequent mintings.

Because of low demand for the coin, in part caused by the Great Depression, no silver dollars were struck from 1929-1933. The production of silver dollars for circulation ceased altogether in 1935.

The peace dollar surfaced briefly, in 1964, when President Lyndon Johnson ordered silver dollar production to resume. Mint officials at Denver began preparations to strike the 45 million silver dollars called for in the new legislation. More than 315,000 cartwheels actually were coined bearing the old peace design and the 1964 date. Nevertheless, before any of the coins could be released to circulation, the rapid price increase in the precious white metal and the decision to remove silver from our circulation coins caused plans for a new silver dollar issue to be dropped.

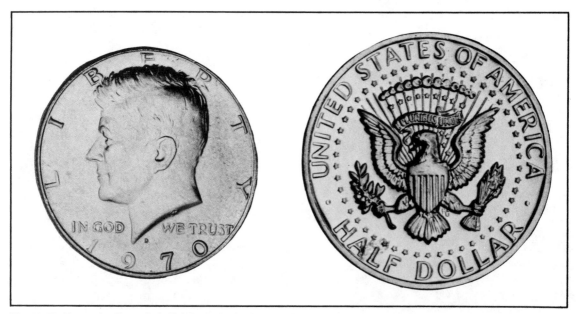

Fig. 13-55. Key to the Kennedy half-dollar series is the 1970-D coin. It was produced only in that year's mint sets.

Fig. 13-56. The peace dollar marked the end of World War I and the resumption of U.S. production of the silver dollar.

The entire mintage was remelted without even a few specimens being saved for the Smithsonian Institution. Hobby rumor through the years persists that a few specimens did escape the melting pot when older silver dollars were mixed into the '64 peace coins. To date, no reputable hobby source has reported seeing a legitimate specimen. If the coin does exist in private hands, it is subject to confiscation under federal law that states no coins not officially released to circulation channels may be privately possessed.

At least one major coin dealer has publicly stated his willingness to pay a large price for a 1964 peace dollar and to challenge government confiscation in federal court.

A new dollar coin finally did emerge in 1971, but it was no longer silver—at least the circulating version. Largely in response to demands from casino owners in Nevada for a coin to replace the silver dollars that had disappeared from their tables, and to new demand for high-value coins from the vending machine industry, the Eisenhower dollar coin made its debut in 1971 (Fig. 13-57). Following the pattern of all coins of the 10-cent and above value, the coin was produced for circulation in cupronickel-clad alloy. A special collectors' edition of the new $1 coin was made available in proof and uncirculated

minting of 40-percent silver (Fig. 13-58). These special versions continued to be offered, at premium prices, through the bicentennial years.

As designed in 1970, the Eisenhower dollar combined a profile of the late general and president on obverse with a reverse symbolic of the nation's recent accomplishments in moon exploration. An American eagle is shown landing on the cratered lunar surface, bearing an olive branch (symbolizing the nation's intent to utilize our space technology for peaceful purposes), with the Earth in the background. The moon remained on the back of the coin in its bicentennial version, designed by Dennis Williams, with the Liberty Bell superimposed on it.

The eagle design returned for the 1977 and 1978 dollar coins. This ended the Eisenhower design and the

Fig. 13-57. After a gap of more than 35 years, a dollar coin was minted—without the silver—in 1971. It honored Dwight Eisenhower and the nation's space program.

UNCIRCULATED 40% SILVER EISENHOWER DOLLAR COIN

These coins are produced in the same manner as coins made for general circulation, the only difference being that they contain 40% silver whereas those made for regular use will be cupro-nickel.

The uncirculated coins, unlike the individually processed proof coins, are minted on high speed presses, moved along conveyors, and run through counting machines. No attempt is made to impart a special finish such as appears on the hand-processed proof coins. The Treasury cannot guarantee that the uncirculated coins will be free from blemishes.

Fig. 13-58. Special collectors' editions of the Eisenhower dollar were made available in proof and uncirculated quality. They featured 40 percent silver content.

old large-size cartwheel dollar coins that had been an American tradition since 1794.

In 1979, the ill-fated Susan B. Anthony "mini-dollar" coin was foisted on the public. Largely unwanted and almost totally unused, the down-sized dollar featured a portrait of the womens' rights champion on obverse. The reverse design was modified from the Ike dollar (Fig. 13-59). The coin was too close in size to the quarter to be a commercial success.

After minting nearly 700,000,000 Anthony dollars in 1979, the coin had become, by 1981, a collectors-only issue. It was included only in that year's proof and mint sets. None was produced for circulation. Because the coin does not circulate in everyday commerce, it is unlikely that new minting will occur in the near future.

20TH CENTURY GOLD COINS

While many collectors believed the denomitization of gold in the United States and its subsequent prohibition of ownership for private citizens from 1933-1974 spelled the end of U.S. gold coinage, such is not the case. The commemorative coinage series for the 1984 Olympics will include a legal-tender $10 gold piece. It is not intended that such a coin be placed in circulation because of the premium price that would surely be attached to it. It will be entirely legal tender (as were its predecessors, dating back to the 1790s).

By the time the twentieth century dawned, all of the odd denominations in the U.S. gold coinage series had come and gone. We were left with the familiar $2.50, $5, $10 and $20 coins. Designs of the Liberty coronet series

Fig. 13-59. The Susan B. Anthony mini dollar was produced for only three years.

Fig. 13-60. Innovative incuse (cut-in) design of the $2.50 and $5 gold pieces, designed by Bela Pratt in 1908, are the only two such currency in American coinage.

were continued until 1907. President Theodore Roosevelt then ordered a redesign of our gold coinage in order to better represent the nation at home and abroad.

For the quarter eagle and half eagle, this meant the adoption of a design the coins would share, from 1908-1929, until production of the $2.50 and $5 gold piece ceased. Both coins featured the design of an Indian in full eagle-feather headdress, on obverse, and an eagle standing on a branch on reverse.

What makes the designs unusual is that they are incuse rather than in relief. Instead of being raised off the surface of the coin, the design on these two coins is cut into the fields of the coin (Fig. 13-60). Public objection was raised to this innovation. Some imaginative souls suggested that germs and other filth tended to gather in these incuse designs and were transmitted from hand to hand to perpetuate epidemics such as the great influenza plagues of the World War I era.

Whatever the reason, the coins were not particularly popular. Coinage was suspended from 1916 to 1924 in the case of the $2.50 piece and from 1917 to 1928 in the case of the $5 piece.

The redesign of the $10 piece ordered by Roosevelt resulted in another Indian-head design. This one is the

more tradition relief type (raised). Otherwise, it was pretty much the same: an Indian in feather headdress and a standing eagle both facing left.

The relatively limited circulation of gold coins by the 1920s, when paper money had achieved public trust and acceptibility, caused $10 gold production to be halted during 1917-1919, 1921-1925, and 1927-1929.

Last struck in 1933, the $10 gold piece of that year is one of the great modern U.S. coin rarities. Although 312,500 were minted, very few were released before the government freeze on gold ownership was ordered in that year. While it is unknown how many of the 1933 $10 gold pieces were issued, they are very rare today and are valued at up to $100,000 in uncirculated condition (Fig. 13-61).

Like the lower denominations, the double eagle came into the 1900s in the same basic Liberty head design it had when introduced in 1849. The redesign of 1907 resulted in a gorgeous new type of coin that featured a representation of Liberty walking directly ahead, as if toward the viewer, holding aloft the torch of freedom and the olive branch. The U.S. Capitol Building appears at lower left. On reverse is a soaring eagle above a sunrise. These were familiar coinage symbols by now (Fig. 13-62). As was also the case in the lower denominations,

Fig. 13-61. A great twentieth century American coin rarity, only a few 1933 $10 gold pieces were released before the U.S. went off the gold standard.

107

Fig. 13-62. Collectors and investors alike pursue the beautiful St. Gaudens $20 gold piece minted from 1907-1933. The first coins produced used Roman numerals for the date, but Arabic numbers were quickly adopted.

the $20 coinage was suspended during the years 1917-1919. It continued uninterrupted through the 1920s and early 1930s—until 1933.

As was the case with the 1933 $10 gold piece, the $20 was struck in relatively large quantity: 445,500. None were officially released before the ban on gold ownership was imposed. A few specimens did get into collectors hands. One went to King Farouk of Egypt (a great numismatist of this century).

Because the coins were not officially released, they may not legally be owned and are subject to confiscation in this country. The few specimens traded outside our borders generally sell for large amounts of money and usually to an American (or his agent) willing to smuggle it back into this country for a well-heeled collector who can't resist the lure of the forbidden.

COMMEMORATIVES

This country has a long history of commemorative coin issues spanning the period 1892 to the present—with several lapses. Commemorative coins differ from regular issue coinage in that they are generally intended to be sold to collectors and souvenir hunters at a premium price over face value. For most of the period 1892-1954, all U.S. commemorative coins were struck by the U.S. Mint and sold for face value to approved sponsoring organizations. Such organizations then sold them to collectors and others at a higher price. The profits made in this way were often channeled into the operation of expositions, the construction of statues and monuments, and—regretably—in the 1930s, into the pockets of greedy speculators who all but killed the commemorative coin program for nearly a half century.

The themes of past U.S. commemoratives vary widely. When the first were struck in 1892, they honored anniversaries and events of national significance such as the 400th anniversary of the discovery of America by Columbus, the World's Columbian Exposition, and the first world's fair, held in 1892-1893 in Chicago. The national scope that should be required to give a commemorative coin legitimacy soon gave way to regional and even local themes that meant nothing to great numbers of Americans—except the numismatists. At its worst, in the midst of the Depression, we had commemorative coin issues for the granting of a city charter to Albany, New York, and the 300th anniversary of the founding of York County, Maine. Interspersed, naturally, were a number of very commendable themes.

With few exceptions, the half-dollar was the chosen commemorative denomination. One of the first exceptions was the coin that was paired with the Columbus half-dollar of 1892-1893 (both dates were produced); this was the Isabella quarter (Fig. 13-63). Struck only in 1893, the Isabella quarter was promoted by the Board of Lady Managers of the Columbian Expo. It was aimed at raising funds to support women's activities at the fair. Because the women tried to get the same $1 per coin that the half-dollar sold for, it was not a big seller and nearly 16,000 of the original 40,000 coins minted were returned to the mint and melted. Melting was the fate of most unsold commemorative coins that were left unsold. In a few cases, they were bought up—for face value or just a bit over face value—by banks or others and released to circulation. This accounts for many of the circulated commemorative coins found in the hobby today. While it was expected that persons who paid $1 or more for a 50-cent coin would not spend it for face value, that did happen in hard times.

The trend toward standardizing the commemorative coins as half-dollars did not start until 1918 when the Illinois statehood centennial commemorative featured a striking portrait of an unbearded Abraham Lincoln—as he appeared in his Illinois days (Fig. 13-64). Prior to that, commemoratives have been a mixed bag of gold and silver coins in denominations from $1 to $50.

A third type of commemorative coin was the first and only commemorative silver dollar (until the 40-percent silver bicentennial dollar was issued in 1975). Struck in 1900, the coin is called the Lafayette dollar by collectors. It marks the erection, of an American-sponsored monument, to Gen. Lafayette in Paris during the Paris Exposition in 1900 (Fig. 13-65). Funds from the sale of the coin went toward the construction of the statue. The statue is depicted in slightly different form on the reverse of the coin than as it was actually constructed. Obverse of the Lafayette dollar featured cojoined busts of George Washington and the Marquis de Lafayette.

Fig. 13-63. One of the nation's first commemoratives, the only commemorative quarter until 1975 and the only U.S. coin to depict a foreign monarch (Spain's Queen Isabella), was the 1893 Columbian Exposition quarter.

Fig. 13-64. One of many U.S. commemoratives to honor statehood anniversaries, the Illinois statehood centennial half-dollar of 1921 features a portrait of a beardless Abraham Lincoln.

In 1903, a pair of commemorative gold $1 coins were produced in honor of the Louisiana Purchase Exposition, marking the 100th anniversary of the Louisiana Purchase from France. Sharing a common reverse design, the tiny gold dollars had obverses depicting Presidents Thomas Jefferson and William McKinley. Jefferson was president in 1803, when the Purchase was made, and McKinley signed the Expo celebration into law. McKinley would have been president at the time of the anniversary had he not been assassinated. In part, the Louisiana Purchase Expo gold $1 with McKinley's portrait might be looked on as a commemorative to the slain president. Nevertheless, a separate gold $1 commemorative was struck in 1916 for that purpose and to raise funds to build a McKinley birthplace memorial in Niles, Ohio.

One of the most interesting commemorative coin series was also our most extensive, to date, in terms of numbers of denominations and designs (rather than just dates and mint marks which became fashionable in the 1930s to lure collectors to buy ever increasing numbers of coins to keep their sets "complete"). This was the five-coin Panama-Pacific Exposition commemorative coinage of 1915 that was struck to celebrate the completion of the Panama Canal.

The Pan-Pac set, as it is often called within the hobby, consisted of a silver half-dollar, a gold $1 coin, a gold $2.50 coin, and two different $50 gold coins, one round and one octagonal in shape (Fig. 13-66). All coins pictured themes emblematic of the canal project and the linking of the oceans. On the big $50 "slugs," that symbolism was in the form of dolphins swimming around the edge of the octagonal coin. The dolphins were not present on the round $50. The design of both coins was otherwise identical. This included a helmeted bust of the goddess Minerva on obverse and an owl in a pine bough on reverse.

Not surprisingly, because they sold for $100 apiece when new, few of the $50 gold commemoratives were sold. Though 1510 of each were coined, the majority were later melted down at the mint. Original sales of $50 coins were 483 of the round piece and 645 of the octagonal. More people presumably chose the octagonal coin because of its unusual shape.

Various anniversaries of statehood and territorial status were cause for commemorative issues for Alabama, Arkansas, California, Connecticut, Delaware, Hawaii, Iowa, Illinois, Maine, Maryland, Missouri, Rhode Island, Texas, Vermont, and Wisconsin.

The sesquicentennial (150th anniversary) of the United States was an appropriate commemorative coinage theme in 1926. The half-dollar prepared in celebration featured the portrait of a living president, Calvin Coolidge, cojoined with that of George Washington (Fig. 13-67).

The Civil War gave rise to commemorative themes marking the 75th anniversary of the Battles of Antietam and Gettysburg. Other issues included a gold dollar for President U.S. Grant and a half-dollar to help fund the monument to Confederate soldiers at Stone Mountain, Georgia (Fig. 13-68).

While collecting commemorative coins (issued prior to 1954) is not inexpensive, even the most common circulated coins—surprisingly these are the oldest, the Columbian Expo halves—sell today for $7 or so. And prices continue to escalate right up to the $50 gold Panama-Pacific slugs that sell for about $35,000 for the octagonal and $50,000 for the round.

In between, there is a lot of ground for the new collector to pick and choose themes, designs or the price range that appeals to him. The current emphasis in com-

Fig. 13-65. The Lafayette dollar of 1900 pictured two great heroes of the American Revolution, George Washington and the Marquis de Lafayette.

Fig. 13-66. It is unusual to see a commemorative coin this well worn; most are saved in uncirculated condition as souvenirs. This octagonal $50 gold piece of the Panama-Pacific Exposition of 1915 was evidently carried as a pocket piece.

memorative coins has been on the highest grade piece of MS-65 and better. Prices of these choice pieces have skyrocketed in the last three or four years and leave the prices for the more commonly encountered MS-60 coins far behind. Many collectors are now beginning to realize that these still attractive, normal uncirculated specimens can be a good value at the current price levels and there is some renewed interest in them. With such a wide range of interests, most collectors eventually succumb to the lure of the U.S. commemorative coinage series and buy at least a piece or two that appeals to them.

Many of the higher-priced commemoratives have been counterfeited in great numbers. It is always worthwhile, when buying a coin in this series, to seek professional and impartial authentication.

PATTERNS

One of the more advanced collectible areas of United States coins is *patterns*. This general term covers a wide variety of experimental, trial, and model pieces either proposed or actually adopted for regular issue coinage.

The standard reference on U.S. patterns, Dr. J. Hewitt Judd's *United States Pattern, Experimental and Trial Pieces,* first published in 1959, defines pattern in the strictest numismatic sense of the word: "pieces which

Fig. 13-67. One of the few instances of a living American being depicted on a U.S. coin, President Calvin Coolidge was honored along with George Washington on the 1926 half dollar marking the sesquicentennial (150th anniversary) of American independence.

Fig. 13-68. The U.S. commemorative series contains several Civil War themes like the 1925 Stone Mountain half-dollar and 1936 Gettysburg half-dollar.

represent a new design, motto or denomination proposed for adoption as a regular issue, struck in the specified metal, and which were not adopted, at least in that same year."

In the coin-collecting hobby today, the term pattern also covers pieces struck from pattern or regular coinage dies in metals other than the official alloy; pieces struck with any convenient die to test a new coinage metal, alloy or denomination; and a group of other pseudocoins that include die trials, unauthorized pieces created by someone inside the mint as a *piece de caprice* or perhaps to sell to a collector, and similar items.

Numismatists view the collecting of patterns as important because these pieces help fill in gaps in our knowledge of the regular coinage. This importance was recognized as early as 1883 when the American Journal of Numismatics carried this quote from Patterson DuBois: "Open for me your cabinet of Patterns, and I open for you a record, which, but for these half-forgotten witnesses, would have disappeared under the finger of Time. Read to me their catalogue, and I read to you, in part, at least, the story of an escape from the impracticable schemes of visionaries and hobbyists—a tale of national deliverance from minted evil. Now, only these live to tell the tale of what 'might have been,' only these remind us of what has been weighed, measured and set aside among the things that are not appropriate, not convenient, not artistic; in short, that are not wanted."

While patterns might not have been wanted by the mint officials and legislators of bygone days, who vetoed the issues of the coinage for which they served as prototypes, collectors want them today. Because of their often beautiful designs—such as William Barber's "Amazonian" Liberty silver patterns of 1872, his "Washlady" silver-dollar design of 1879, and George Morgan's "Schoolgirl" design for the proposed 1879 silver dollar, combined with familiar size, weight and feel of normal U.S. coinage—patterns have found favor with many collectors who seek out the extraordinary (Fig. 13-69).

On the other hand, there can be found within the pattern series designs carried over from the regular coinage series, but struck in different metals. Many numismatists find irresistible the lure of an Indian-head cent or Liberty seated "silver" dollar struck in aluminum, or a $20 "gold" piece struck in copper. Such patterns, called regular dies trial pieces, are another popular specialty in the pattern field.

There are such interesting creations as the gold "ring" dollar. This was intended to solve the loss and handling problems of the tiny gold dollar coin of the 1849-1889 era by making the coin larger in diameter with a hole in the center.

By normal coinage standards, all U.S. patterns are rare. Even the most common, such as the 1856 Flying-Eagle cent, are not known to exist in numbers much greater than 1000. It is not uncommon for pattern pieces to have been struck in editions of only a handful or, at best, a few dozen. How many of them survive today is unknown.

Patterns were freely sold and traded by the U.S. Mint for much of the nineteenth century. By 1916, however, the practice was halted and legislation passed making it illegal for the private collector to possess pattern coinage made after that date. The ban was not totally effective, however, nor is it strictly enforced. Many types of later patterns, particularly in the commemorative series, are known in hobby circles.

Fortunately, for those who would become interested in collecting patterns, prices for these items are not in comparison to regular U.S. coinage of identical rarity. For instance, compare the 1804 silver dollar (really a pattern under the strict definition) of which 15 are known, and which currently regularly sells in the $200,000 range, to a pattern even as popular as the Schoolgirl silver dollar. With about 15 known, the Schoolgirl sells today for a top price of "only" about $10,000. Many other pattern coins sell for well under $1,000. A few undamaged pieces can be found for less than $200 or so.

Even if you don't intend to collect pattern coins, you would probably enjoy borrowing or buying a copy of the Judd catalog for your numismatic reference library. The most recent editions are well illustrated and updated; they make interesting reading.

CONFEDERATE STATES OF AMERICA COINAGE

While certainly not issues of the United States government, the few coinage issues of the Confederate States of America are often collected as part of the American coinage series.

Actually, there was no Confederate coinage produced for circulation. The few known types were pattern issues for proposed coinage. The Confederacy never found itself solvent enough or with sufficient gold and silver bullion available to strike coins for circulation. With the exception of the 1861-D gold dollar coins produced at the captured Dahlonega Mint, and most of the 1861 half-dollars produced at the New Orleans Mint, these Confederate patterns had their own designs. It was apparently intended that they be produced to the same size and metallic standards as the U.S. coinage.

In 1861, a set of dies was ordered to produce a Confederate one-cent coin. The order was filled by a Philadelphia engraver who produced a dozen specimens in copper-nickel. This was the same alloy used for the U.S. cent at the time. Fearing arrest for trading with the

Fig. 13-69. Two popular pattern dollars are those known to collectors as the schoolgirl (top) and Amazonian dollars.

enemy, the die-sinker kept the dies and the coins. They were hidden until after the war. Then they were purchased by Capt. John W. Haseltine, a prominent numismatist of the day.

Haseltine used the original dies to restrike the Confederate cent in gold, silver and bronze. Because the die pair was originally designed to work with the thicker planchets of the copper-nickel cent, they broke during the restriking. Only seven gold, 12 silver, and 55 bronze restrikes were made. In the 1960s, during the Civil War centennial, the original dies surfaced again. They were again used to create restrikes. These 1962 restrikes can be easily discerned from the original coins and the first restrikes because they featured raised fracture lines and bumps of raised metal where the dies had broken (Fig. 13-70).

The design of the Confederate cent featured a bust of Liberty facing left, wearing a Liberty Cap, with the words "Confederate States of America" around the top, and the date 1861 below. On reverse was a wreath of tabacco, cotton and corn. A bale of cotton surrounds the denomination 1 cent.

While there are occasional offerings or references to so-called Confederate nickels, dimes and quarters, the origins of these pieces in any official capacity of the Confederacy is doubted.

The Confederacy did strike some half-dollars at the New Orleans Mint in 1861, using the regular U.S.A. dies. The more than two million 1861-O halves, struck by order of the State of Louisiana or the Confederate Government, are indistinguishable from the recorded 330,000 struck by the United States. Collectors generally attach no special value to the coin as a Confederate issue.

There was a distinct Confederate States of America half-dollar, though again, only a pattern piece, in an issue of four. The half-dollar pattern used the regular seated Liberty obverse of the U.S. coinage, mated with a new reverse that depicted the Confederate shield with a Liberty Cap and Pole, and a wreath made of one cotton plant and one corn plant.

Three of the four Confederate half-dollars went to high government officials, including President Jefferson Davis, and to influential New Orleans citizens. The chief coiner of the New Orleans Mint kept the fourth, along with the reverse die.

After the war, the die for the Confederate reverse came into the possession of Scott's, a New York City coin and stamp firm, that acquired 500 original 1861-O half dollars, planed the reverse off them and restruck the Confederate half-dollar with the original die. These restrikes can be differentiated from the four original coins

Fig. 13-70. Restruck from broken dies actually used to produce the Confederate States of America one-cent coins, these pieces were sold as souvenirs during the Civil War centennial 1961-1965.

because the thinner, shaved planchets used for the restrikes required greater press pressure to produce the Confederate reverse design. This somewhat flattened the details of the original obverse.

Besides these 500 restrikes with 1861-O obverses and Confederate reverses, the firm produced another 500 pieces in white pot metal using the Confederate reverse with a new obverse die bearing the inscriptions: "4 Originals Struck By Order of C.S.A. in New Orleans 1861 ******* Rev. Same as U.S. (From Original Die Scott)."

These pieces are known in the hobby as Scott tokens. Even they have a collector value of $100 or more. The restruck Confederate halves will often sell in excess of $1,000. The value of the original quartet cannot be established because it has been so long since one of them has been publicly offered for sale.

HAWAIIAN COINAGE

Another sideline collecting area closely related to the U.S. coinage is the coinage struck for the Kingdom of Hawaii before it was a territory and then a state. The nineteenth-century numismatic history of one of our current states is interesting to many collectors (Fig. 13-71).

Hawaii's first sovereign coinage was a large cent issue of 100,000 coins struck, in 1847, by order of King Kamehameha III. These copper cents are the same size and standards as the U.S. copper cent of the era. Obverse of the Hawaii cent features a bust of the King in military jacket, with date below. Around the top is the legend "Kamehameha III Ka Moi (the King). On reverse, a wreath surrounds the denomination Hapa Haneri (part of one hundred), with Aupuni Hawaii (government of Hawaii) above. The whole of the reverse design is copied from the U.S. large cent of the era. While original Hawaiian cents are valued from $175-$2,500, depending on condition, the collector should be aware that replicas

Fig. 13-71. The Kingdom of Hawaii issued coins under two monarchs: Kamehameha III (cent at top) and Kalakaua I (dollar at bottom).

of the coin continue to be struck to this day as souvenirs for tourists. Most of the replicas have the words "souvenir Alii of Hawaii" on the reverse bottom, beneath the wreath, but by no means are all of the fakes so marked.

The next Hawaiian coinage came, in 1881, in the form of a pattern five-cent nickel struck under King Kalakaua I. Neither this coin nor a pattern 1/8th dollar (12½ cents) of 1883 were adopted for regular issue. In 1883, however, regular silver coinage of the dime, quarter, half-dollar, and dollar denominations were produced.

United States coinage standards were adopted. Designs of all values were similar. They had a right-facing portrait of the bewhiskered monarch on obverse. Re-

verses featured various royal symbols, crests and coats of arms along with the denominations in English and Hawaiian: one dime—umi keneta; quarter dollar—hapaha; half-dollar—hapula; and dollar—akahi dala.

Along with these regular-issue coins and official patterns, a number of spurious patterns and pieces have surfaced in the past century. These include supposed patterns for a silver dollar and gold $20 coins under Queen Liliuokalani and Princess Kaiulani.

Also collected with the regular Hawaiian coinage is a group of token issues, mainly plantation tokens, issued in payment to workers for use in company stores, etc., dating from the period 1862-1887. While these were not legal tender in the Islands, they did achieve a modicum of local circulation in the relatively closed economy of the Kingdom. Surprisingly, many of the tokens are valued more highly by current collectors than the actual coins of Hawaii.

Like the Hawaiian cent of 1847, the Hawaiian silver dollar of 1883 is often encountered as a souvenir replica. It is usually marked as a souvenir and it is not of silver composition.

U.S. PROOF AND MINT SETS

Virtually from its earliest days, the U.S. Mint has made available specially struck specimens of its coinage. In the early years, these proof specimens were generally reserved for gift presentations to domestic and foreign dignitaries. Later, the mint began to make such coins available to coin collectors. These were usually sold at face value or for just a small premium over face value.

All of these early presentation coins are rare and valuable today. They were distinguished generally because they were made available singly rather than in prepared sets. While it was certainly possible for the numismatists of the day to go to the mint and obtain proof specimens of every coin from half cent through double eagle, they were usually purchased singly.

This differs from modern proof-set practice whereby these special coins are made available only in sets. Proof coins are special editions of regular U.S. coinage. They are made from planchets that are specially selected to be free of flaws and specially polished to a mirror finish. New dies, also specially polished, are used to strike and proof coins. Rather than being struck a single time with the dies, as is the case for circulation-quality coinage, proof coins are double struck to produce a deeper relief to the design. The coins are then handled with gloves and packaged in plastic to avoid fingerprints and other marring before they are sold at a premium price to collectors.

The term *proof* is indicative of a method of manufacture, rather than a condition of a coin. This is a point often confusing to the beginning collector. Proof coins can be mishandled, and even circulated, to the point of wear. When a proof coin is not in perfect condition, it should be described as to its degree of wear. Examples are Proof-55, using numerical grading, or VF proof, using adjectival grading.

Prior to 1968, all proof coins were made at the Philadelphia Mint and they bear no mint mark (except the war nickels). Since 1968, the San Francisco Assay Office has produced the proof coinage for collectors. They bear the familiar "S" mint mark.

Collectors define the modern proof set era as beginning in 1936 because, after a 20-year lapse, the coins were again made generally available at the Philadelphia Mint. In 1942, with the change from the copper and nickel five-cent piece to the silver-content war nickel, both types were available to collectors in proof form before proof sets became a casualty of the war. It was 1950 before the sets again became available.

In 1955, the mint changed their method of packaging the proof coins. Previously, each coin had been sealed in a plastic pouch and placed in a cardboard box. This allowed the collector freedom to pick and choose from among the denominations. In practice, most chose the full set. In 1955, the mint began to package the coins, cent through half-dollar, in a single plastic pouch containing compartments for each coin (Fig. 13-72). To differentiate between the two types of sets available in 1955, collectors call them the *box* and *flat pack*.

The flat pack continued in use through 1964. In 1964, proof coinage was suspended at the time silver was removed from our coinage. In place of proof sets, so-called "Special Mint Sets" were sold in the years 1965-1967 to meet collector demand for special coins. They were not of comparable quality.

When the sale of proof sets was resumed in 1968, they came packaged in new, hard plastic cases. These cases better and more permanently protect the coins.

Mint sets, though of similar nature, are different from proof sets in that the coins come from normal minting processes, though they are specially chosen to be defect-free. The mint sets differ in that they offer collectors, altogether in one package, one specimen of each denomination from each issuing mint of the current year's coinage. Coins struck only as proofs, such as the S-mint cents of 1968-date, are not included.

Prior to 1947 when this service began, collectors would have trouble acquiring such specimens from the different mints. Collectors on the East Coast would rarely see the coins from Denver and San Francisco in their normal everyday change. The reverse was true in the West. Like the proof sets, the mint sets were sold at a premium.

From 1947-1958, the uncirculated coin sets sold by the U.S. Treasury contained two specimens of each regular issue coin, mounted in a cardboard holder, with obverse and reverse of each coin visible on a side. Without further protection, the coins were subject to tarnish.

In 1959, the same type of protective plastic envelope that was used in proof set packaging was adopted, along with the concept of selling only one coin of each denomination (Fig. 13-73). In the face of declining demand by collectors, and rising costs, the mint announced in 1981 that there would be no further uncirculated coin sets

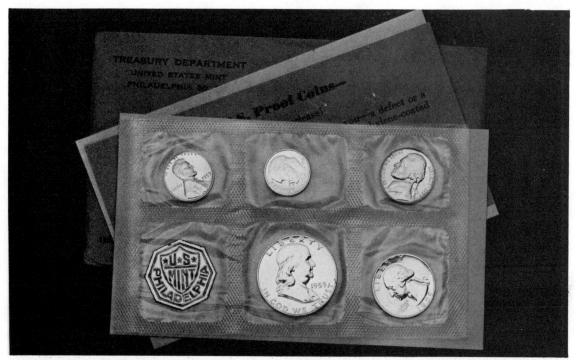

Fig. 13-72. Prior to being packaged in hard plastic cases, U.S. proof sets came in cellophane envelopes.

Fig. 13-73. Uncirculated coin sets, sold directly by the mint, allowed collectors to easily obtain a specimen of each denomination from each minting facility each year.

produced. The 1981 mint set had already gained some degree of numismatic value because it contained three Anthony dollars, one each from the P-D-S mints, and none of the coins were struck for circulation. The same situation was created in 1970, when the Denver-minted Kennedy half-dollar was only struck in sufficient quantity for inclusion in that year's mint set. This created an instant collector's item.

ERROR COINS

The chapter would not be complete without an inspection of a popular specialty—*error coins.* While some collectors prefer to call them *varieties,* mostly in deference to the feelings of the mint officials responsible for quality control, they are more widely known as errors (Fig. 13-74).

Error coinage covers a wide range of mishaps that can befall a coin on its way through the minting process. Most error collectors define the minting process as having been completed at the time the coin leaves the striking dies. Anything that happens to a coin after that stage is merely thought of as valueless damage.

Types of errors range from partial coins struck on clipped or broken planchets to wrong-metal coins, caused when a planchet for one denomination gets mixed in with those for another, to off-center coins and multiple struck coins.

It is a tribute to the production skills of the U.S. Mint that so very few error coins are produced from among the billions of coins manufactured each year, let alone are not caught in the various quality control steps and melted down. Few of the general public have ever seen an error coin. If they have, they have not known what they were looking at. Many of the errors that do escape the mint in the sewn bags of freshly struck coins are caught in the local banks by tellers when the coins are wrapped. Some of the most advanced collectors of numismatic errors have inside contacts at banks whom they pay a premium to be on the watch for error coins.

Many error coins are truly impressive. Examples are nickels, half-dollars, or even dollar coins struck (actually only partially struck) on cent planchets or blank planchets that have received no coinage impression at all. Other types of errors, such as die breaks, produce less noticeable results and it takes a trained eye to spot them.

One of the biggest misconceptions that the general public and beginning collectors have of error coins is that, because they are so rare and unusual, they must be of great value. Such is just not the case. There is relatively little demand for them. Even the most outstanding error types rarely sell in excess of $1,000, and many dozens of minor minting varieties can be purchased for a quarter or a dollar or two. Error collecting is one of the biggest challenges left to the collector who likes to look for his

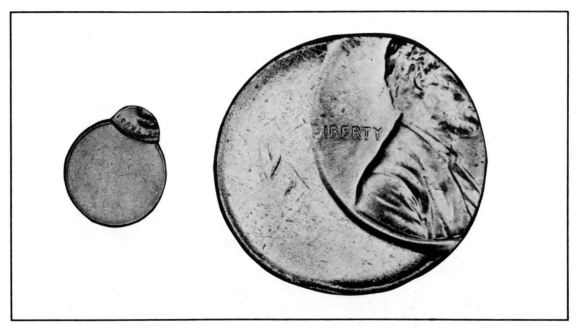

Fig. 13-74. Error coins are a popular collector specialty. One of the more dramatic, yet surprisingly inexpensive types, is the off-center coin. These cents show different degrees of misstriking.

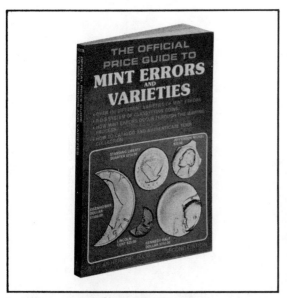

Fig. 13-75. Like many specialty collecting areas of numismatics, a good reference book is necessary equipment for the beginning collector of mint errors.

Fig. 13-76. One of the most famous U.S. error coins is the 1955 double-die cent that shows doubling of the lettering on the obverse.

coins in pocket change, bank rolls, or even mint bags of coins.

The beginner should obtain one of the several books on error and variety coinage—such as that authored by Alan Herbert—and study the subject thoroughly before jumping in and making large purchases (Fig. 13-75). Almost every type of error that can be made in the mint can be, and has been, duplicated outside the mint by fakers looking to cash in on the value of the real item. *Numismatic News* columnist Alan Herbert offers weekly advice for the error collector in his "Odd Corner" column. He also serves as a clearinghouse for the authentication of error coins. He recommends that the budding variety collector learn all he can about the minting process so as to better understand how an error can legitimately occur.

Some of the more famous and popular varieties of modern U.S. coins, coins with high values, are actually error coins. These include the 1955 and 1972 "doubled die" cents (Fig. 13-76). These are actually the result of a double image on the hub that creates the dies. The "3-legged" Buffalo nickel resulted from too heavy polishing of the die. The overdate coins such as 1942/1 dime and 1943/2 nickel also fall into the variety category. They were obviously not intended to look like that when they left the mint.

In recent years, several specialty organizations have been formed, on the national level, to serve collectors of mint errors. They provide valuable services such as cataloging, the issue of informative newsletters, and authentication of suspect coins.

Chapter 14

U.S. Paper Money

WHILE THEY WERE ORIGINALLY ISSUED BY widely differing authority, with widely ranging acceptability and over the course of nearly a century, the early paper money of America—a combination of Colonial and Continental notes—are today generally collected together. As the name implies, Colonial currency is that paper money issued by order of the various Colonies during their days as part of the British Empire or in the post-July 4, 1776 era during the fight for independence.

The use of paper money in the area which would become the United States of America actually predates its use in many parts of Western Europe and most of the rest of the more "civilized" world. While paper currencies had been in use in China since the seventh century, when it was known as *flying money* because of its light weight and ability to circulate widely with ease, it was not until the late seventeenth century that the Western world began experimenting with nonmetallic currencies.

The North American continent had its first paper money, issued by 1685, when the military commander of New France (Canada) issued promissory notes hand printed on pieces of playing cards to circulate as money until the arrival of the delayed paymaster. The Massachusetts Bay Colony followed suit soon after, issuing in December, 1690, 7000 pounds worth of the first publicly

authorized paper money notes in the Western world. They were used to pay the expenses of a border war with Canada. This publicly authorized character was an important step because previous paper currency issues in Europe and North America had been by banks or were emergency issues not authorized by any governing body.

Following that precedent, by the turn of the eighteenth century, other colonies were printing paper currency as needed to keep moving their chronically specie-short economies. By the end of the Revolutionary War, all 13 colonies had issued some form of paper currency.

Beginning in May, 1775, the Congress of the newly unified former colonies began the issue of Continental currency to finance its fight for freedom. The Continental currency was plagued by increasing public distrust. The Continental paper dollar was able to hold its value at par with a specie dollar only until October, 1777. By that time, widespread counterfeiting by British, Tories and opportunists conspired with the natural inflationary nature of a printing-press economy and increasing uncertainty as to the outcome of the war to push the exchange ratio of the Continental currency to $11 in paper for $10 in coin.

After that point, the devaluation accelerated. By the

next year, October, 1778, the ratio was 4.66 to 1. The low point was reached in April, 1780, when a dollar in silver or gold was worth $40 Continental. These were the *official* exchange ratios adopted by the Congress and many of the states to offset rampant inflation. In actual commerce, the Continentals were all but worthless. George Washington lamented that it took a wagonful of Continental currency to purchase a wagonload of supplies for his army. A truer measure of the value of the government's paper currency could be found in the fact that by October, 1787, amid speculation that the Continental currency might never be redeemable in cold cash, it was selling at the rate of $250 paper for $1 specie. Eventually, the government did come up with a plan to restore some value to the Continental currency. In 1787, the government issued 6-percent interest-bearing bonds to holders at the rate of $1 for each $100 of Continental currency turned in.

Issued concurrent with the Colonial and Continental currency notes were numerous privately printed paper monies from banks (as early as 1732 in Connecticut), utilities, merchants, individuals, and even churches. Most of the early American paper currency was crudely produced on thick, rough paper. Some types were ornately engraved and even printed in two colors.

Much of the lure of Colonial and Continental paper money is because many of the fledging nation's most promising figures were directly connected with the notes. Some, like Benjamin Franklin and Paul Revere, were actually engaged in the printing of the notes. Revere, a skilled metalsmith, engraved copper plates for several Massachusetts currency issues of the Revolutionary Era. Franklin, a printer by trade, produced the notes for several colonies in the 1700s. Putting his inventive genius to the problem of counterfeiting, Franklin created an anticounterfeiting measure that involved transferring the delicate images of leaves to the back of the notes. This made them difficult to reproduce. Many early notes of the 1740-1760s era, from the colonies of Pennsylvania, New Jersey and Delaware, bear the notation on reverse: "Printed by B. Franklin." See Fig. 14-1. Most notes of the era also have an inscription "Death to Counterfeit," or something similar, indicative of the serious nature with which the crime was viewed in those days.

Colonial currency can be found printed in values that reflect the use of both the English pound sterling system and the American dollar that was derived from the Spanish real. Some colonies, like Connecticut, denominated their currency in pounds, shilling, and pence right up through 1780. Others, like Maryland, adopted the dollar system, as early as 1767, even though the dollar amounts were odd—$1/9, $1/6, etc.—conforming to six-

pence and ninepence. Whole dollar amounts were also issued in values of $1, $2, $4, $6 and $8 in that 1767 issue.

Continental currency was denominated in dollar values from the first. It included some unusual denominations, such as $2/3, $7, $8, $30, $40, $55, $70, and $80.

Most of the Colonial and Continental currency issues were counterfeited. Surprisingly, collectors today do not differentiate much between the original notes and contemporary counterfeits (at least in terms of price). Many issues are unknown as genuine surviving specimens and numismatists have been left with only the fakes.

Modern replicas have no collector value. Since the early 1970s, the hobby has been deluged with a series of replicas of Colonial, Continental, and other types of paper currency printed on relatively thick paper that has been artificially treated to appear aged. The edges are usually stained a deeper brown. To the noncollector, the item looks amazingly like it could actually be 200 years old. No collector will be fooled by such a fake if he has the chance to see and handle a few genuine specimens. One telltale sign, besides the quality of the paper, is the fact that the modern replicas are *printed* entirely in black ink. There is no difference between the ink on the date, signatures, and serial number of the fakes than in the rest of the printing. On genuine notes (and even contemporary counterfeits of the day), the date, serial number, and signatures were all hand-signed individually and often done in a different color or shade of ink than that used for the body of the printing.

The early notes of the Bank of the United States have been particularly heavily reproduced in this manner. They can be found in all denominations from $1,000 to $1,000,000. Several persons in different parts of the country, and even abroad, have turned up with these modern fakes that say on their face the Bank of the U.S. promises to pay $10,000 or a million *in gold*, and demand such payment. This is despite the fact that the bank has been out of business for more than a century. Often the "lucky" holder of these notes has a fantastic tale—such as of finding the note in a family Bible that has been in an unopened trunk for 125 years—to tell.

The notes have become so notorious among coin dealers and coin columnists that the Bank of the United States fakes are known collectively as "Old 8894," for the serial number that virtually all of the denominations bear. Naturally, on genuine notes, that serial number would change from note to note.

Collectors with an interest in the Colonial and Continental currency series might be pleasantly surprised to discover that prices of many types and specimens are

PRINTED BY BENJAMIN FRANKLIN

Colonial Pennsylvania note issued June 18, 1764. It is one of 4,000 notes in denomination of 5 shillings. Back of bill carries warning, "To Counterfeit is DEATH," along with hallmark "Printed by B. Franklin and D. Hall. 1764."

Fig. 14-1. One of the lures of Colonial currency is that some of the notes were engraved, printed, or autographed by famous American patriots (like this note printed by Benjamin Franklin).

quite modest. Because none of the notes has any exchange value, face value is generally not a consideration in pricing. Condition is all important. If the collector is determined to own only "Gem Uncirculated" notes, he will find few are available at any price. Those that are available are priced well into the hundreds or thousands of dollars.

By concentrating on still-respectable lower grade notes, the early American currency specialist can build a representative collection for $25 or less apiece. For further research, the definitive catalog on the subject is the 1976 edition of Eric P. Newman's *The Early Paper Money of America* (Fig. 14-2).

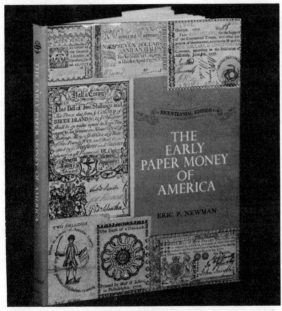

Fig. 14-2. The definitive reference work on Colonial and Continental currency is Eric Newman's *The Early Paper Money of America*, 1976.

U.S. LARGE-SIZE CURRENCY

The War of 1812, with Great Britain, and the Mexican War, of the late 1840s both spawned federal currency issues in the form of relatively high face-value notes that paid interest to the holder. Virtually all of these notes were redeemed. Specimens are extremely rare in the collector market today. Many collectors would never see an example if it were not for the unissued specimen (sample) notes of some of the issues that have been handed down.

The government got back into the note-issuing business on a permanent basis, in 1861, when the enormous financial strain of the Civil War quickly forced the United States to suspend payment of gold and silver to domestic accounts and issue paper money in its place. The specie was reserved for use in international trade.

Despite two issues of interest-bearing U.S. Treasury notes in the last prewar days of 1860-1861, the opening guns of the Civil War found the United States short of the necessary funds with which to wage a protracted war.

Congress moved swiftly in response to the national emergency to authorize the issue of $60 million worth of paper currency. While today's collectors generally assume that these first notes, the *demand notes* of 1861, were backed by nothing more than faith in the government, this was not entirely true. By the terms of the authorizing legislation, the demand notes were not payable in gold, but they were declared payable in coin and were so redeemed by the government prior to Dec. 21, 1861, when the paying of specie by the United States was suspended.

For a short time in 1861, the demand notes were quoted on a par with gold. As the war progressed, in most parts of the country the demand notes—and all other forms of U.S. paper currency—were acceptable in everyday trade only at a discount. This was true even though they were receivable for all payments to the government, including taxes and duties.

The demand notes took their names from the statement on the front that the United States promised to bear the bearer "on Demand" the face value of the notes (Fig. 14-3). In the 1860s, the notes were more often called *greenbacks*. The nickname was taken from the color of their back designs. The name was subsequently applied to virtually every other form of U.S. currency. The term remains current today as does the use of green ink on the back of U.S. paper money.

The demand notes of 1861 also set a standard size for U.S. paper money that would be followed on basically every note issued by the federal government until 1928. The size, a holdover from the bank note private issues of the period 1840-1860, was approximately 7¼" × 3". In comparison to the current size notes, this is known to collectors as large-size currency.

Following the demand notes, the government issued several other major types of paper currency. Although each type of note might have had the same face values and been authorized by different legislation, with different backing, all were basically spendable and sound.

Some, such as the interest-bearing notes and compound interest treasury notes of the Civil War years, even paid interest at the then-high rate of 7 percent a year

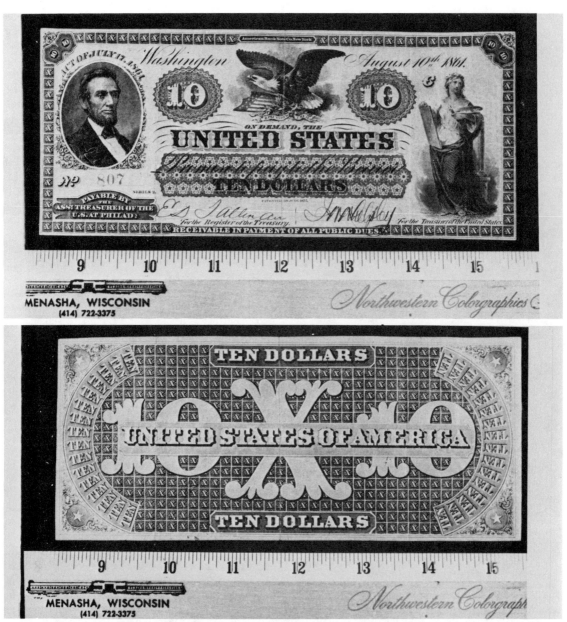

Fig. 14-3. The first U.S. paper money issued for general circulation were the Demand Notes of 1861. These Civil War-era notes, because of the color of their back designs, gave rise to the term "greenback."

(and higher). Issued only in relatively high denominations of $10-$5,000. These notes were actually not intended to circulate as money (although they could). Theoretically, the notes actually gained in face value every six months as interest became due and payable. Naturally, most specimens of these interest-paying currencies have long since been redeemed. Some outstanding examples do remain.

It is falsely assumed by some collectors that the surviving notes can still be cashed in for the interest. For one thing, many of the surviving notes are unissued specimens that never had any legal tender status. More

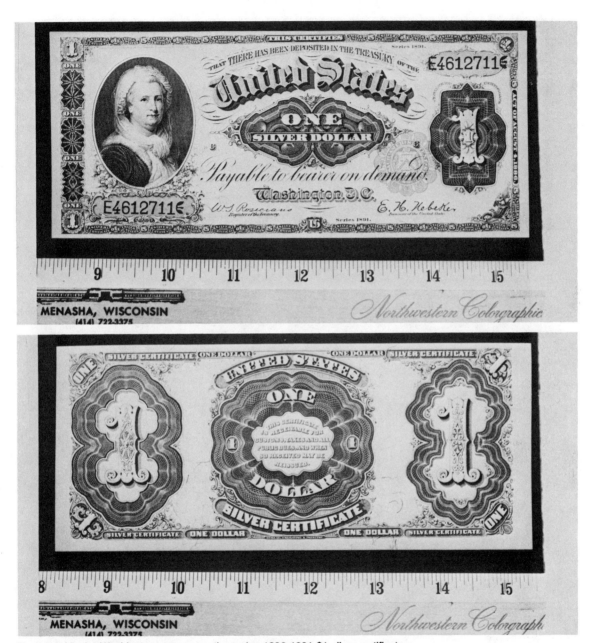

Fig. 14-4. Martha Washington appears on the series 1886-1891 $1 silver certificate.

importantly, however, the interest payments stopped at maturity for these notes (anywhere from one to five years). Some of the higher value notes of this type carried interest coupons attached to the side of the note. These could be torn off by U.S. Treasury officials when the interest on the face value was collected. At 7 3/10 per-

cent per annum, the interest on a $50 note was 1 cent per day; the interest on a $5,000 bill was $1 a day.

The longest-lived type of U.S. paper money, the United States note, also called legal tender note because of the wording of the promise to pay, was first authorized during the Civil War, in 1862, and remains current today

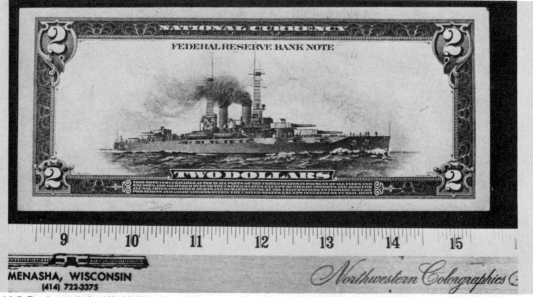

Fig. 14-5. Produced during World War I, the ship on the back of this series 1918 Federal Reserve bank note gave it the hobby nickname of battleship deuce.

even though none have been printed since 1969.

The subject of major Constitutional debate at the time of their issue, the notes did much to pave the way for future issues of U.S. currency backed only by the credit of the government. Specifically, the inscription on the back of the notes, when first issued, said: "This note is a legal tender for all debts, public and private, except duties on imports and interest on the public debt, and is exchangeable for U.S. six per cent twenty year bonds, redeemable at the pleasure of the United States after five years." While the notes are no longer even redeemable for the government bonds, they do remain "legal tender."

Not all early United States currency was backed only by faith. At least three types—the silver certificates, treasury (or coin) notes, and gold certificates—have been at various times redeemable in coin or bullion. While the notes are still legal tender and fully redeemable, you can no longer receive gold or silver for them. You will receive current-issue Federal Reserve notes or base metal coinage.

Other types of federal currency issues in the large-size note issuing period from 1861-1928 included re-

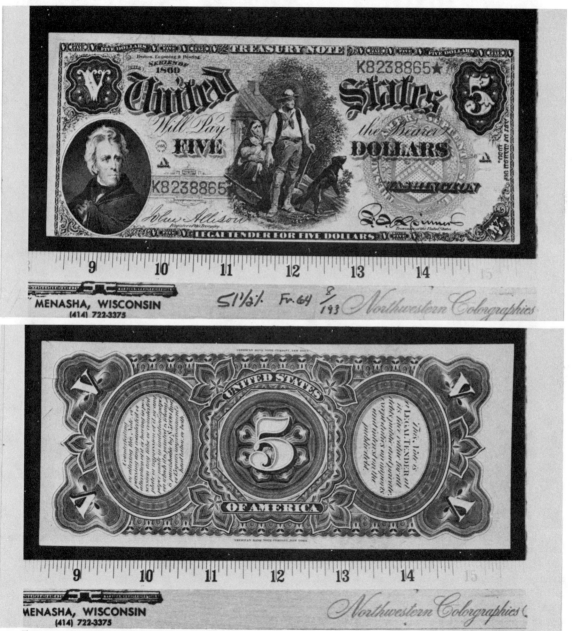

Fig. 14-6. An American pioneer family, depicted as the central vignette of this large-size $5 U.S. note, makes it popular with collectors.

Fig. 14-7. Five silver dollar on the back graphically demonstrate the denomination and backing for this series 1886 silver certificate. The motto on the coins' reverses was the first appearance of In God We Trust on U.S. paper money.

funding certificates, Federal Reserve notes, Federal Reserve bank notes, national bank notes and national gold bank notes. Other than the national bank notes, there does not seem to be any particular favorite type of large-size currency among collectors. Rather, each collector of these notes has his own personal favorites.

Because of their larger size, the old *horseblankets*, as the large notes are sometimes called, were often very beautiful examples of the epitome of the engraver's art in the nineteenth century. Virtually every type of large notes had its own design. This is in contrast to the modern currency period where all types of U.S. paper money shared the same basic designs.

Many collectors are surprised to find that George Washington was not the first man to appear on the U.S. $1 note. That honor went to Salmon P. Chase who was Secretary of the Treasury at the time of their issue, and later chief justice of the Supreme Court. His portrait appeared on $1 United States notes until 1869. Then George Washington took his familiar place on the face of the $1.

Although George Washington was a fixture on the $1 legal tender notes from 1869 on, he shared the denomination with others on different classes and types of notes. For instance, Martha Washington appears on the first $1 silver certificates (1886) (Fig. 14-4). On the 1896 silver

Fig. 14-8. The majestic Indian portrait on this series 1899 $5 silver certificate makes it among the most popular U.S. currency notes with collectors.

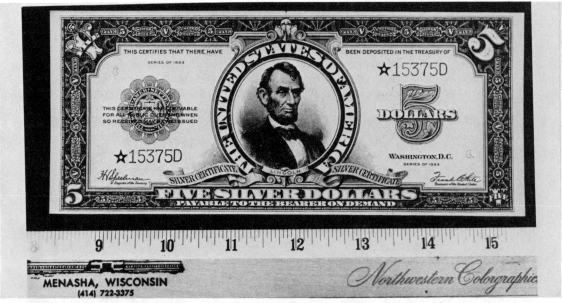

Fig. 14-9. Called the Lincoln porthole note because of the shape of the border around his portrait, this series 1923 $5 silver certificate was the last of the large-size notes.

certificate $1, George and Martha share the back. The face of the note presents an allegorical scene of "History Instructing Youth," part of the very popular (and expensive "Educational" series of $1, $2 and $5 silver certificates of 1896).

From 1899 to 1923, neither George nor Martha was

on the $1 silver certificate. They were replaced by a bald eagle and small portraits of Abraham Lincoln and U.S. Grant. In 1923, George Washington appeared on the $1 silver note. He continued to do so in the small-size period from 1928 until the silver certificates were abandoned in 1963.

Thomas Jefferson was only one of many famous Americans to appear on the $2 bill. The first was Alexander Hamilton. Others included Civil War Generals Winfield S. Hancock and James Birdseye McPherson, inventors Robert Fulton (steam boat) and Samuel Morse (telegraph), statesman William Windom, direct ancestor of the actor and an almost perfect double, and even George Washington, who appears on the 1899 silver certificate.

The list of famous Americans, allegorical figures, and persons who are today only footnote figures in the

Fig. 14-10. Another popular design is the "Buffalo Bill," series 1901 $10 legal tender note. It was issued, some say, to commemorate the Lewis and Clark Exposition that opened in 1904.

nation's history continues throughout the denominations of the large-size currency. Among the most popular type notes with collectors are the following.

Federal Reserve Bank Note, $2 Series of 1918. Known to collectors as the *Battleship note*, this $2 bill carries on its reverse design a dynamic representation of an American naval battlewagon under full steam (Fig. 14-5). The note was issued in the World War I era so the martial theme is understandable.

Legal Tender Notes, $5 Series of 1869-1907. Called the *Pioneer family* note, this type features a central vignette of the idealized American pioneer family bravely facing the wilderness (Fig. 14-6).

Series 1886, $5 Silver Certificate. The back of this note carries a design of five Morgan silver dollars. The obverse of one bears the 1886 date. It is interesting for many collectors to find that this note was the first American paper money to carry the national motto "In God We Trust," as shown on the Morgan dollar reverses (Fig. 14-7). The motto was not officially placed on U.S. currency until 1955.

Series 1899, $5 Silver Certificate. This series is called the *Onepapa* note as a corruption of the name of the tribe of the Indian depicted on the face (Fig. 14-8). Actually, the Indian's name translates to Running Antelope. It is from the Uncpapa Sioux clan. The portrait of the Indian, in full native headdress, beadwork, etc., is considered to be the finest representation of the American Indian on any numismatic item.

Series 1923, $5 Silver Certificate. Popular because it is the last of the large-size silver certificates, it is also the first $5 bill to use the portrait of Abraham Lincoln. The use of Lincoln's portrait became standard on that denomination in the next 50 years. Collectors know the type as the Lincoln *porthole note* because the round frame of the portrait makes it appear as if Lincoln is looking out of a ship's porthole (Fig. 14-9).

Series 1901, $10 Legal Tender Note. The *Buffalo Bill* is how most collectors know the Series 1901 $10 legal tender note. Issued just prior to the Lewis and Clark Exposition (in Portland, Oregon, in 1905), the note is thought by some collectors to have been a form of commemorative note to mark the expo and to honor the explorers who helped open the Pacific Northwest. Explorers Meriwether Lewis and William Clark are pictured on the sides of the note's face, but it is the big, bold vignette of the American Bison that gives the note its nickname and basic popularity (Fig. 14-10).

Certainly many of the higher denominations of large-size currency have designs that are also appealing, but because of their high face value few collectors have been able to seriously collect them. Currently large-size notes, into the $100 denomination, are commonly made part of many paper-money collections. Even the $500, $1,000 and occasional $5,000 or $10,000 note that becomes available find ready homes.

As with all numismatic items, the collector is better off to buy the finest condition he can afford when collecting large-size paper money. While uncirculated notes routinely run into the several hundred and several thousand dollar category, nice circulated specimens can be found for quite reasonable figures.

SMALL-SIZE U.S. PAPER CURRENCY

In 1928, several years after studies had been done to determine the feasibility of "downsizing" the nation's paper money, and following just such a change in the American-controlled Philippine Islands, a new size of paper currency was issued in the United States. Collectors use the terms *small size* or *modern* to describe these notes. These are the very same type of notes you now have in your wallet.

The small-size currency, measuring just over 6¼" × 2½", is some 32 percent smaller in area than the large-size notes they were intended to replace. The idea was to save money on printing costs and to provide currency that was easier to handle in everyday commerce.

All of the currency types that were current at the time of the changeover were continued into the small-size, note-issuing period: the United States notes, silver certificates, gold certificates, national bank notes and the Federal Reserve notes. Later the Federal Reserve bank notes were carried over.

With the change to smaller-size currency came a standardization of design. They are the same basic designs we use today. The authorizing legislation was still different for the various classes of notes. The silver notes continued to be redeemable in silver and the gold certificates were still redeemable in gold.

While each of the note classes featured some subtle differences in wording and placement of design elements, they were standardized in terms of portraits and back designs. The most noticeable differences between the classes of notes is in the color of ink chosen for the U.S. Treasury seal and serial numbers.

The U.S. (or legal tender) notes were given a red seal and serial numbers. Small-size U.S. notes are almost universally known to collectors as *red seals*. The silver certificates received a blue seal and number. The gold certificates have gold-colored ink (naturally), the national bank notes and Federal Reserve bank notes shared brown seals and numbers because the FRBNs were an emergency currency issue that was printed on national-bank-note stock during the "bank holiday" of 1933. The Federal Reserve notes adopted the green seal and serial numbers that they carry to this day. While the U.S. notes are still officially current, and could theoretically be printed at any time, only Federal Reserve notes have been printed since 1969.

The very earliest small-size notes had two major design differences from those of today. The first $1 notes, silver certificates and legal tender notes, had on the back a large word "ONE," with the full value "One Dollar" across it, and numerous figure and word representations of "one" in the corners and at the sides (Fig. 14-11). It was not until 1935 that the familiar $1 back design of the national seal at both ends of the note, with "ONE" in center, was adopted.

On the early $2 bills, issued only in U.S. notes until the series 1976 Federal Reserve notes were introduced during the bicentennial, the back has a scene of Monticello, the home of President Thomas Jefferson. That design continued until 1966 when the last of the $2 red seals were printed. When the denomination reappeared a decade later, in its ill-fated reincarnation as a Federal Reserve note, the back had been changed to depict the signing of the Declaration of Independence, from a painting that hangs in the nation's Capital.

Other small changes have marked the other denominations. An example is the redesigning of the $20, back in 1946, to show the remodeling of the White House and the maturing of the trees and shrubs.

Like the large-size currency which it replaced, the small-size notes were originally printed in denominations

Fig.14-11. The earliest small-size U.S. notes featured a back design different from that which we encounter every day.

Fig. 14-12. As an emergency measure in WWII, currency used in Hawaii received a special overprint. The notes would have been devalued if the Japanese had invaded and captured the islands.

of $1, $2, $5, $10, $20, $50, $100, $500, $1,000, $5,000, and $10,000 for circulation, and even a $100,000 gold certificate for bank-to-bank transfers of large amounts of money. No denominations larger than the $100 bill have been produced since 1949. There has even been a lot of legislative agitation in recent years to do away with the C-note.

There are many ways to collect small-size currency. Many people collect a high-grade set trying to obtain uncirculated specimens of each class of notes. Because relatively low denominations can be chosen, and because there are only six notes to complete the collection, this is a popular way to collect.

Others collect one or more of the classes of notes by series. They attempt to obtain a specimen of each of the many issue series produced, generally in the $1 denomi-

nation. For the $1 silver certificate, this requires up to 20 notes, without any consideration of minor varieties.

A smaller, but still enthusiastic group, collects $1 Federal Reserve notes by serial groups or blocks. They obtain one note of each prefix and suffix letter combination from each of the 12 Federal Reserve banks. Lately, the Bureau of Engraving and Printing has begun to skip-number currency issues. This results in thousands of block combinations to challenge collectors.

Besides the regular issue small-size notes, collectors will find a large group of experimental, test, and emergency issues if they decide to specialize in small-size notes. The most popular and best known of these varieties are a trio of World War II era issues that are highly sought after today.

Two different issues of currency were specially produced for use in overseas areas that were thought to be subject to invasion. These are known to collectors today as *Hawaii notes* and *North Africa notes*. The theory behind each was that these distinctly marked notes would take the place of normal U.S. currency circulating in the area. If war reverses resulted in the areas falling into enemy hands, these special notes could be declared invalid. This way the enemy would not have its hands on great stores of American cash.

The first issue was produced for use in Hawaii. Early in 1942, all then-circulating U.S. currency was recalled and specially overprinted currency was issued in its place. These special notes came in denominations of $1 silver certificates and $5, $10 and $20 Federal Reserve notes (San Francisco district). In place of the normal-color, U.S. Treasury seal and serial numbers, these notes had those elements in brown ink. More prominently, the word "HAWAII" was overprinted in black block letters at both ends of the face of the notes and in big outline type on the backs (Fig. 14-12).

A similar issue was prepared for use in North Africa and the Mediterranean theater of operations when U.S. troops invaded those Nazi-held areas. American troops were relieved of their normal money and given in its place special $1, $5 and $10 silver certificates. These notes were not overprinted like the Hawaii emergency currency. They had only a yellow U.S. Treasury seal to distinguish them from normal Federal Reserve notes. The serial numbers remained blue. It was not necessary to recall these notes. They remain legal tender today. Many of them came home with servicemen as souvenirs of the war.

A third type of special currency issue, brought on by the war, was introduced in 1944. Special runs of $1 silver certificates were used in an experiment to see if the paper content of U.S. paper money could be changed without harm in terms of vulnerability to counterfeiting and wear. Those notes printed on normal paper received a red letter "R" overprinted in the lower left corner. The notes printed on the experimental paper were overprinted with a big red "S."

The results of the experiment were not conclusive. No change in the paper stock was made, but collectors were left with two interesting varieties. Collectors should be aware that normal Series 1935A $1 silver certificates have been recently overprinted with red R's and S's. You should have such bills authenticated before buying them as genuine. The serial numbers of the genuine notes are documented and available in several of the specialty books on small-size currency.

For the collector who wants to study the modern U.S. currency series further, I recommend the newest edition of Chuck O'Donnell's reference work, *Standard Handbook of Modern United States Paper Money*. The newly revised seventh edition was published in 1982 and should be available from many coin dealers.

NATIONAL BANK NOTES

Because of their great popularity and the manner in which they are collected, national bank notes transcend the boundaries of large-size and small-size notes. This is true even though they were issued virtually from the beginning of the large-size era, in 1863, and continued to be printed through 1935 in the small-size era.

In the 72 years of their issue by more than 14,000 "home town" banks across the nation, the $17 billion worth of national currency issued between December, 1863, and May, 1935, represent the most popularly collected series of United States paper money in the hobby today.

Their long historically, as well as financially, interesting life began when the National Currency Act was signed into law by President Lincoln on February 25, 1863. The dual aim of the legislation was to provide a ready and steady market for the sale of U.S. bonds issued to finance the Union's war, and to create a sound bank currency that would replace the generally insecure issues of the state banks then in circulation.

While national bank notes were only one of seven different classes of U.S. paper currency circulating virtually simultaneously during and after the Civil War, they represent more interesting types of variations than any other. For more than half a century—from the implementation of the National Currency Act in 1863 until the creation of the Federal Reserve System in 1914—the national bank notes were an important part of the paper money circulating in this country. The composition of these notes, and the individual histories behind each of the issuing banks and its officers who signed the notes, present unlimited fascination for today's numismatist.

The National Currency era came to an end in May, 1935, when the U.S. bonds that secured the value of the national bank notes then in circulation were called in for redemption. This ended nearly three-quarters of a century of an important era in "Main Street Banking."

Six distinct series make up the national bank note issues (four in large size and two in small). Large size nationals are comprised of the original series, the series of 1875, the series of 1882, and the series of 1902. In

Fig. 14-13. This diagram locates the important features of a national bank note. Currently, this is the most popularly collected area of U.S. paper money.

small size, there are the series of 1929, type 1 and type 2. Within each of the large-size series, there are several major varieties and subtypes.

Alternatively, nationals are sometimes referred to by collectors according to the charter period of their issue, thus: first charter—original series and series 1875; second charter—series 1882; third charter—series 1902, and small size.

The terms *charter period* and *charter number* are particularly important to national bank notes. They refer to the issuing authority for each particular bank. The original National Currency Act of 1863 provided that banks organized under its provisions be chartered as national banks for a period of 20 years.

In anticipation of the expiration of those first charters in February, 1883, an act was passed on July 12, 1882, extending the banks existence for another two decades. A similar extension was granted in 1902. In 1922, just before the next expiration date, the National Currency Act was amended to provide 99-year lives for all national banks. Five years later, this was amended to endow perpetual succession of their corporate identies on national banks. A better understanding of national bank notes as collectors' items can be gained by studying the several components of the national currency issues (Fig. 14-13).

Charter Number. Upon approval of its organization as a national bank, the comptroller of the currency would issue each bank a charter number designating its place on the roster of all such banks. Charter No. 1 was issued to The First National Bank of Philadelphia in June, 1863. Charter No. 14320, the highest to appear on a national bank note, was issued in early 1935 to The Liberty National Bank & Trust Company, Louisville, Kentucky. The very earliest original series national bank notes did not have their charter number printed on the notes.

It was soon discovered that notes being presented at the U.S. Treasury for redemption could not be easily sorted. As a result, the act was amended, in 1874, requiring the charter number to be overprinted twice on the face of the note. Further revision, in 1882, called for the charter number to be engraved on the border of the note's face in six different locations. This was to facilitate the redemption of partially destroyed notes. The act also required the overprinting of the charter number on the face and its placement in large numerals on the back. This gave rise to the popular series 1882 brown-back notes. New legislation in 1908 dropped the requirement to have the charter number on the bank. This created the second charter date back and value back series.

The small-size nationals that debuted with series 1929 were no longer printed from plates that had been specially engraved for each bank. Rather, for the type 1 notes, the charter number was overprinted twice in black on the face of the note, along with the bank, city and state names, and the officers' signatures. On the type 2 small-size nationals, the charter number was printed an extra two times on the face, in brown ink, matching the U.S. Treasury seal and serial numbers.

Bank Title. Each national bank's title, once approved by the comptroller of the currency, was engraved on the printing plates for that bank's notes during the large-size period, and overprinted during the series 1929 issues. On large-size notes, the bank name, together with the city and state of the bank's location, is printed in a variety of bold and interesting type faces and arrangements in the center of the note. Many collectors center their national bank note collections on notes with interesting or unusual bank titles such as The Asiatic N.B. of Salem, Massachusetts, The Brother of Railway Clerks N.B. of Cincinnati, and The Rhode Island Hospital N.B. of Providence.

Date. While the engraved date near the title on the face of all large-size national bank notes remains something of a mystery to collectors, it is now generally believed to have been chosen by the comptroller to represent the approximate date of issue for the note. Because this does not represent an absolute date of issue, however, collectors attach no significance to the date.

Treasury Serial Number. From the first issues of national currency on December 21, 1863, to August 22, 1925, all national bank notes carried a U.S. Treasury serial number on the face of the note. On all notes except the first charter $1s and $2s, the U.S. Treasury serial number appears somewhere in the upper right of the note. On those two notes, it appears vertically at the left center of the face. After August 22, 1925, the U.S. Treasury number was replaced with a second impression of the issuing bank's serial number.

Bank Serial Number. Found on all national bank notes, except for type 2 small size notes, this number indicates how many impressions of a particular printing plate configuration had been printed for the bank of issue. For type 2 small notes, the bank serial number is an indication of how many notes of a particular denomination had been printed by that bank.

Treasury Signatures. On all national bank notes, the engraved signatures of the register of the treasury and the treasurer of the United States appear on the face, usually just above center. The register's signature is to the left of the bank title, and the Treasurer's signature is to the right. There are exceptions to this placement. The particular combination of these signatures can pinpoint the period in which the plate was engraved for a specific bank.

Bank Officers' Signatures. The original National Currency Act of 1863 required that each national bank note be signed by the issuing bank's president or vice president, and cashier. These signatures, whether pen autographed, rubber stamped, or engraved, always appear at the bottom face of the note (cashier to the left and president to the right). These signatures gave a local "stamp of approval" to this type of currency. This was probably an important consideration when it was first issued at a time when paper money was usually viewed with distrust.

The thousands of persons whose signatures appear on national bank notes help give each individual note a history not found in other forms of U.S. currency. Collecting famous signatures on national bank notes is another interesting hobby sidelight. On these notes can be found the autographs of such famous millionaires as J. Pierpont Morgan and Andrew Mellon; pioneers of the auto industry such as Ransom E. Olds and Charles Nash, as well as countless otherwise anonymous bankers who helped build the nation's economy.

There are even signatures of bank officials who gave their lives in the days of Jesse James and John Dillinger. Some were killed in the line of duty protecting the assets of their depositors. On the other hand, there were signers of national bank notes who became embezzlers and absconded with the depositors funds.

Treasury Seal. Found on the face of all national bank notes, the U.S. Treasury seal was overprinted as a final government authentication of a note. This gave each piece of national currency its validity as circulating money. Generally found on the right side of the note's face, it varied, through the national currency period, in color (red, brown, blue), in size, and embellishment (8 or 12 scallops, 34 or 40 rays).

Geographic Letters. From 1902 to 1924, large block letters were overprinted with and near the bank's charter number on each national bank note to facilitate sorting at central redemption points. Each letter stood for a particular geographic area of the country in which the issuing bank was located: N for New England, E for Eastern, S for Southern, M for Midwest, W for Western and P for Pacific.

Plate Position Letters. On all large-size national bank notes, a letter from A through D appears twice on the face of the note to indicate from which position (top, second, third, or bottom) on a printing plate the note had been produced. Because of the great variety of plate configurations used—$10, $10, $10, $20; $10, $10, $20, $20; $50, $100, etc.—collectors attach little significance to plate letters. Among small-size nationals, the plate position letter is part of the serial number. On series 1929 nationals, the prefix letter of the serial number is the plate position. Because 1929s were printed six to a sheet, the plate position prefix letters run from A through F.

Denominations. National bank notes were authorized, over the course of their history, in denominations of $1, $2, $3, $5, $10, $20, $50, $100, $500, $1,000 and $10,000. No notes of the $3 or $10,000 were ever printed. No surviving $1,000 nationals are known;

nevertheless, the U.S. Treasury reports 21 still outstanding. Only three, of a reported 173 outstanding, $500 nationals are known to be in collectors' hands. It should be noted that not all banks issued all denominations in all series.

Circulation. While the original National Banking Act of 1863 authorized state as well as national banks to issue circulating currency upon deposit of U.S. bonds with the U.S. Treasury as security, no state banks took advantage of this privilege before it was withdrawn in 1864. This left the national banks in a monopoly position. The 1863 legislation allowed national banks to issue notes to a total face value of 90 percent of the market value of the bonds they had placed in security. That figure was changed to 100 percent in 1900. The circulation privilege for national banks was effectively withdrawn in favor of the Federal Reserve bank system in July, 1935, when the last of the note-issuing security bonds was called in. By not issuing bonds of the type specified by legislation, the government has prevented the issue of national bank notes since that time.

Closing. A national bank could wind up its affairs in one of three ways specified by law. A bank that violated provisions of its charter or current governing legislation or that refused to or was unable to redeem its notes, could be placed in charge of a receiver by the comptroller. If it could be proved sound, it could be allowed to reopen. If not, the receiver liquidated the bank's assets to meet the greatest amount of liabilities. A bank could also go into voluntary liquidation on a two-thirds vote of the stockholders. This was often done to allow the bank to buy out or to be purchased by another bank. After 1918, a bank could also close its door by such a merger without the formality of liquidating its assets.

Types of National Bank Notes. Although the first charter period ran from February 25, 1863 to July 11, 1882, notes from the first charter period were issued until 1902 (a 40-year period). Banks were chartered for a 20-year span. Once a bank was chartered in a particular period, it continued to issue notes of that period for two decades despite the fact another charter period might have come into effect (July 12, 1902) during the course of that time. When the bank's original 20-year life expired, and it was rechartered under the second (or even third) period, it would begin the issue of notes appropriate to that extension.

During the first charter period, two different series of notes were issued: original series and series of 1875 (Fig. 14-14). Notes of the original series appeared in $1 to $1,000 denominations. They are distinguishable principally by their lack of overprinted charter numbers. Some banks did issue original series notes with charter numbers surcharged. The nearly identical 1875 series notes have red (or in rare cases, black) charter numbers imprinted, along with the notation at the left of the bank title "Series 1875." Serial numbers of first charter notes appear in either red or blue; blue is the scarcer color.

Three distinct note issues make up the national currency of the second charter period (July 12, 1882 to April 11, 1902). These type differ principally in their back designs. Collectors have evolved the nicknames of *brown back, date back,* and *value back.*

Like the notes of the first charter period, the second charter currency was issued for a span of 40 years (until 1922) when all charters had to be renewed.

The series 1882 brown backs were placed into circulation in that year and continued to be issued into 1908. They take their name from the large charter number printed at back center, in a geometric design, all in brown ink, that matched the predominant color of the notes' faces.

The second issue of series 1882 notes is called date back. Large dates (1882-1908) appear in the center of a green back design. They were issued only by banks that had issued brown backs, and whose charters remained in force. Those banks whose charter expired in the 1908-1916 period were rechartered and issued notes of the third charter period. Date backs were issued in denominations of $5-$100 from June, 1908 to July, 1916, with the $50 and $100 notes continued current in this type until 1922.

The third type of series 1882 notes is called value backs. As implied, the name comes from the large spelled-out indication of denomination in the center of the backs where the dates and charter number had earlier appeared. As a type, they are the rarest of national bank notes. They were issued in the period 1916-1922 by banks that had issued the date back type and whose charter was still effective. Naturally, this number dwindled each successive year as banks were rechartered and their notes issued in third charter designs.

Passed to extend the life of those national banks whose charters were coming to expiration beginning in 1902, the Currency Act of April 12, 1902, created the third charter period and the three distinct types of national currency issued thereunder. In 1922, Congress did away with the need for continual renewal of charters every 20 years by granting perpetual charters.

Issued from 1902 until they were replaced by the small-size national currency in 1929, the third charter nationals represented a change in design to distinguish them from the notes of the second charter period. The

Fig. 14-14. Produced only in the first charter period, the $2 national bank notes are called "lazy deuces" by collectors because of the large red numeral two that appears to have fallen asleep on its face.

first issue of third charter notes was the popular and often-rare red seals, issued only from 1902-1908, for a shorter time and by fewer banks than the other third charter notes. Their scarcity, and the fact they were issued by every state and territory, except Hawaii, make them a challenge among collectors who seek to build a state set of this type.

The latter two issues of the third charter period both feature blue U.S Treasury seals. They are principally distinguished by their backs. The 1902 series date back carries the date 1902-1908 in the white space at upper back. They were issued between 1908-1915; the $50s and $100s were produced until 1926. The third type of third charter note, called the *plain back* because of the lack of dates on reverse, was issued from 1915-1929. They were superseded by the small-size issue. They are most plentiful of all national bank notes.

When the rest of the U.S. currency was reduced in size, in July, 1929, the national bank notes were included. Their designs were standardized with all other classes of currency in the same denominations.

Two separate types of small-size national bank notes were issued. Type 1, current from July, 1929 to May, 1933, is distinguished chiefly by the appearance of the bank charter number only twice, on the face of the note, in heavy black numerals. Type 2 notes have the same two charter numbers, but they feature an extra pair in brown ink alongside the serial numbers. They were issued from May 1933 to May, 1935.

Survivors. Of the approximately $17 billion worth of national currency issued between 1863-1935, it is estimated that some $50 million worth remains outstanding. Most knowledgeable observers are in agreement

that the surviving amount is about equally divided between large- and small-size issues, representing about three-tenths of 1 percent of the total issue. From this tiny pool of surviving specimens, collectors form the basis for many diverse specialty collections of these notes. The most popular type of national bank note collecting is by geographic area of the issuing bank.

A good way to begin collecting these notes is to start with those notes issued in your own home town. That's fine if you live in a medium size town or city, but not too great if you live in Iola, Wisconsin, which never had a national bank, or in New York City, which had more than 135 note-issuing banks.

Most towns and cities had anywhere from one to a half dozen banks of issue. If you complete a collection of your home town—most collectors try to obtain only one note per bank—you might want to expand to the country or even the whole state. By the time they reach the level of collecting an entire state, many advanced collectors begin to try to obtain one note of every type and every denomination from each bank. That is an impossible task because surviving specimens are unknown for many banks. It is nevertheless interesting because the search for newly surfaced notes is never-ending. There is always the hope that the last note needed to complete a segment of such a collection will turn up in the next hoard.

Besides geographic collecting, there is the collecting of national bank notes with interesting names. This field is virtually limitless; it is bound only by your own interpretation of what makes a name interesting. Some people collect notes with people's names as towns, like Enid, Oklahoma, Douglas Arizona, Holly, Colorado, etc. There are Indian names (Pueblo, Colorado, Cheyenne,

Fig. 14-15. There are as many ways to collect national bank notes as there are collectors.

Wyoming), color names (Painted Post, New York, Blue Earth, Minnesota), and just plain unusual names, like Sour Lake, Texas, Slippery Rock, Pennsylvania, and Lone Wolf, Oklahoma.

One fellow collects nationals by bank or city names related to his own first name, Peter, as in St. Petersburg, Florida. You can collect national bank notes signed by women officers of the banks—a real research project—or you can collect nationals by charter number. Some people try to get a specimen from every bank with charter number under 100. Others try to get an example of every charter number over 14,000.

How about my own personal specialty? I collect national bank notes that could have been in the tellers' cages when the banks were robbed by Jesse James, Butch Cassidy and the Sundance Kid, John Dillinger, Bonnie and Clyde and other infamous robbers (Fig. 14-15).

If you put your mind to it, there is no limit (other than that imposed by your wallet) to building a national bank note collection. That is what accounts for the ever-growing popularity of this specialty area.

NATIONAL GOLD BANK NOTES

A distinct class of currency that was separate from, but related to the national bank notes, were the *national gold bank notes*. Gold and the American West have been inseparably linked as part of this nation's history since the discovery of the precious yellow metal at Sutter's Mill in 1848. The short-lived, national gold bank notes were a contemporary part ot "The Golden West," and today

trade on that romantic image, and the rarity of the notes, to derive their popularity and value among collectors.

Authorized under an 1870 law, the national gold bank notes were quite similar to the national bank notes. Similar in design, the NGBNs had a back design that consisted of a vignette of a pile of U.S. gold coins in all denominations from $1 to $20. To reinforce the image, the notes were printed on yellow paper instead of white (Fig. 14-16).

Besides design, the principal difference between the two classes of notes is that the national gold bank notes were payable—and prominently said so on their face—in gold coin. This was a concession to the traditional mistrust by Western Americans in paper money and the California area's long history of gold as the principal medium of exchange.

Like other national banks, national gold banks had to deposit U.S. bonds to secure their circulation. They could, however, issue notes only to the extent of 80 percent of the face value of those bonds. Additionally, it was required that each bank have gold coins actually in its vaults to a total of 25 percent of the notes outstanding.

This gold redemption property gave the notes the necessary credibility and they circulated at par with specie at a time when most paper money in the West could not. They circulated so extensively that surviving specimens are generally found in conditions so low that most collectors would find them unacceptable in other U.S. currency types. No uncirculated specimens are known today. The average condition of national gold bank notes is good to very good.

In all, 10 national gold banks were chartered. There were nine in California, and the Kidder National Gold Bank in Boston, Massachusetts. While the nine California banks all issued notes, the Boston bank did not.

In the period 1870-1878, exactly 196,849 national gold bank notes were issued. Their face value was $3,267,420. Today, official U.S. Treasury records indicate 6,639 notes remain outstanding (this includes four $500 notes unknown in any collection). A recent comprehensive survey of collectors indicates only about 275 specimens known from all banks in hobby hands.

OBSOLETE BANK NOTES

In the period circa 1830-1865, which overlaps the late Colonial currency era and the U.S. government currency issuing era, the only paper currency circulating in the nation was what collectors today call *obsolete* or *broken* bank notes. Not all of this currency was issued by banks.

In the pre-1861 era, the issue of paper currency was a matter of concern for states rather than the federal

Fig. 14-16. Rare and valuable today, the national gold bank notes featured a pile of U.S. gold coins depicted on the back. They were circulated only in California.

government. Each state had its own laws relative to the issue of paper currency. Some permitted no such issue. Others allowed only state-chartered banks to circulate currency. Still others had no laws at all; this opened the way for issues of currency to virtually anybody with access to a printing press. None of this currency was legal tender. It could not be tendered to the government in payment of taxes or even forced on a private merchant for settlement of a purchase.

Whether or not these individual currency issues circulated at all, or circulated at a discount from their face value, was a matter of negotiation between the person holding the note and the person whose goods or services were being sought. A bank note of this period could be as good as gold or worth only the paper on which it was printed. Most fell somewhere in between.

Notes that were issued by banks known to be sound generally found ready acceptance in their immediate locale. There are no guarantees that a note issued by a Boston bank would be acceptable in Cincinnati, and vice versa. Because of the costs involved in sending notes across country for redemption, they were often acceptable only at a discount far from home. A $1 note from New England might buy only 85 cents worth of goods in the South.

Because of their remote locations on the American frontier, notes from what is now the Midwest—Wisconsin, Michigan, Illinois, etc.—came to be called *wildcat notes*. If the holder of one of these notes wanted to redeem it at the bank of issue, he had to go out into the wilderness—among the wildcats—to try to find it. As often as not no such bank existed. The currency was an entirely fabricated issue. The name itself actually comes from one well-known Michigan fraudulent bank note of the era that pictured a wildcat as its central vignette. For similar reasons, this type of currency was also known as *yellow dogs* and *red dogs*.

Today, collectors more often designate the class as broken bank notes, indicating most of the issuing banks went broke, leaving the holders of the notes stuck for payment. More accurately, the term *obsolete American currency* is becoming popular. Not all notes of the era were issued by banks and not all of the banks of issue went broke. Notes in the mid nineteenth century were issued by railroads, canal companies, druggists, and others (Fig. 14-17).

Collectors generally attach lower value to obsolete bank notes than to national currency. This is simply because the obsoletes no longer have any exchange value and were not U.S. government issues.

Collecting specialties for the notes are quite similar. Many people collect the obsolete issues of their home state. With the exception of Alaska and some of the far Western states, most have a good number of notes to choose from. Many other collectors like to collect obsoletes by topic. There are thousands of different designs of the notes in the era (each bank or issuer chose his own designs). People collect trains, animals, soldiers, children, ships, slaves, and many other subject categories (Fig. 14-18).

Obsolete notes can be found in all conditions from torn and dirty rags to crisp uncirculated notes that are as clean and bright as the day were printed (usually because they were never actually placed in circulation). Such unissued notes are referred to as *remainders* in the hobby. Even uncut sheets of notes from some banks are available at a relatively inexpensive price.

The low cost of many obsoletes is a big factor in their popularity. Nice collectible specimens can be purchased for $3 to $5 each. Many hundreds more are available in the $10 to $20 class. Even the top rarities in this field generally do not sell for more than $1,000.

Fig. 14-17. In the days prior to the Civil War, there were few restrictions on the issue of paper money. This note is actually a railroad ticket good for 125 miles passage. It was worth $5.

Fig. 14-18. Many collectors of obsolete bank notes specialize by subject matter of the vignette(s) in the design. Animals are popular. This Kansas note features horses, pigs, and peacocks.

CONFEDERATE CURRENCY

With virtually every gold and silver coin in the Confederacy needed to buy supplies from overseas, the Confederate government resorted to a printing press economy at home. The disasterous results were runaway inflation and increasing mistrust of the notes. The first Confederate paper money issues were produced, in 1861, when the Confederacy was headquartered in Montgomery, Ala. The notes were designed and printed by the American Bank Note Company. They hid behind the guise of the Southern Bank Note Company so that they would not be prosecuted for trading with the enemy. After that first issue—in denominations of interest-bearing $50, $100, $500 and $1,000 notes—all notes were produced in the South by various contract printers and in various degrees of quality. Some were little more than woodcuts. Others were quite finely engraved (Fig. 14-19).

All Confederate paper money, along with the allied issues by the state governments of the Confederate states, are popular with collectors and most specimens are quite reasonable in price. While the early Montgomery issues will sell for several hundred dollars or more, as will a few rare types of Confederate notes, most are available in the $10 to $20 range. Many are available for less than $5.

There have been many reproductions of Confederate currency. They range from contemporary counterfeits to modern souvenirs. Many of these are marked "facsimile," but many are not so marked and the collector should take care until he has become familiar with the genuine article.

FRACTIONAL CURRENCY

During the Civil War and the years immediately afterward (1862-1875), the nation was hit with a chronic coin shortage. Precious-metal coinage was hoarded in those uncertain times. To allow the wheels of commerce to continue to turn, the U.S. government instituted several series of postage and fractional currency. The issues were in denominations from 3 cents to 50 cents and they replaced the silver coinage that disappeared at a rate faster than the mint could turn it out.

The earlier issues are known as *postage currency* because they were perforated, like stamps, and they carried on their face designs of then-current U.S. stamps. Later, different engravings were chosen and the notes more closely resembled our other paper money. Because of their small denominations, the notes were smaller in size than the paper money of the day. Generally, they were about half the size of the present $1 bill. The sizes did vary with denomination and type.

Fig. 14-19. Confederate currency ranged in quality from sublime engravings early in the war, like this rare Montgomery $100, to crude woodcut-produced notes later as the treasury's resources dwindled.

The *fractional currency* series is a paradise for the advanced collector or the variety specialist. The notes were printed in hundreds of minor design, paper, watermark and other varieties that are still being cataloged. The more casual or beginning collector, however, can stick to the main type of notes and build a nice collection at a fairly low cost. Many fractionals are available for under $10 if the buyer is willing to take circulated notes.

The unusual 3 cent and 15 cent denominations help make the fractionals interesting to collectors (Fig. 14-20). Besides those values, the notes were issued in denominations of 5, 10, 25 and 50 cents.

An interesting related item in this field is the frac-

tional currency shield. Issued by the U.S. Treasury Department, these shields were sold to banks to be used as counterfeit detectors. They had specimens of all then-current fractional notes, face and back, mounted under glass. Included was a 15-cent note with the portraits of Union Generals Sherman and Grant that was never issued. The shields now sell for $1,000 and up.

ENCASED POSTAGE STAMPS

Another attempt to relieve the coin shortage was the privately issued encased postage stamps invented by John Gault of Boston. Because they combine a genuine U.S. postage stamp with a hard metal-backed, windowed case, these items are popular with both stamp and coin collectors. They are most often collected by paper money collectors as an adjunct to the fractional currency series.

Mr. Gault bought the stamps and enclosed them in his cases. He minted the cases with advertising messages of sponsoring merchants on the back. The mica window protected the stamp from wear and tear and these coinage substitutes were well received. While the sponsoring advertiser paid Gault 1 cent apiece over the face value of the stamp, he had the benefit of having an advertising message passed from hand to hand all over the country (Fig. 14-21).

Some of the merchants who took advantage of this new medium included dry goods stores, insurance companies, patent-medicine peddlers, hotels, haberdashers, brewers, and wine sellers. While not all merchants issued encased postage stamps in all denominations, they were produced in every value corresponding to the available postage stamps of the day: 1, 2, 3, 5, 10, 12, 24, 30, and 90 cents.

Generally, the higher values are the rarest today. An exception is the 2-cent issue that was only produced by Gault on a trial basis. The idea caught on nation-wide and encased postage stamps were issued from such places as New York to Rhode Island, Cincinnati, Chicago, and even Montreal. Very rare today, even the most common combinations of issuer and stamp value retail for more than $100 if it is in undamaged condition.

MILITARY PAYMENT CERTIFICATES

Kind of a descendent of the emergency Hawaii and North Africa U.S. paper money issues of World War II, the military payment certificate (MPC) issues of the U.S. Military Forces was a phenomenon of the occupation years that lasted through our involvement in Vietnam.

The theory was not so much to provide overseas troops with currency that could be declared worthless, if captured, as to help control the black market in the countries where our troops were stationed. Servicemen in most overseas locations were paid only in MPC, rather then U.S. currency, and the MPC could be spent *only* by servicemen.

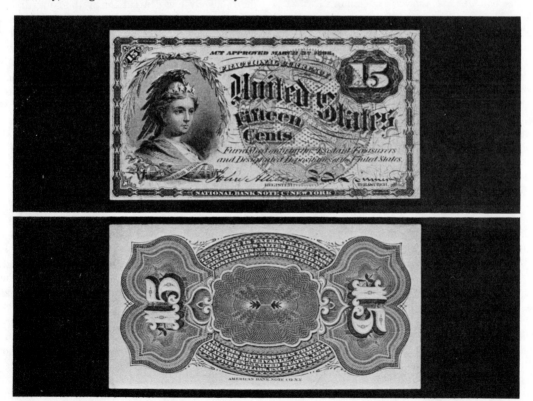

Fig.14-20. The Civil War spawned a coin shortage that resulted in the U.S. Government issuing fractional currency in such denominations as 15 cents.

Fig. 14-21. Another paper coin substitute during the Civil War was the encased postage stamp. They are popular today with stamp collectors as well as numismatists.

This effectively kept American money out of the hands of the native populations and was supposed to keep a lid on black-market activities. While the first issues of military payment certificates were quite plain, the later issues used a wide range of appealing designs from American Indians and animals to portraits of idealized servicemen and even to showcase our military hardware. One popular Vietnam-era $10 MPC shows a Green Beret in action on one side and a tank on the other. Other MPC notes depict jets, submarines, and space exploration themes (Fig. 14-22).

The various MPC series were usually recalled and replaced on a surprise basis (with all personnel restricted to base). This left the black marketeers holding worthless, obsolete MPC issues, while legitimate holders (servicemen) could get new series for old on a dollar-for-dollar exchange. Because the old series then became worthless, little of it was saved. This makes the whole area challenging for collectors. The current emphasis is on top-grade specimens that are all but unavailable for some early types. Even the later types in uncirculated condition are scarce, and they sell for up to several times their face value. Military payment certificates were issued in a wide range of denominations, from 5 cents to $20.

STOCKS, BONDS AND CHECKS

Even though they never had any legal tender status, stocks, bonds and checks—because they were stores of value and closely resemble paper currency in manner of production and issue—are becoming popular sidelight collectibles with many collectors. Few of these financial instruments in collectors hands retain any cash value. Most of the stock and bond certificates in the hobby have been redeemed and cancelled, were never issued in the first place, or have become worthless as the issuing firm

went bankrupt. Still, it happens occasionally that a collector acquires a share certificate that is still "good" on the books of the company that issued it or one of its successors.

The stock and bond craze has been stronger in Europe than in this country, but it is a growing field here. Because of their large size and often intricate engraving work, these beautiful examples of the security printing art are real showpieces. The storage or display of large numbers of them is a problem.

Railroad stocks and bonds are far and away the most popularly collected certificates (Fig. 14-23). Usually combining big, beautiful train scenes with a lot of local and national history—and often the signature of a famous American financier or railroad tycoon as president—they were issued by hundreds of American lines, large and small, throughout the nineteenth century and well into the current century. Mining stocks are also popular.

The value of stocks and bonds is generally dependent more on its design than any other factor. While they are undoubtedly generally scarce in terms of numbers, the relatively low demand among the hobby has kept prices reasonable. Those stocks autographed by famous Americans like Wells & Fargo, Thomas Edison, the Vanderbilts, or the Rockefellers naturally are more highly sought after. Prices range from $1 to over $1,000. About $3,000 is the top price paid for an American certificate.

Besides the American stocks and bonds, there is a whole world of foreign material that is often equally beautiful in design and execution, and made somewhat the more fascinating by the foreign languages in which they were issued.

Checks are collected much like national bank notes or obsolete bank notes, generally by geographic location of the bank of issue, or for the vignettes on them. Personal checking accounts were virtually unknown prior to World War II. Before that, persons who had need of a check used an instrument provided by the bank. Often, as an advertisement for the bank itself, the checks were imprinted with fine engravings of a bank building or other local attraction (Fig. 14-24).

Because almost everybody used checks at one time or another, many checks are valuable collector's items because of the autographs of persons signing or endorsing them. Checks are known to have been signed by presidents of the United States as far back as George Washington. One collector has made it his goal to complete a set of checks, one signed by each of the presidents. That is a formidable goal.

The discovery several years ago of a hoard of old checks, dating back to the 1830s, in a Cooperstown, New

Fig. 14-22. Their military and space themes help make the later military payment certificates popular with collectors.

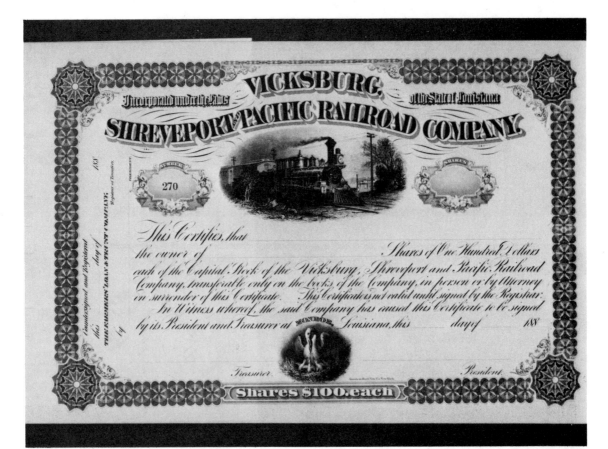

Fig. 14-23. Antique stocks and bonds are a relatively new collectible field in the broad spectrum of numismatics. Century-old stocks can be purchased for as little as $2.

York, bank provided collectors with numerous examples of the autograph of famous American author James Fennimore Cooper.

Combining his interests in numismatics with the sports memorabilia field in which Krause Publications also has periodicals, Chet Krause collects checks signed or endorsed by baseball players. These include payroll checks issued by the teams. Checks of Babe Ruth and Ty Cobb are often encountered in this manner and they always bring a good price.

The era of greatest collector interest in old checks dates about from 1830, when vignettes were first used on checks, through the 1930s. By that time most checks had once again dropped the use of engraved illustrations.

While checks that have been used have a greater historical interest in many cases, collectors today do not seem to differentiate between used and unused checks as far as collecting interest or value. Some paper money

dealers feel that checks are one of the last great untapped collectibles in the field. They believe interest in check collecting has not even begun to reach the proportions it eventually will develop. Most checks are available for under $5 unless they bear a famous autograph, and it would be hard to pay more than $20 for a check (again without a famous signer). When compared with bank notes of the same era, this might some day be realized to have been a groundfloor opportunity.

ERROR NOTES

The Bureau of Engraving and Printing annually produces some four billion U.S. currency notes. Given that enormous quantity of output, it is indeed remarkable that so few error notes ever make it into hobby channels.

In the years since about 1977, the numbers of currency errors finding their way past BEP inspectors has greatly increased in the $1 denomination. This is mostly because of the great numbers of $1 that must be produced each year to satisfy demand from the public and to replace specimens that wear out. In today's economy, the average $1 bill has a street life of only about 18 months. A coin has a street life of about 15 years. That was the major reason the government tried to replace the $1 bill with the Anthony dollar in 1979.

Because of sheer volume, the $1 notes do not receive a great deal of electronic or human inspection. Errors are generally related to the overprinting, or third printing, done by Currency Overprinting and Processing Equipment (COPE).

Paper money in the U.S. today is printed in three separate press runs. On the first time through the press, the backs are printed. The majority of the face design is done on the second press run with the notes still in 32-subject sheets. After the second printing, the sheets are cut into two 16-note panes and fed into the COPE. The COPE adds the third printing. This consists of the green U.S. Treasury seal and serial numbers and the black Federal Reserve bank seal and district designator

numerals in the four corners. Without ever being touched by human hands again, and virtually without inspection, the panes go directly from the overprinting stage through equipment that cuts them into individual notes, stacks them, and wraps them for delivery to the proper Federal Reserve bank.

In recent years, spectacular errors have resulted from the use of COPE as the bugs were worked out of the system. Among the better-known types are notes (in all denominations) with the overprinting applied to the back or upside-down on the face. These notes sell for between $125-$250 over face value in uncirculated condition (Fig. 14-25).

The value of error notes is almost always dependent on the error rather than on the denomination of the bill affected. For instance, in the case of inverted overprinting a $1 note will generally sell for $125 or so. Yet, a $100 bill might bring only about $250, even though it is much rarer, and most of that extra value comes from the higher face value of the note.

The $2 bill, because it circulated for so short a time

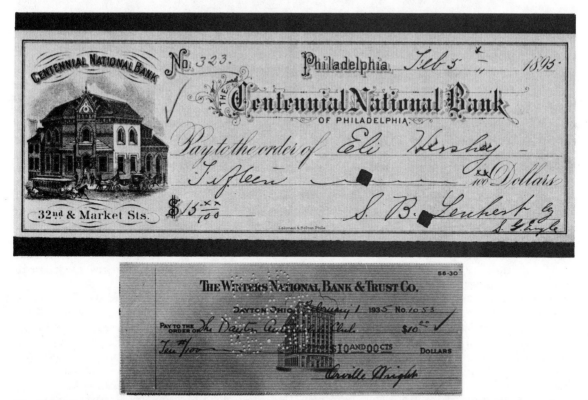

Fig. 14-24. Another new collecting area in the field of fiscal paper is checks. Some feature elaborate engraved vignettes. Others have famous autographs, such as the bottom check, signed by aviation pioneer Orville Wright.

149

Fig. 14-25. While these two $5 bills might look normal at first glance, they are both error notes. The note at top has mismatched serial numbers. The note at bottom has the overprinting applied upside down.

and has not been printed for so long, is the most popular denomination in the current series error notes. An inverted overprinting on a 1976 series $2 may well bring $250. Generally, the higher denominations do not achieve significantly greater value simply because fewer people collect them. Because almost all type of errors can be found on a $1 bill as well as a $10, $20, or $100, the average collector prefers not to tie up his hobby funds in the higher face values.

Other errors that are now being found more often include totally missing printings. This generally happens when two sheets are fed into the press at the same time with the bottom sheet getting no ink. This has resulted in notes with no back printing, no overprinting, or—perhaps the most striking—only the overprinting on the face (with the rest of the face design—portrait, borders, etc.— missing). Values here are currently about $300 over face value.

Perhaps the most commonly encountered error note is the offset error. At first glance, this usually appears as

if part or all of the face design has been printed on the back of a note or that the back design has been printed on the face. When more closely examined, you will see that the "wrong side" impression is actually reversed—a mirror image. This is an offset impression whereby ink has gotten onto the hard rubber rollers of the printing press (in normal image) and then been transferred to the wrong side of the next sheet through the press (in reverse image). The ink usually gets on the roller as a result of a sheet of notes not feeding into the press, or folding up once inside that stage of the print operation.

When an entire sheet fails to feed, the whole printing plate impression will be transferred to the next sheet. The result is up to 32 offset error notes. If the sheet was only folded, just parts of a few notes might be affected. The offset will transfer to the next several sheets that pass through. The first will receive the darkest impression, with each succeeding sheet receiving lighter transfer of ink, until it is gone from the roller.

While inspectors catch many of these errors when

the full sheets are inspected, after both face and back printings, many others escape into circulation. Value of offset errors is dependent on how dark the offset is (the darker the better) and how much of the side of a note is affected. Full offset transfers are the most valuable—up to $200 each—while partial offsets might be worth only a few dollars over face value. This is especially true if the note is in circulated condition.

As is the case with virtually every numismatic item, the condition of error notes is very important in determining their value. Uncirculated notes are preferred by the vast majority of error collectors.

The list of error types is virtually endless. Many one of a kind notes are well known to hobbyists. An example is the famous "Band-Aid $5" of a few years back. During the printing of a $5 Federal Reserve note sheet some years ago, the plastic backing from a Band-Aid fell into the press and onto the sheet being printed. The high pressure with which currency is printed in the intaglio (engraved) bank note process apparently held the Band-Aid piece in place, right through the overprinting stage, and it received parts of the face and overprinting details. When the note reached a local bank, the strip loosened and it was noticed by a teller. The note eventually found its way into the hobby. Such error notes are called *intercepted printings* and they are valued according to how much of the printing was intercepted, by what, and whether that item is still attached to the note.

The king of paper money errors is the double-denomination note. This type of error occurs when notes that have received the back printing for one denomination are given the face printing for another. This has resulted in many famous notes as far back as the nineteenth century national bank notes: at least three notes are known to have been printed with $50/$100 combinations, face and back. Other types of this error have continued. Fairly recent years, several $1/$10 Federal Reserve notes mismatchings surfaced. The value of such errors runs from several thousand dollars for relatively modern specimens to $20,000 or more for some of the early nationals.

Collectors should be warned that many types of errors that can legitimately occur at the Bureau of Engraving and Printing can be duplicated on the outside with such things as electronic erasers. Avail yourself of the error note authentication services of *Bank Note Reporter's* expert Alan Herbert. Always buy your error notes from a reputable dealer.

The most commonly encountered "error" note is the wrong color back printing. This is not a legitimate printing error because it did not occur at the BEP. The back color of all U.S. modern currency is green. There has never been a verified case of the wrong color ink being used to print either the face or back of a note. Yet, sometimes U.S. notes show up with backs in blue or yellow.

While the early large-size gold certificates sometimes used yellow back printing, none has been done since 1928. The blue or yellow backs sometimes seen on modern U.S. paper money is the result of bleach or alkali being applied to the note. This can happen on purpose to create a fake error or as innocently as being in the washing machine when bleach is used. These chemicals break down part of the green ink and leave either the blue or the yellow components. Such notes, as is the case with all phony error notes, have no collector value.

Chapter 15

World Coins

WORLD COINS ARE GENERALLY COLLECTED EIther by topic or country. I will concentrate here on collecting by country. It is an impossible goal to attempt to collect the whole field of world coins. Even if you started today with the intention of obtaining a specimen of each new issue in each denomination, you would never catch up. There are simply too many new issues each year. We do not hear about some of the issues in this country until years after they have entered circulation.

The most logical way to collect world coins is to specialize in one or more countries that appeal to you. Many numismatists choose the country of their ancestors, grandparents, or parents. Other collectors choose a country they have visited during military service or on vacation; perhaps they have picked up the beginnings of a collection at that time. Still others choose a country to collect for no reason they can logically explain. Perhaps they think it is an exotic land. Perhaps it has been in the news lately or it might be of special historical significance.

Whatever the reason, specialization is definitely the way to go in the world-coin field. The best place to start is to pick up a copy of the *Standard Catalog of World Coins* from your local library or coin dealer. Paging through the massive book, you will be able to judge the scope of any

nation's coinage issues from the mid-1700s to today. You might decide that a nation has issued too many coins for your tastes, too few coins to be challenging, or too many coins of great rarity and high value.

Once you have a basic idea of what the scope of your collection will be, you will probably want to purchase a specialty catalog. Many countries are covered in small, specialty catalogs that go into much greater detail than the *Standard Catalog*. Perhaps the nation of your choice had coinage prior to the eighteenth century. It will almost certainly have varieties and related issues of interest. To determine what books might be available for your specialty, consult a numismatic bibliography or the library catalog of the American Numismatic Association. If your country is one of the more modern, popular nations, your local coin dealer might be able to help you off the top of his head.

While it would be impossible to survey the entire world-coin arena in this space, I will discuss three of the most appealing countries for many beginning collectors: Canada, Mexico, and Great Britain.

CANADA

Because of its proximity, many American collectors become interested in the coins of Canada. The similarity of

Fig. 15-1. Canada's recent regular coinage of commemorative silver dollars has been the envy of collectors in the United States. This proof 1981 .500 fine silver dollar marked the centennial of the Trans-Canada railway.

the coinage systems in our neighboring countries also contributes to this popularity. In addition, before the mid-1970s, when the Canadian dollar became worth only about 85 U.S. cents, the coins of Canada circulated rather freely in the Northern states. Many collectors from Washington to Wisconsin to Maine began to build Canadian collections from coins picked up in circulation.

Canada's coinage history is much shorter than our own (at least in terms of official government issues).

While colonial French coinage circulated as early as the late 1600s, the first Canadian decimal coins did not appear until 1858. Then 1-, 5- and 20-cent coins were issued in the name of the Province of Canada (Ontario and Quebec, today).

The first truly national Canadian coins were offered, in 1870, following the confederation of Ontario and Quebec with Nova Scotia and New Brunswick in 1867. Both of the latter had their own distinctive coinage in the early 1860s. Prince Edward Island had a single issue of 1-cent coins, in 1871, prior to entering the Confederation in 1873. A coinage of Newfoundland was also initiated in this period, 1865, and continued through 1947. That British dependency moved into the confederation in 1949.

In contrast to the .900-fine standard of American silver coins, Canadian silver was originally launched on the sterling system. Such coins have a fineness of .925 and they are slightly smaller in size. In 1920, Canada changed to an .800-fine standard. In 1967, a .500-fine coinage was adopted. A year later, all silver was taken out of circulating Canadian coinage. Nickel was used instead.

Canada's 1-cent coin also contrasted with United States 1-cent coins. Canada's first cents, in 1858, were of

Fig. 15-2. Mexico's coinage legacy is centuries older than that of the United States, a mint of the Spanish Empire was built in Mexico in the sixteenth century to turn out the gold and silver cob coinage (known today as gold doubloons and pieces of eight).

the large-size, bronze composition then in use in England. This size was used until 1920. Then small cents, with the same standards as those of the United States were adopted. The Canadian cent took an unusual twist in 1982 when it was announced that beginning in March, the denomination would be issued in a redesigned 12-sided shape.

When Canada's dominion coin issue of 1870 was introduced, the 1858 provincial issue of a 20-cent coin was abandoned in favor of the 25-cent coin. The move was made, in part, because of the confusion of the 20-cent piece with the United States 25-cent coin, which circulated freely in Canada. A similar fate would befall the United States' own 20-cent coin a few years later.

Although tentative steps aimed at the creation of a dollar coin were instituted in 1911, it was not until 1935—the year silver dollar coinage was halted in the United States—that Canada launched the issue of a silver dollar.

The first Canadian silver dollar was a commemorative of the Silver Jubilee (25th year of monarchy) of King George V. From the beginning, Canada's dollar series has been frequently employed as a vehicle for the commemoration of national events. This has been to the envy of American collectors (Fig. 15-1). Such popular themes as the Calgary Stampede rodeo, the Royal Canadian Mounted Police, and early railroading have been marked with Canadian commemorative dollars in recent years.

Since 1971, Canada has issued a special commemorative .500-fine silver dollar each year. In 1973-1976, the nation issued a long series of gold and silver commemorative coins to mark the 1976 Olympic Summer Games at Montreal. There have been other commemorative coins, in the 5-cent and 25-cent denominations, as well as the entire range of Canadian denominations. This includes a special $20 gold piece, in 1967, to celebrate the centennial of Confederation.

In the early years, Canada's coins were struck by the British Royal Mint in London or Birmingham. Since 1908, Canada has operated its own mints, at Ottawa, and, since 1968, at Winnipeg. Some pure nickel composition dimes were struck for Canada at the U.S. Mint in Philadelphia in 1968.

MEXICO

With a coinage history dating back to Spanish colonial days in the 1500s, Mexico has a rich numismatic legacy that many American collectors are now finding appealing.

From the irregular *cob* coinage struck at crude colonial mints from the vast silver and gold treasures of Mexico, to today's modern circulating coins produced at one of the world's finest minting facilities, Mexico's coinage is quite interesting (Fig. 15-2). Along with the coins issued by colonial monarchs, there are issues from several revolutionary authorities and today's constitutional government. Coinages of the Republic era and the current United States of Mexico trace their heritage to Spanish dominion days and also through the centuries of many state and local issues.

Many collectors begin their interests in Mexican coinage with the period of King Charles III (1760-1788). This roughly parallels our own Revolutionary era coinage. Because the government and economy of Mexico were very stable during that era, their coinage issues

Fig. 15-3. The entire realm of Mexican numismatics has been cataloged for easy reference by the beginning collector in Krause's *Standard Catalog of Mexican Coins, Paper Money, Stocks, Bonds and Medals.*

Fig. 15-4. While the world of British coinage dates back to pre-Christian days, through Henry VIII, and into Shakespearean times, many collectors begin with the reign of King George III, depicted here on a two-penny coin.

were frequent and numerous. The late 1700s coins can be purchased for only a few dollars in a wide range of denominations.

While specialists might go in for the various state and local mint marks and assayers initials and other varities, the more casually interested collector will find plenty of challenge in the issues of the Republic (1823-1864), the Maximilian Empire (1864-1867), the Republic decimal issues (1869-1905), and the Estados Unidos Mexicanos since 1905 (Fig. 15-3).

The Mexican coinage of all eras is rife with national heroes, native designs, and commemorative themes.

Fig. 15-5. The long reign of Queen Victoria spanned the height of the days of the British Empire. The reverse of this crown silver piece shows St. George and the Dragon.

GREAT BRITAIN

Because of our nation's colonial ties to England, and the Anglo-Saxon heritage of many Americans, Great Britain remains one of the more popular countries of specialty for U.S. numismatists.

While the origins of coinage in England go back well into the first millenium with the coins of Saxon kings and Viking raiders, most collectors begin with a much later era, the coins of King George III are popular. See Fig. 15-4. For many others, the long reign of Queen Victoria (1837-1901), with its several changes of official portrait to show the graceful aging of the monarch, is a favorite (Fig. 15-5). In the more modern era, the stationing of many American servicemen in England during World War II and since gives still other collectors personal ties with English coinage of the George VI (1936-1952) monarchy and that of his daughter, Elizabeth II.

The strange denominations of farthing (¼d), shilling (12 pence), florin (2 shillings) and others, combined with English-language legends, gives additional appeal to British coinage.

While there are many rarities in the series down through the centuries, a very nice type set of monarchs and denominations can be built up with little trouble and no great expense. For those of historical bent, coins of famous British kings and queens are not all that expensive, for coins going back to King Henry VIII, Elizabeth I, and others.

There are annual specialty catalogs covering British coinage and an excellent monthly magazine. Details on these publications can be obtained from a world coin dealer in your area.

Chapter 16

Tokens and Medals

T HE TERM *EXONUMIA* IS A RECENT INVEN-
tion to describe the field of nonmonetary collectibles that nevertheless fit into the numismatic field by
virtue of their use as coinage substitutes or as metallic
commemoratives of a noncoinage nature. The word is
derived from the Greek *exo*, away from, and *numis*,
money.

The field broadly covers everything from wooden
nickels and merchants tokens to official government-
issued commemorative medals and military decorations
and orders of a commemorative nature (Fig. 16-1).

Generally, a token is considered to be an item that
was intended to circulate, in lieu of money, in an
emergency coin shortage. Examples are the Hard Times
tokens of the 1832-1844 era and the Civil War tokens of
the 1862-1865 era. Both of these were privately minted to
replace 1-cent coins that were being hoarded or for advertising or trade stimulation purposes. Examples are the
many thousands of "Good For . . ." tokens issued by
merchants in this country for more than 100 years.

Other major categories of collectible tokens include
transportation tokens that were sold for use on buses,
trolleys, trains, and subways (Fig. 16-2). Some items that
are today commonly known to collectors as tokens served
no real currency function. These include political tokens,

used in the nineteenth and early twentieth century to
promote candidates for public office or to run down the
opposition satirically; fraternal tokens, used for identification by lodges and organizations; coal and wood tokens,
paid out as wages to miners and loggers and exchangeable
for cash (sometimes) or goods in the company store; and
even love tokens, regular-issue U.S. coins (sometimes
Canadian and English, also), that have one side smoothed
off and re-engraved with the initials or name of a loved
one.

The term *medal* is generally reserved for a metallic
item of a commemorative, souvenir, or presentation nature. This can include the various privately struck local
and state centennial medals, medals struck to mark the
anniversary of a corporation or local store, medals presented to distinguished citizens by the governments at
local, state, or national levels (Fig. 16-3), and medals
presented by the military for valor or service.

If an item was ever produced that was metallic in
nature, carried a picture or inscription, was intended to
serve as money or a commemorative, it is collectible
under the heading of exonumia. Most collectors find that
they have to specialize in such a wide area. They collect
on the basis of geographic location—medals and tokens
from their town or state—or subject matter. Examples

Fig. 16-1. British military decorations are popular with exonumia collectors because the name of the recipient is engraved on each. The soldier's history is easily looked up in reference books. This medal dates to the Boer War at the turn of the century in South Africa.

Fig. 16-2. A popular token collecting area is the transportation field.

Fig. 16-3. The U.S. government issues many official medals such as this 1980 release. An original gold specimen went to the Duke's family, but collectors may buy a bronze reproduction for about $3.

include exonumia pertaining to automobiles, prison tokens, famous American soldiers, livesaving medals, and British war decorations.

The greatest appeal of exonumia for many collectors is that it is a relatively uncharted field. Many areas have never been adequately cataloged. With relatively little idea of what is rare and how many people are collecting, prices have remained generally reasonable throughout the field.

Junk boxes abound where the collector can pick and choose from among hundreds of exonumia items for a dime or quarter each. Many areas of this collectible specialty consider an item expensive if it sells for more than $10. There are, however, certainly many rare and popular items that are valued into the hundreds and thousands of dollars. This is particularly true for Hard Times and Civil War tokens. Membership in the Token and Medal Society is recommended for the beginning exonumist.

Chapter 17

How to Collect

THERE ARE NO RIGHT OR WRONG WAYS FOR you to collect coins and related numismatic items. You are always entirely free to buy or not buy a coin on the basis of whether you feel it will fit into what you have chosen as the parameters of your collection. In discussing the many and varied types of collectible numismatic items in the previous chapters, I suggested some specialized ways in which many of them could be assembled into interesting, meaningful, and potentially profitable collections. In this chapter, I delve into the mechanics of building a collection by the three most popular methods: date and mint mark, type, and topical.

A few words of general advice apply to all of your coin collecting endeavors. They will be beneficial to you no matter how you choose to pursue the hobby. The first suggestion, and one of the hardest for the beginning collector to heed, is not to try to buy everything that comes along. This applies to new issues as well as to older, scarcer coins. Unless you are one of the fortunate few to whom money is no object (in a hobby like numismatics, nobody is that well off), you can't begin to afford everything at once unless you have chosen your collection on a very elementary level.

A big mistake some beginning collectors make is in thinking they have to buy the first rare coin they see or they will never get another chance—at least at current price levels. This is simply not usually the case until you get into some of the highly specialized areas of paper money or token and medal collecting. Most coins that collectors collect were struck in relatively large numbers. Many of those have survived to this day and they are in the hands of fellow collectors or dealers.

Even with truly rare numismatic items, you can be almost assured that if you miss one another will be along soon. John Hickman, who is the nation's premier expert on national bank notes, has developed a theorem in that area that, by extrapolation, applies to all other areas of numismatics with which I am familiar.

It is Hickman's observation that even if there are as few as half a dozen known specimens of a particular national bank note (or other numismatic item), the numismatic market is such that one of those specimens will become available every three years or so. It is my observation that this is accurate even for such rarities as the 1913 Liberty nickel or the Brasher doubloon. While there might be gaps of considerably longer than three years between transactions for these rarities, it does seem to have averaged out over the recent decades. And there are fewer than six known examples of each which are not forever interred in a major museum collection.

The lesson here is not to panic and mortgage the farm when you see a particularly scarce coin come to the market that you would like to have for your collection. At the same time, when the truly scarce items do become available at a time when their purchase might conveniently fit into your hobby budget, it is a good idea to buy them. The hobby's better items tend to increase in price steadily. If you pass up the chance today, the next time around the item will surely be carrying a larger price tag. You must strike a harmonious balance between building your numismatic collections and carrying on the rest of your life's affairs.

In line with some of the above guidelines is the golden rule of building a collection of any type of collectible: buy the best quality you can afford. Not to infringe upon your rights to collect whatever you want, but long hobby experience has shown me that the beginning collector is better off to start buying high-grade specimens than to try to upgrade them at a later date.

If you are working on a type collection of United States coins, and you have decided to make that your hobby goal, I would advise you to build that collection slowly by buying top condition coins. You should not try to build it swiftly by buying lower-grade pieces. By top grade, I don't necessarily mean "Gem Uncirculated." That's another one of your personal collection choices. You might have decided that because an uncirculated type set of U.S. coins is out of your financial grasp, that you will collect a set of circulated examples. Fine, but follow my advice and buy high-grade circulated specimens. If you have $10 to spend on this collection, buy an extremely fine common-date Indian-head cent rather than half a dozen good or very good cents or nickels.

That XF Indian will likely retain a bit of original mint luster, will show virtually all of its original design details, and in general will be a credit to your collection. The lower-grade coins that you might have bought will someday have to be replaced by higher-grade pieces as your collecting tastes mature.

The same is true if uncirculated-type coins are your favorite. Buy MS-65 quality rather than MS-60. In both cases, the value of your collection will grow faster when it is built of high-grade specimens because that is a fact of numismatic life. The highest-grade coins are the most in demand and the pieces which will rise more rapidly in price. By buying the better coin today, you save yourself tomorrow's price increase while you allow that price rise to accrue to the coin as it sits in your own collection.

MINT MARK COLLECTING

The most widespread and popular collecting form today remains, as it has always been, date and mint mark collecting (Fig. 17-1). That is the assembling of a collection of every date and mint of issue for a particular U.S. coinage series. Date/mint mark collecting is not currently extremely popular in world coins. This is largely because most nations' coinage has been issued on an erratic schedule. Few nations have more than one mint striking their coins.

In the United States, however, our traditions of a 200-year-old monetary system, regular production of most coinage denominations, and the use of branch mints to provide coins for our commercial needs have created a great number of coin series that lend themselves well to collecting by date and mint mark.

Without exception, all United States carry a date indicative of their issue. While there are scattered cases—including the very famous 1804 silver dollar—throughout our numismatic history in which coins have been struck in a year other than that which appears on it, collectors universally ignore the actual date of striking or issue in favor of the inscribed date. Likewise, each U.S. coin is imprinted with an initial or initials symbolic of the mint that actually produced the coin. While the "P" mint mark has been returned to all coins except the cent that is struck at the Philadelphia Mint, it has been a tradition since the 1790s that coins produced at the "Mother Mint," the nation's first coining facility, did not carry a mint mark. This tradition was broken only once before 1980. That was during the World War II years when the five-cent "nickel" was struck of an emergency composition of silver (35 percent), copper (56 percent) and manganese (9 percent) during 1942-45. The mint mark on all nickels was placed conspicuously above the dome of Monticello on the reverse, including a "P" for those war nickels struck in Philadelphia.

United States branch mints followed the nation's expansion all over the continent. When gold was discovered in the Carolinas and Georgia in the 1830s, U.S. Mints were established in Charlotte, North Carolina and Dahlonega, Georgia. They began turning out coins with "C" and "D" mint marks, respectively (Fig. 17-2). By 1840, another branch was operating in New Orleans; it produced coins with an "O" mint mark. While the Charlotte and Dahlonega Mints did not survive the Civil War, the New Orleans branch continued to turn out silver coins until 1909.

Hard on the heels of the California gold rush of 1848 came a U.S. Mint at San Francisco. The distinctive and popular "S" mint mark, though halted and restarted a time or two in its history, continues to appear on coins struck even today. The Comstock silver lode, discovered in

Fig. 17-1. Filling the penny board is the most basic form of assembling a date and mint mark collection. The most popular way to collect U.S. coins is the route taken by most beginning numismatists.

Nevada in the late 1860s, brought another branch mint to the West. This one was in Carson City, Nevada, where miners converted their silver strike into freshly minted coins with the "CC" mint mark (Fig. 17-3).

By the time the last of the mints was opened in Denver in 1906, taking advantage of the proximity to Colorado copper country, the "D" mint mark, that had once marked the gold coins of Dahlonega, could be used for Denver production without fear of mixup. The old Georgia mint had struck its last coins nearly 50 years earlier.

Because each of the U.S. Mints was intended to strike a different proportion of our national coinage needs at the time of its operation, not all mints turned out coins of every denomination in a given year. It has only been in very recent years that such has been the case.

The presence (or absence) of a particular mint mark can be very influential on a coin's value. The first-year

Lincoln cent is the classic example. On those 1909 Lincoln cents, which feature the prominent designer's initials V.D.B. (Victor David Brenner) on the back and no mint mark, indicative of a Philadelphia origin, the premium for a good condition specimen is $2. The very same coin, bearing the San Francisco "S" mint mark under the date, sells for $300 in the same good grade. The reason is relative rarity; nearly 28 million such coins were produced in Philly. The total mintage of the piece at San Francisco was just 484,000.

Such striking difference in coinage value are what helps make collecting by date and mint mark a great challenge. And therein lies the lure for many collectors. Since R.S. Yeoman produced the first coin board, which later evolved into the familiar Whitman blue coin folder and the latter-day albums, generations of American collectors have grown up with the date/mint mark method of collecting. Most collectors today remember getting their

Fig. 17-2. Mint marks were created to identify the product of U.S. branch mints after national expansion put the Philadelphia Mint out of reach of many citizens. The Charlotte (N.C.) mint began coining operations in 1838.

start by searching their pennies for just the right combination of issuing date and mint to fill another hole in their collection of 1909-1940 or 1941-date cents.

All that is required to start a date and mint mark collection is to decide which one or more of your favorite U.S. coins types you will collect in this manner, and to get one of the myriad special holders with which to house your collection. By nature, the limits of your collection are laid out clearly in front of you. By choosing to collect a particular coin type by date and mint mark, you have predetermined to seek out each of a limited number of coins.

Beyond one or two ultrarare specimens that you can encounter in some series—such as the 1913 Liberty nickel if you decide to collect that series—you have an attainable goal in sight from the moment you start that collection. You can work toward that goal with a single-minded determination. Such is not necessarily the case when you decide to form a type collection. There are many more decisions to be made when going this route.

TYPE COLLECTING

A *type collection* is a collection of coins in which only one specimen of a piece is collected, without regard to the date or mint of issue. This allows the collector, in cases where a coinage type may contain some rare examples, to

acquire a coin of the same design, but a more common date and mint mark (Fig. 17-4).

The type collector is blessed (or cursed) with a relatively open-ended collection. Instead of limiting his scope to one specimen each of each date and mint mark for a particular coin design, he is free to choose from a wider array of coins. But he must make that choice wisely to avoid making his collecting goal too easy or too difficult.

One of the basic decisions a potential collector of U.S. type coins must make is what his personal definition of *type* will be. There are no hard and fast collecting rules to help or hinder you. A coinage "type" is generally regarded as a coin of a particular design and composition, but different collectors have different viewpoints on what consists difference in these areas.

An example is the Lincoln cent series. Many type collectors are content to consider their type collection of Lincolns complete with two examples: one featuring the Wheatback design, in use from 1909-1958, and another featuring the Lincoln Memorial back, in use since 1959. Many others will add a third coin to their Lincoln type set, one of the zinc-coated steel cents of 1943, because its white finish causes it to stand out in such contrast to the rest of the series. But still other type collectors will argue that there are several more types of Lincolns necessary to complete a type collection here. They would cite the V.D.B. reverse cents, the "shellcase" cents of 1944-46 made from metal salvaged from used cartridge cases, and the new 1982 cents of copper-coated zinc composition as separate types. Where you draw the line is strictly up to you. If you are like most type collectors, you will continue to add types to your set, indefinitely, even after your original collecting goals have been met.

Perhaps the biggest decisions for the type collector is how many denominations to include in his type set and how many years to include. A currently popular type collection is the twentieth century type. This helps limit the coins needed for completion to a relatively easy-to-manage number and it gives the collector great flexibility in choosing around the scarce and rare dates. It is still an extremely wide and varied collection in terms of numbers

Fig. 17-3. The historic mint mark of the Carson City (Nevada) coining facility is CC. It is most commonly found on silver dollars produced from ore mined from the Comstock Lode.

164

of denominations—from cent all the way through $20 gold, if you like—and different designs.

Other type collectors limit their sets to one metal such as all U.S. gold coins, or the bronze and copper issues, or just the nickels. They allow their sets to span the entire range of that particular metal's coinage history in this country. This allows you to represent within the scope of your collection up to two centuries of U.S. coinage.

One big advantage of type collecting is that you can bypass the scarce or rare date or mint mark in favor of a common coin while still maintaining the "integrity" of your set. If, for example, you are collecting a type set of U.S. 1-cent coins, you need not buy an 1856 flying eagle cent for $3,000 in uncirculated grade, when an uncirculated 1857, 1858, or 1859 piece can be had for $450.

Before deciding to build a full type collection of U.S. cents, you should consider that our very first cent type, the flowing hair large cents of 1793, with chain reverse, begin at about $1,000 in collectible grades. You might, in

such a case, be better off to limit yourself to the type cents of the nineteenth and twentieth centuries.

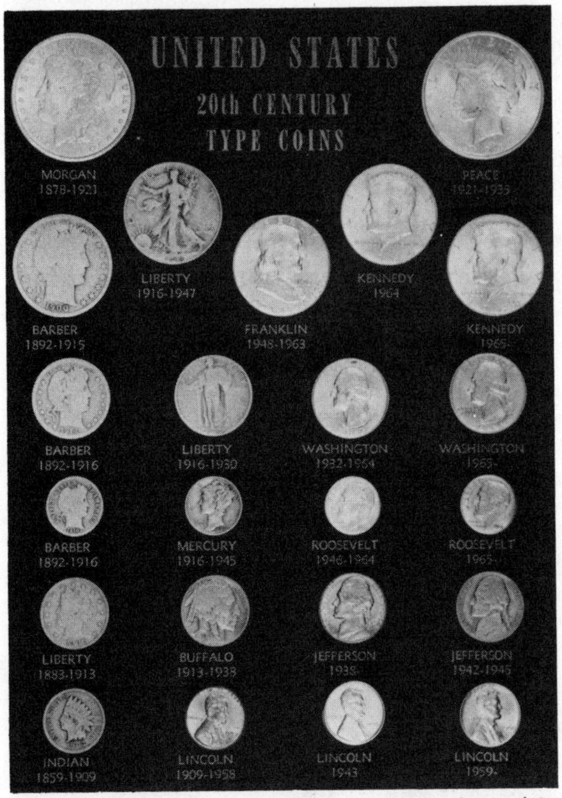

Many collectors seek to construct their type sets of uncirculated coins. Such a set is indeed eye catching, but you don't have to collect uncirculated coins to form a type collection. To the untrained eye, a nice type collection of extremely fine condition coins, chosen for their original luster, will present as nice a picture as a true uncirculated set. And it will cost a lot less.

Certainly a type collection is more impressive to a noncollector than a date and mint mark set. To the non-numismatist, an album full of Mercury dimes looks just like a book of 10-cent pieces. There is no apparent variety to the untrained observer. The real type coin fanatic will tell you that this is the best reason to collect by type.

The same money spent assembling a complete set of Mercury dimes would buy dozens of different type coins, from half cents through double eagle gold pieces, each one different in size, design, and color from the others. If you are the type of coin collector who is captivated by a single beautiful coinage design, the potential variety of type collecting might not appeal to you, but type collecting is rapidly becoming the most popular way for the advanced numismatist to collect.

Even the investment advisors favor type collecting. They reason that, by putting your money into as many different coinage types as possible, you minimize the risk of sticking your investment dollars into a single coinage series that could turn unpopular. The other side of that argument is that, if you have faith in your own judgment, the date and mint mark collection you build of a given U.S. coin series might be worth a big payday someday if that series all of a sudden becomes hot.

TOPICAL COLLECTING

The third major way to collect coins and other numismatic material is by topic. The topical collection is built of coins, paper money, medals, tokens, etc., that share a common design theme. Because U.S. coins and currency have been relatively staid and traditional in design, and do not change frequently, topical collecting is much more popular among world coin and note collectors. The true topical collector, however, knows no geographic or economic bounds in his collecting pursuit. Additionally, the vast U.S. commemorative coinage series has an abundance of topical material from which the collector can draw to build his personal theme collection.

Perhaps the most popular topical theme, here and abroad, is animals. If you look only to regular-issue U.S. coins, most collectors are stymied after the eagle (all gold and silver coins) and the buffalo (5 cents of 1913-1938).

Fig. 17-4. A popular collector or investor alternative to date and mint mark collecting is type collecting. One specimen of each major design is assembled.

165

But if you move into the U.S. commemorative series, you can add the bear, horse, beaver, turtle, dolphin, whale, calf ox, etc. There are even such mythological creatures as the mermaid and hippocamus (half horse, half fish).

In the field of world coins, there is no end to the "zoo" you can create from coinage designs. So widespread is topical collecting, that many foreign governments have taken notice of this collecting phenomena and begun to issue special coins in designs created to appeal to the topical collector. Birds, animals and flowers, many of them are very rare species, have recently shown up more and more often on world coinage. This is especially true for the expensive gold and silver kind coins.

Certain popular national events give rise to commemorative coinage issues create new topical collectors. In 1981, the wedding of the Prince of Wales led to more than 70 different legal-tender coins from England, her colonies, Commonwealth allies, and friendly nations the world over. And that doesn't even count the medals struck for the occasion.

Topical collecting can be a good deal like type collecting in that many topical collectors limit themselves to one representative example rather than trying to buy everything. For example, the collector of birds on American coins will likely buy only one coin with an eagle on it. This might be any denomination from 25 cents to $20. The collector might narrow his scope from the larger world of birds to, for example, chickens. Then he would attempt to get one type of each coin ever issued with a chicken on it (and there have been several dozen different types), but usually without regard to date and mint mark.

Virtually any topic that strikes your interest will make an excellent topical coin collection: bridges, trains,

Fig. 17-5. Paper money is usually included when building a topical collection. The birds on coins can't begin to compare with the larger, more colorful designs of bank notes—like this Indonesian 10 rupees.

sports, nudes, boats, soldiers, native costume, mythological figures, etc. You can limit your topical collecting to legal tender coins or even to coins that were actually intended to circulate in their country of issue. Surprisingly, a large number of Third World coins have never seen their "native" land. They are created, designed, minted, sold, and collected strictly within the borders of the U.S. or a Western European nation.

Most topical collectors eventually expand their areas of interest to include paper money or commemorative medals and tokens. By including paper money in your topical collection, you open up an even wider area of choice. With their larger surface and capability for color printing, currency notes offer topical collectors some of the finest collectibles in their particular areas of interest. Native birds are so much more attractive when they appear in natural color on a nation's currency than when they are shown in reduced size and in metallic rendering on a coin (Fig. 17-5).

Similarly, if your collecting interests are in some of the more modern areas, such as airplanes, you'll find more to collect in world paper money because it is a newer form of money.

Topical collecting is probably the most open-ended of all types of numismatic collections. Besides deciding what to collect in the way of subject matter, and the parameters of issuing nations, periods, and currencies, there is the continual watching of the new coin and note issues columns of *World Coin News* to see if some new country or regime has issued a coin or bank note with a design that appeals to your specific topical collection. In that way, your collection is never "complete."

While world coins have been well cataloged and photographed, many of the world's paper money designs are still unfamiliar to the average collector. Even the telephone-book sized *Standard Catalog of World Paper Money* does not show the face and back of every major note type. There is always something turning up in your field of topical interest that you never knew existed. These finds help make topical collecting fun for even the most veteran numismatist.

All it takes to begin a topical collection is to decide what you want to collect. Then spend a few evenings' time browsing through the *Standard Catalog of World Coins* and the companion paper money volume. By the time you have gone from Afghanistan through Zaire in these catalogs, you will have a fair idea of what you are looking for in the marketplace. Then it's up to you to seek out the specimens you want.

A topical collection is probably the easiest way to begin branching out from collecting only coins to collecting some of the other numismatic items. For instance, if your topical interest is in railroads, it will be relatively easy to find some one dozen world coins that show different types of trains (from old steam engines to modern diesel streamliners). There are several world bank notes that depict modern railroad equipment and you will find that dozens of older foreign currency notes show antique engines.

Those older world notes might lead you into the field of U.S. paper money. In the area of obsolete bank notes, you can find hundreds of century-old American bank issues showing trains. Many of them provide the finest examples of the engraver's art that have survived in any form. There are even two U.S. government-issued currency notes of the early twentieth century that depict trains and are available relatively inexpensively.

From the field of coins and paper money, the train collector can move on to stock certificates and bonds. From the early 1800s right up through the recent decades, hundreds of railroads and related companies around the world have issued securities to their investors. These securities have vignettes of trains and other railroad-related subjects. Because of the larger size of these stocks and bonds, most of the vignettes are far larger than on currency notes. Consequently, their greater detail makes them that much more attractive to collectors. Of all the antique stocks and bonds being collected today (a relatively new numismatic specialty), railroad items are far and away the most popular in the United States and Europe. In Europe, the stock and bond collecting craze is even stronger than in the United States.

The railroad topical collector will also find endless numbers of medals and tokens relating to his subject specialty. There are commemorative medals issued to mark the inaugural runs of special trains, historic medals from United States and worldwide government and private mints, and railroad anniversary medals. Their are fare tokens that were redeemable for train rides (the modern subway token is a direct descendant of this type), and tokens the railroads gave to wood and water suppliers along the track who provided the ingredients necessary to propel the steam engines.

In the Southern United States in the nineteenth century, a number of railroad tickets were issued as a type of currency. When railroad transport was the only viable long-distance travel medium, railroad fare currency circulated freely in widespread areas because the holders knew they would be needing it sooner or later for travel.

While these fare ticket currency notes were denominated in amounts of 1, 5, 10, 20, etc., a closer look shows the word "dollars" was not used. The notes promised to pay the bearer in the form of train rides of specific mileage lengths. This was often in odd distances such as 2½ miles. As with all forms of topical collecting, the railroad collector can never hope to have a "complete" collection. Too many items pertaining to railroads have been issued over the past 150 years. But the challenge is what makes topical collecting fun for most numismatists.

Chapter 18

Grading

THERE HAS BEEN NO SUBJECT MORE CONTROVER-sial in the numismatic hobby/industry in the past 15 years than that of grading. Grading is nothing more than providing a written (or verbal) description for a coin that accurately reflects its state of preservation. The purpose of doing so is to allow the coin (or other numismatic item) to be bought, sold, or traded fairly when the two parties involved are not face to face in a situation where the coin can be viewed. An example, is when you are dealing by mail.

Anyway, that *used* to be the purpose of grading a coin. Today, a coin is graded so that a "correct" value can be placed on it. The difference between seemingly identical coins, one of which is labeled "Choice Uncirculated MS-65," and the other "Gem Uncirculated MS-67," can easily run into hundreds or even thousands of dollars. The same situation is true for notes that are "Crisp Uncirculated" or "Gem Crisp New."

If there is anything that turns new numismatists away from the coin collecting hobby faster than the confusion and controversy that surrounds the grading of coins, it would be the high prices that such disorder has promoted and justified. In the next few pages, I think I can help bring some order to this chaos and cut through some of the rhetoric about grading.

The condition of a coin or any other collectible item is the greatest factor in determining its value. For two coins of identical type, date, and mintage, the better-condition piece will always sell for a higher price. This is simply because most collectors want to obtain specimens that are in as good a condition as possible and they are willing to pay more for them.

If it is your sole intention, as a numismatist, to collect coins for the pleasure and hobby benefits alone, you could skip this discussion of grading and acquire the items for your collection without regard to the con-dition/price correlary. If the coin you are looking at pleases you with its state of preservation and price tag, you can buy it without worrying whether it has been labeled a "Choice" or a "Gem" specimen. Collecting in this manner makes the hobby much more fun, but, sadly, it cuts down on the profits if and when the time comes to sell.

For most of us, to whom the hobby is both a pastime and something of an investment medium, grading has to become part of our numismatic stock in trade. Whether or not you are buying choice or gem material, you must be concerned with paying the right price for it. And that is what the *new* definition of coin grading is all about—the bottom line.

If all your price guides tell you that the coin you want to buy sells in top condition for $35, you want to make darn sure that if you spend $35 for that coin you get a piece that is in top condition. It's that simple and it applies whether you are talking about $35 or $3,500, or $35,000. It also applies at all ends of the grading scale. If a top-grade coin is $35, and an extremely fine coin is $10, you don't want to pay $10 for a very fine coin (and so on down the grade scale).

When I pay a premium for a coin's condition, that coin better make the grade or it goes back to the seller. That's the attitude you should develop in your own best hobby interests. It's too easy for the beginning collector to ignore the reality of coin grading or to put up with shoddy grading by others. In the long run, such an attitude costs you money and will surely sour you on this great pastime.

It's better for all coin collectors, right from the very start, to take a realistic approach to the subject of grading. Decide now what your own grading standards are going to be, learn to grade by other widely accepted standards, and learn to correlate those standards to your own. It's easier than it sounds. Once under your belt, you can proceed confidently to some of the more interesting and pleasing aspects of the hobby.

I recommend the American Numismatic Association (ANA) standard for grading simply because it is the most widely used. The ideal in coin grading, of course, would be for everybody to use the same system. Even if every collector in the country graded by ANA standards, there would still be problems because coin grading is an art/ science.

The advantage of going with the ANA system is that, once you become comfortable with it, you can easily pick out the dealers you want to do business with and the coins you want to buy. For example, you are a collector of Buffalo nickels and you are assembling an investment grade set of MS-60 or better coins. You need only know a few key rules about grading coins of this type to ascertain if they come up to ANA MS-60 form. You'll know where to look on the Indian (cheek) and the buffalo (shoulder, hip, tip of tail) for the first signs of wear that take a coin out of the uncirculated class. All of this is clearly spelled out in words and pictures for you in the pages of the ANA grading guide. The same is true for all coin types listed in the book.

You don't even have to memorize the grading guide. Once you learn how to use it and how to relate the drawings and descriptions to a coin held in your hand, you will be able to quickly and confidently grade coins. You will often hear and read that grading coins is a skill that takes many long years to develop after looking at thousands of coins. Don't believe it. That old saw might have been true in earlier days when there were no estab-lished and published coin grading standards. Today, any coin collector who can read, has normal eyesight and intelligence, and is willing to be honest with himself and with fellow hobbyists, can grade coins. The real skill in the hobby's past, in regards to coin grading, was in estab-lishing a personal standard for condition at a time when there were no universal standards. Today there are rec-ognized standards on which to base your own personal system of grading.

No collector is forced to grade coins by ANA stan-dards or any other system. Like all other parts of the hobby, you are free to set your own rules when it comes to grading. For example, as a collector of "Extremely Fine" U.S. type coins, I do not totally agree with ANA standards for that grade. The ANA grading guides call for a "Choice Extremely Fine-45" condition coin to appear "with light overall wear on the coin's highest points," with all design details "very sharp," and "Mint luster is usually seen only in protected areas of the coin's surface, such as between the star points and in the letter spaces."

It is my personal collecting choice not to pay XF-45 prices for coins that do not exhibit considerably more mint luster than just between the spaces in the lettering. I know that they exist, that they are readily available, and that they can be priced right.

Those three contingencies are the basics for any grading system whether it is "official" or your own. It is no use setting your grading standards at impossibly high levels. Nobody will ever succeed in completing a collec-tion of MS-70 anything. There seldom is such a thing as the perfect coin, with infrequent scattered exceptions. Even attempting to collect only MS-65 or better coins in such series as eighteenth- and nineteenth-century half-cents and large cents is impractical. While you can cer-tainly find the occasional type coin in such lofty degree of preservation, it would be virtually impossible to ever assemble a date set of such pieces.

Besides this availability, you have to exercise a bit of reason. You can't expect to buy "Very Good" condition coins that still exhibit mint luster; they just do not exist. If a coin with VG design details *does* show luster, it has been tampered with. My choice to demand a bit of luster in my XF-45 coins is based on years of experience and observa-tion that tell me it is not a totally unreasonable standard.

The third part is price. It's easy to pay more than an XF-45 price for a coin exhibiting mint luster; you just buy an "About Uncirculated" coin. The whole point of my wanting to pay the XF-45 price is to get a bargain. By diligent searching, a bit of cherry picking, and some haggling, it has been possible to buy these coins that fit my personal grading standards while not paying more than "book" prices in most cases.

The price is the bottom line of grading. It doesn't matter what you call a coin; it matters how that coin is priced. I could easily build on my collection of choice XF coins by buying from certain dealers with a reputation for less than accurate grading on merchandise they sell. They know that they can take a nicely struck, lusterous XF-condition coin, buy it for bid price from another dealer, repackage it in their own 2×2 with a "new" grade or "Uncirculated," and a new price.

By pricing that coin at what would be a bargain price for a true MS-60 specimen, they hope to lure the unwary buyer. Because their price is often not too far off the retail for the coin if it was being properly graded and presented, I could quite often make a good buy with a bit of dickering and some cogent commentary about the true grade of the piece. Nevertheless, I refuse to do business with such persons as a matter of principal.

The point is that reputable coin-price guides present an accurate summary of current market levels for accurately graded coins. There is no excuse to pay too much for a properly graded coin. Similarly, there is no excuse for a seller to give away his coins at bargain prices if they are accurately graded.

Besides working with a grading guide, you can sharpen your coin-assessment skills by seeking out the aid of a more experienced collector or friendly dealer. If you can get such a person to share some of their expertise with you by going over actual coins, it will often help drive home the points made in a grading book. When looking at such coins, it will be helpful for you to attempt to grade them on your own. Then ask for help of somebody whose knowledge and judgment you respect.

If their grading differs greatly from yours, ask for an explanation. Remember that grading is subjective. Each observer sees different things on a coin. Some are more observant of degree of wear on design elements, others are quick to pick up a bag mark or an edge nick, while still other collectors get an overall "feel" for the grade of a coin based upon observation of all of this and more.

It is not unusual for two people to differ by a half a grade or even a whole grade when evaluating the same coin. If your grading is consistently off by more than this, you should probably think about adjusting your standards or going back to the book for a refresher. Not surprisingly, there are also a number of formal classroom coin grading courses and seminars available around the coun-

try. The American Numismatic Association's annual summer seminar, held in Colorado Springs, Colorado, and at one other traveling location each July, offers a grading course that is very popular. A number of the private college and pseudocollege extension numismatics courses also offer grading classes. Details on these are regularly announced in the numismatic press.

It has recently become popular for knowledgeable numismatists to offer short coin-grading courses at large coin conventions in conjunction with educational forum activities. While these are not especially comprehensive, they are usually free and well worth the couple of hours spent. The final word on coin grading has to be *consistency*. If we were all consistent graders, we'd have few grading problems. The beginning collector sometimes does not realize that coin grading makes no allowance for age or metallic composition of a coin. There is no tolerance in grading based on the age of a piece. A coin, whether it is 300 years old, three years old, or three days out of the mint, is either "Uncirculated" or it is not. Similarly, a bag mark or scratch cannot be explained away on a gold coin just by saying that gold is more easily marred than harder metals. If a coin grading description calls for a coin in MS-67 condition to have *no* scratches or nicks, it doesn't matter whether the coin is made of gold, silver, or bronze, if the coin is scratched, it is not MS-67.

Another form of grading inconsistency you should be aware of—because it is one that is likely to hit you in the wallet—is the sometimes-seen difference in a coin's grade when it is bought and when it is sold. It is surprising the number of coin dealers who will tell you a coin is MS-65 when you are buying it and charge you an MS-65 price for it; yet, when you come back to sell it to the very same dealer, he will tell you it is only MS-60 and offer you a price commensurate with the lower grade.

Such dealers usually have a number of "good" reasons when you point out the discrepancy. He might tell you that an assistant graded the coin the first time around or he might accuse you of mishandling or switching the coin. One large, well-known, but not particularly respected firm, recently attempted to explain away such a situation to a disgruntled buyer by saying that grading standards are different depending on market conditions. The buyer had purchased a coin as MS-63 when the coin market was booming in late 1979. When he went to sell the coin to the same dealer two years later, he was told that the much slower market conditions had somehow "transformed" his coin into a much less desirable and less valuable MS-63. While it is certainly true that patterns for coin demand and prices on coins will change in a fluctuating market situation, the actual grade of the coin itself cannot change unless it is subjected to additional wear or damage.

The way a coin dealer grades is the surest indication of his legitimacy. It will be well worth your time and effort to search for those dealers whose own grading standards are compatible with yours, and to throw your business their way.

Chapter 19

Housing Coins

HOUSING A COIN, CURRENCY, OR RELATED COLlection is a concern the beginning numismatist has to face almost immediately upon entering the hobby. After all, you can't throw your coins into any old desk drawer or brandy bottle and call it a collection. Choosing an appropriate method of storing your coins makes them easily accessible to you, gives form and order to your collection and, ideally, should protect your numismatic treasures from wear and contamination.

The most frequently encountered coin housing is the familiar Whitman blue folder. Usually three cardboard sections taped together and capable of being folded into a book, it is the least expensive and easiest method of storing coins as a collection. Properly sized holes are diecut into the boards and labeled with date, mint mark, mintage, and perhaps other information. When the coin is acquired, it is merely inserted into the proper hole with a little thumb pressure. Until the coins have been taken out and put back several times, they usually fit quite snugly in the holes and they are relatively secure. They are unprotected on their face and the back is not available for viewing.

Such folders are not suitable for valuable coins or uncirculated specimens because the surface of the coin is brought into contact with the cardboard of the folder, with

fingers when being inserted, and, if the folder is improperly folded, with the surfaces of other coins. All of this can result in abrasion, wear, or unsightly marking of your coins.

For several decades, the Whitman blue coin folders have been the staple accessory of the beginning collector. They were an improvement over R.S. Yeoman's original printed cardboard sheets with holes drilled all the way through. While both sides of the coin could be viewed, they were also prone to drop out while being handled. Today, the old Whitman coin board of the 1940s is something of a collectors item in its own right (Fig. 19-1).

A third generation of Whitman coin album maintains the book style, but it provides greater visibility and protection at a modest increase in price. These albums have thick cardboard for the pages. The cardboard is generally just a hair thicker than the depth of the coin which they are designed to hold. Holes for the coins are drilled clear through the cardboard and a paper layer that is attached to each side of the cardboard page. All information about the coin is preprinted on the paper. To hold the coin and protect it from rubbing while in the album, clear plastic slides are provided (top and bottom). The plastic slides are inserted between the paper and cardboard layers of the album page, sandwiching the coin between. By using a

Fig. 19-1. While the old Whitman coin folders were convenient, they gave little actual protection to the coins they held.

bit of care when inserting and removing the coins, your collection is quite well protected against wear and damage in such an album (Fig. 19-2).

Both the folders and the bookshelf albums are made for all popularly collected U.S. coin series and in several of the more popular Mexican, Canadian and European denominations and types. They are also made in non-labeled versions so that you can use them for tokens, medals, and foreign coins. For example, many commemorative medals are made in silver-dollar size. An album with 38.1 mm-holes can be readily used for such a purpose. The unlabeled version of the cent folder or album makes a fine housing for Civil War tokens.

The principal drawback to the folders and cardboard albums is that they are not suitable for archival (long-term) storage. Some of the acids used to make cardboard and paper will, after a period of years, react to the metallic composition of some coins and cause them to tone or even become spotted. Oil, from contact with human fingers, adheres to the surfaces of the coin and enhances this effect. Spotting often takes the shape of a fingerprint that is distinct enough to be entered into evidence in a court of law.

Many collectors use a rubber glove, when handling high-grade or expensive coins, and avoid the use of paper albums for long-term housing. For the length of time most collectors keep a coin, such albums, especially those made in very recent years, are perfectly safe.

There is another type of album that is unsafe for any length of time beyond a few weeks. This type of album contains plastic pockets for coins and it is marketed under the Harco "Coinmaster" label, among others. These albums contain pages made of heat-stamped polyvinyl chloride known—and feared by numismatists—by the initials PVC. PVC is a plastic compound made pliable through the use of various chemicals, nearly all of which are dangerous to coins, paper money and nearly every other subject they come in contact with.

For a number of years in the 1970s, PVC albums were very popular because they had a clean "modern" look and were relatively inexpensive as plastic coin housing went. By the late 1970s, it was discovered that the agents used to soften the plastic in compounding PVC were "migrating." The chemicals leave the plastic and adhere to whatever was being housed therein. On coins and other metallic items, especially those of nickel and bronze, the damage took the form of a green film or even hard "crud" deposit on the surface of the coin. While it could be cleaned with certain chemicals, the cleaning damaged the surface of the coins and ruined the value of high-grade pieces.

On paper money, the damage was in the form of direct soaking up of the oily plasticizer. This turns currency notes into greasy messes. Currency and stamp collectors were particularly hard hit because there were

Fig. 19-2. The newest generation of coin album from Whitman is their bookcase series. It offers plastic sheets to protect each side of the coin while leaving it open for viewing.

173

great numbers of PVC albums in use in those hobbies. The larger size of currency and stamped envelopes made the use of safer plastics too costly.

While there are chemical tests to determine whether a substance contains PVC, it is enough for the beginner to know a few characteristics about the substance. While certain other plastic compounds share these characteristics, you would be better off not putting your valuable coins or currency in them even if they are not PVC. The same type of softening agents were likely used as a plasticizer.

One of the key things to look for is softness. PVC is an extremely pliable form of plastic. The chemical compound of polyvinyl chlorida contains various substances that make the whole chain flexible. You can easily bend an album page or currency holder, made of PVC, over double and it will return to original shape without any damage. If you try this with the more rigid, safer, plastics, they will crack or break or a white line will permanently appear at the point of the band. That's because such plastics are not softened.

Another good test for PVC is to look at and feel the substance. PVC is not a crystal clear type of plastic. There is an opaqueness to it that you would notice if it were compared to other "clear" plastic coin holders. The big give away is the feel. PVC actually feels oily. Most of the safer plastics have a hard, cold feel to them. PVC has a distinctive "greasy" feel even though it is not actually exuding plasticizer.

While PVC might not harm your coins in a short period, it is better not to risk its use at all. Manufacturers of coin albums, individual "flips," and other numismatic accessories use different types and quantities of plasticizers in their formulas and some begin to break down much more quickly than others.

Krause Publications was the first voice in the coin hobby to sound the warning on PVC albums and holders. Research done and articles written by various staff and contributors alerted collectors to the danger as early as 1978. Shortly thereafter, the firm instituted a policy of requiring sellers of PVC-compound hobby accessories to carry a disclaimer in their ads warning buyers of the potential hazards of storage in contact with PVC. If it is advertised in the Krause coin papers and magazines without a warning, it is safe.

There are a number of very safe plastic coin and currency holders available. While they will eventually break and perhaps damage what is being held, the time span for the expected break down is measured in centuries. For all but museum or time capsule storage, certain plastic accessories now available are perfectly safe for collectors.

The best of these are polyester and acetate. Polyester is preferred by most collectors because of its superior clarity. Polyester is better known as Mylar, that is the trade name of Du Pont's specific polyester formula. It is also marketed by Celanese under the name Celmar. Mylar coin and currency holders are more expensive than acetate, but they also have greater resistence to tears, they are more flexible and they come in a wider variety of sizes and shapes. If you see the words Mylar or acetate in conjunction with an advertised coin holder, you can feel perfectly safe in choosing it for your own use.

The very hard plastic cases, tubes, and other housing material can be considered safe. These are all made of compounds that have little or no softening agents that can damage your coins or paper money.

Many coin dealers continue to use the PVC "flips" to hold their stock. These are essentially two pockets joined together at the top. One pocket holds the coin; it can be easily viewed obverse, reverse and edge, and easily slid out for inspection. The other pocket generally holds a 1-inch square of paper or cardboard with a written description of the coin, grade, and price. Because most dealers turn over their stock frequently, or might want to change prices of the inserted card often, they do not mind the risk of using these flips for short term storage. After buying a coin housed this way, the wise collector or investor will transfer it to something safer as soon as possible.

One of the most widely used means of housing individual coins, both for dealers and collectors, is known to hobbyists as the 2×2. The 2×2 is a hinged piece of cardboard, die cut with a hole of coin size, with a thin piece of acetate or Mylar glued in. A coin can be inserted between the layers of cardboard, which are then folded over and stapled or taped shut, effectively sealing the coin. Pertinent data can be written right on the cardboard portion of the holder. Both front and back of the coin are easily viewed. The edge is hidden. Such holders are extremely inexpensive, disposable, and popular with dealers. In their standard 2-×-2 size, they allow coins of all sizes, right up through silver dollars, to be conveniently housed or carried in a single box (Fig. 19-3).

Perhaps the biggest danger in dealing with 2×2s is simple human carelessness. The very thin plastic sheet over the coin does not provide much protection from nicks. Many coins have been ruined when collectors slipped with the staple puller, jackknife, or nail file while trying to open the things. The protruding staples can also

Fig. 19-3. There is a wide range of envelopes, pockets, and cases for storing and displaying coins. Some of them are sate. Some can actually damage your coins.

be hard on the coins' surfaces if they are carelessly handled in a group such as in dealers' junk boxes, etc. For these reasons, many collectors prefer to use tape to seal the three open sides of the 2 × 2. By using different colors of tape, they can also color code their collections to record the purchase date or the grade.

Individual coin envelopes are another popular means of storage. While some are made of relatively inexpensive paper that gives off a sulphuric acid vapor over time and might harm coins. Other paper is of archival quality and it will do no harm at all to coins even after hundreds of years of storage. Unfortunately, there is no way for the layman to tell one paper from another. In order to be sure, you must buy your envelopes from a reliable coin dealer or directly from the manufacturer. Most accessories are available from coin shops, hobby shops, or through advertisers in the numismatic periodicals. The disadvantage with envelopes, naturally, is that they do not allow the coin to be seen.

In the early days of numismatics, collectors did not use albums, 2 × 2s, or even envelopes. Because most coin collectors of the nineteenth century and earlier were relatively wealthy to begin with, they had coin cabinets custom constructed for them. Generally, about the size of an end table, but taller, a coin cabinet was a usually ornate piece of wooden furniture that was, in essence, a box containing a number of thin drawers or trays (Fig. 19-4). The drawers were arranged into compartments or drilled to hold coins. They were usually layered with velvet or other plush fabric as much to enhance the appearance of the coins as to protect them from sliding around and bumping into each other. This has given rise to a sometimes-heard euphemism in the hobby—*cabinet friction.* While the term would seem to denote slight rubbing of a coin's high points by being slid around in a coin cabinet—and while that may actually have happened in the past—the term today usually means that someone is trying to pass off a slightly circulated coin as uncirculated. The obvious wear is claimed to have resulted from many years storage in a rich man's coin box. It does give the coin a more romantic air than merely saying it is "About Uncirculated."

There has been a resurgance in coin cabinetmaking and use in recent years. Antique coin cabinets are widely sought-after by numismatists. Such a cabinet might sell for well over $1,000 in an infrequent appearance at a coin auction.

A good way for a beginner to see an old coin cabinet is to look at how a museum houses the coins it does not have on public display. When a collector donated his collection to a museum or library, they often got the cabinet as well. Many still use them today.

Besides the various boards, albums, flips, and 2 × 2s designed to hold individual coins, there are a number of specialized holders for coin collectors and investors. One of the most popular is the tube; it is used for holding entire rolls of coins. Because the traditional paper rolls with which banks have been wrapping coins for most of the twentieth century can cause tarnishing of the edges and end coins in a roll, collectors who want to store quantities of coins safely often use plastic tubes made especially for that purpose. The hard, opaque plastic tubes have round cylinders to hold the proper number of coins—50 cents, 40 nickels, 50 dimes, etc.—but they are square in shape overall so that the rolls can be stacked, stood on end, and otherwise more conveniently stored.

The paper-money collector has a wide variety of storage options open to him; all of them have relative safety, viewing, and cost merits. In storing paper money, avoid the PVC plastic so commonly used in currency albums in recent years. A number of smaller albums, about the size of gentlemen's wallets of the last century, are popular today. They generally have a dozen acetate pockets and they can store 12 or 24 notes (depending on whether or not you want to view both sides). They are bound with a spiral comb so that they will lay flat no matter what page is being viewed.

When choosing a paper-money holder, the collector has to be extremely careful. Just inserting a note in a holder can be a dangerous job. Trying to force a note into a new plastic pocket can result in a bent corner or a wrinkled bottom edge. Such defects can easily cut in half the worth of a note. When putting a note into a holder, it is best to "open" the holder first by sliding a piece of cardboard cut to size into the holder and out a few times. Once the note is all the way in the holder, tap the bottom of the holder on a table a few times to settle the note far enough down (most holders are conveniently oversize) for complete protection.

Besides the commercially made coin and currency holders, many collectors use a diversity of custom-produced housing for their collections. A particularly attractive line of coin and currency holders is available from Capital Plastics, an Ohio firm that has been serving the numismatic hobby for many years. Check a current issue of *Numismatic News* for information on ordering a catalog of the firm's products.

Capital Plastics makes a wide range of ready-to-use coin holders from extremely thick (up to ¼-inch) plastic. Their holders are generally the sandwich type that has two pieces of clear plastic with a piece of colored plastic between (Fig. 19-5). The colored plastic is die cut to fit

Fig. 19-4. Wealthy collectors of past years stored their coins in custom-made cabinets. A Smithsonian curator displays some of the cabinets used by pharmaceuticals magnate Eli Lilly to store his coins.

coins of all sizes and shapes. The clear plastic on each side holds them in place. All of this is put together with plastic screws to allow access. While the firm's product line includes large boards for entire date/mint mark sets of popular U.S. coins, they also have 2-×-2 constructions that hold a single coin.

Custom engraved lettering is available on all Capital Plastics products. Also available is complete custom design of a holder specifically seated to an individual's needs.

Paper money collectors are big customers of Capital Plastics because the firm offers properly sized holders that are little more than two crystal clear boards of heavy plastic screwed together and custom engraved. This little assembly is a veritable fortress for a currency note. Once screwed between those layers of plastic, there is little that can harm a note—beyond lengthy submersion in water. Inevitably, when you see a $50,000 or $100,000 piece of paper money displayed at a coin show, it is encased in one of these sturdy holders. These custom plastic holders are not inexpensive, but when protection is the object, rather than price, most collectors and dealers opt for this type of storage.

If you have some manual dexterity and the proper tools, there is no reason you can't make your own custom coin and currency holders. While working with plexiglass or similar hard plastics is not as easy as woodworking, it is not much more difficult if you take your time and realize the material's tendency to crack under strain when you are dealing with thinner pieces.

Many collectors mount and frame their collections much like prized paintings. This allows them to display their coins with other objects, such as antique engravings, or in special groupings that aren't available in commercial coin holders. There are many books on picture framing or you can work with a custom framer to design and build what you want.

I use store-bought frames in the standard sizes to display some of my numismatic items on the walls of my home and office. It is not a good idea to hang anything too expensive or hard to replace on the walls. Still, many of the historic items of coinage, currency, and medallic art that have caught my attention are displayed in frames with photos and a short caption explaining their historic significance.

When done with a watchful eye on the materials

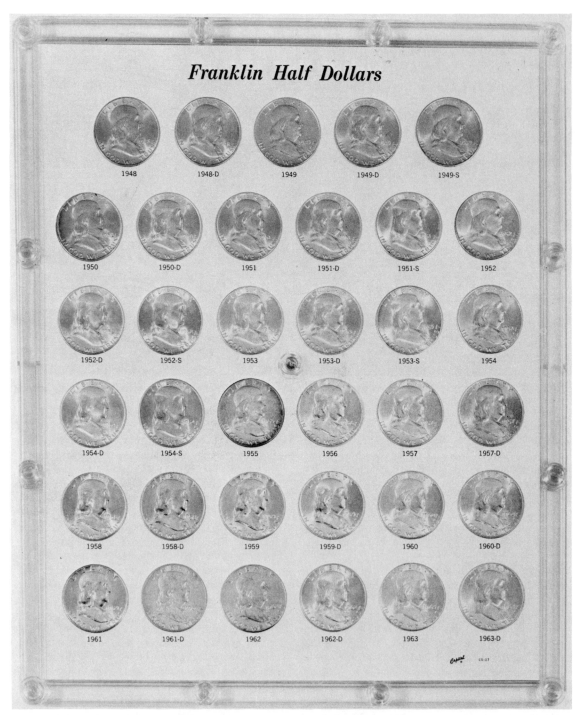

Fig. 19-5. Capital Plastics makes an excellent line of hard plastic coin holders. They will customize one to the collector's specifications.

used, and especially toward keeping the item safely and securely anchored in the frame, home-made housings can be very attractive. They keep your coins or currency well protected. For many, the idea of stapling a coin in a 2 × 2 and throwing it into a safe deposit box is not appealing. They prefer to have their numismatic items on display where they can be seen and enjoyed. Even if coins and currency are hanging on a wall of your den or bedroom where few people will ever see them, it gives you a great deal of personal satisfaction to house treasures in a manner that is safe and attractive.

A helpful hint in constructing your displays is to make the special effort to acquire museum wax. This substance is used by museums to mount all manner of material without harm. Even the rarest and choicest coins can be mounted directly with it. While it is difficult to locate, you should be able to get a lead from your local museum, library, or historical society.

Chapter 20

Cleaning Coins

THERE ARE VERY FEW CASES IN WHICH CLEANing a coin or currency note will enhance its value. Sure, collectors like their coins bright and shiny, but only only if they are in that condition because of proper care and lack of exposure to circulation and debilitating natural elements. There is little in the numismatic world that is less attractive than a well-circulated coin that has been artificially cleaned, and shined, dipped, buffed, or whizzed (wire brushed) in any other manner to make it appear to be something it is not. Most collectors would prefer an honest tarnished coin or a dirty coin to one that has been cleaned. Some highly principled collectors refuse to even consider a cleaned coin or note—no matter how rare.

An acquaintance of mine is a well-known collector and historian of U.S. territorial national bank notes. His greatest goal in life is to own a complete set of such territorials (a worthy goal, because only one complete set is known). He is so much opposed to washing, pressing, trimming or otherwise "doctoring" a piece of paper money, that he will refuse to purchase a cleaned specimen no matter how much it will further his collecting goal. He and many others like him feel that a bank note gets dirty, wrinkled, and torn from good, honest circulation. Any attempt to cleanse away that human element is

an assault on the note itself, and to the collecting fraternity as a whole.

Whizzed coins were the hobby's biggest problem before overgrading. Even more of a problem than outright counterfeits, whizzed coins were processed "Extremely Fine" or "About Uncirculated" coins that were made to appear uncirculated. By treatment with chemicals and an electrically operated fine wire brush, small nicks could be polished off the surface of a coin while the original luster was being replaced by an artificial shine. These buffed-up beauties victimized many collectors and investors before the ANA took a tough stance on those who dealt in such coins. The ANA went so far as to prosecute several people for mail fraud. Convictions and prison sentences were obtained.

While these whizzed coins remain at large today, they are seldom encountered in dealing with reputable professional numismatists. When they are, they will be labeled clearly as having been whizzed.

A process somewhat akin to whizzing, but which does not involve the displacement of any metal on the surface of the coin, is termed *dipping*. A dipped coin is treated by immersion in any one of several types of commercially packaged chemicals to remove tarnish. It is just like using silver or brass polish, but without the abrasives and resultant fine scratches. The process takes its name from the fact that coins are usually dipped right into the jar. Sometimes the dipper doesn't even bother to rotate the coin where he is holding it by the edge and a dipped coin will exhibit two tarnished areas on opposite sides of the rim where fingers held it.

It takes a practiced eye to discern a dipped coin, but most coin dealers can pick one out in a second. It would do the collector well to learn the same technique. While dipping is not looked upon with nearly the degree of loathing as other forms of cleaning, it has begun to be considered unfavorably by many numismatists.

The big danger a beginning collector faces with dipped coins is buying—as I once did—a dipped coin thinking that it is original luster that makes the coin shine. Silver dollars and the U.S. commemorative series have been particularly prone to dipping in the recent past. No denomination or metal is exempt from the practice.

The practice of dipping began when dealers discovered that tarnished or unattractivly toned coins did not sell well, and that the simple application of a little Jewelustre or similar product would approximate the original gleam of a new coin. These dipped coins found ready homes and a marketing technique was born.

Today, the trend might just be moving in the opposite direction. Many collectors and investors prefer the original toning to a dipped coin. There was some talk in the American Numismatic Association in 1981 of making the presence of dipping part of the consideration for grading an uncirculated coin, but that died out without any results.

Generally, cleaning of coins can be recommended only in specific instances where the coin is pitted or contaminated with a substance (such as PVC residue) that will worsen if left untreated. Cleaning of coins should always be done with the mildest possible solutions and least amount of rubbing to avoid abrasion of the surfaces. Carbontetrachloride is a popular cleaning agent. It is safe to use, but always try good old soap and water first. If a coin is really badly encrusted, such as are some buried treasure pieces that have reacted to salt water, you might consider taking them to the high school or college physics lab and asking the teacher to clean them with a ultrasonic cleaning device. A large retail jeweler might also have a ultrasonic cleaner at his disposal. Such devices are perfectly harmless to coins if they are not used in conjunction with abrasive or acidic chemicals.

When properly done, a cleaned coin should be undetectable. This goes under the assumption that the piece has not been cleaned in an effort to make it appear to be of a high grade. No knowledgeable coin collector will be fooled by someone trying to pass a cleaned coin for a better-condition coin. They take on an unnatural look that the collector will soon recognize as artificial. After observing many different types of coins in all states of preservation, you soon learn what genuine untampered specimens look like. A worked-over piece is going to stick out like a sore thumb.

While there are occasions that call for the cleaning of a coin, there are none that I can think of for cleaning paper money. Coins can be cleaned without being detectable, but not so with paper money. In every case, a currency note is better left dirty than cleaned.

Even the application of pure soap and water to most notes will cause them to take on a laundered look. Dirt is washed away from all parts of the note. When the folds of the paper have been washed in the case of a circulated note, they take on an unnatural whiteness that turns off most collectors.

In the case of older bank notes—those that featured hand-signed autographs of the president and cashier of the issuing bank—washing might well remove the signatures even if all the other printing is left intact. There is simply no way of knowing, short of expensive analysis, what type of ink the bank official's used when signing their currency. Inks that might appear indentical will often react very differently when they come into contact with water or other cleaning agents.

Just as with coins, there are other ways of improving a note's appearance, but collectors find them universally distasteful because they are always done with the intention of making the note look better than it actually is. A favorite technique is to starch and iron a note to give it body (particularly after it has been left limp by washing).

The great numismatic investment boom of the late 1970s brought with it an influx of people who wanted nothing but perfect specimens even in nineteenth century U.S. paper money. By the nature of the production methods used, such money was imperfect. A good example is that few buyers of "investment grade" material would consider an untampered-with, large-size U.S. note. They thought they looked wrinkled because they did not lie perfectly flat on the table. In that era, notes were printed while wet and the pressure of the printing press and the effects of being weighted down while drawing caused the paper to stretch and shrink unevenly. The result was notes that do not now, and never did even when new, lie perfectly flat.

Still, because there was a demand by unknowledgeable investors for perfectly flat old U.S. currency, a supply cropped up. Persons eager to fill the demand merely starched and ironed the old notes. Viola! Perfectly flat, they surely would be worth lots more money than the untreated original note. Sadly, these doctored notes are now coming back onto the market. Their owners are realizing that they have been had and they cannot realize top dollars from their supposed "Gem" notes.

A good way for the collector to detect such processing is to take the note out of whatever holder it is in and lay in on the table, if it is perfectly flat (any note other than modern paper money that is), be suspicious. Smell the note. If you are familiar with the odor of starch, you might be able to detect it in the note. A final test is to hold the note under a black (ultraviolet) light. Starch in a note will glow brightly under such lighting.

I have even heard on one note "doctor" who painted in starch the word "sucker" on the notes he tampered with. If the chump ever got suspicious, he would see that final bit of ridicule when he examined the note under black light.

Chapter 21

Organized Numismatics

SOME NUMISMATISTS ENJOY THE FRATER-nal aspects of the hobby by joining some form of organized numismatic group. These can be as specialized as coin clubs at your place of employment, the local coin club, or a national or international organization. All of these have a different appeal and different benefits and responsibilities.

What is surprising is that great numbers of coin collectors do not join any such groups. The advertised membership of the American Numismatic Association, the world's largest coin collectors group, is only in the 30,000s. It is doubtful that all the rosters of all the coin clubs around the nation could produce another 30,000 members. Best estimates are that there are some 10 million coin collectors in this nation. It would appear that many interested numismatists prefer to enjoy their hobby alone. This is borne out by diminishing membership for most numismatic clubs in the past decade.

The principal advantage to the average coin collec-tor of being a member of his local club is that it allows him to make contact with his fellow numismatists in his im-mediate area. Detractors of clubs will also tell you that this is the local club's single greatest disadvantage. Whatever the case, the beginning coin collector would do well to at least investigate the possibility of joining a local club.

Most clubs welcome new members enthusiastically. Some will require that you be brought to your first meet-ing as a guest of an established member. In this way, many clubs feel they can avoid subjecting their members to possible theft or robbery by at least knowing who is sitting in on their meetings. Many clubs have their meet-ing date, time, and location published in the local paper (often in a Saturday or Sunday coin and stamp column). You can also find out about local clubs by asking a coin dealer in your town. If your town isn't big enough to have a coin dealer, it probably doesn't have a coin club either.

The (generally) monthly meetings of a local coin club usually center around a business meeting of rather short duration. This is generally to conduct business pertaining to the annual coin shows most clubs have or the banquet, picnic etc., that is part of the social structure of the club. The rest of the evening might be taken up with a slide lecture, a visiting speaker, a show-and-tell program, a club auction, or merely with an unofficial bourse where members and member dealers buy, sell, and trade.

As is generally the case in all clubs of this nature, most of the work will be done by a few enthusiastic individuals. Most of the griping about why things aren't done right will be done by the rest. For the casual numis-matist, the local coin club can be an important source of hobby news and local gossip. For the beginner, it is a good place to meet fellow collectors from whom you will be able to gain the benefit of years of collecting experience if you keep your eyes and ears open and your mouth shut (except to ask questions).

The principal function of any local coin club these days seems to be that of putting on an annual coin show. Whether this is a 10-table affair held in a church basement, a respectable 40-dealer event at the local VFW Hall, or a two-day, 120-dealer extravaganza in a real convention center or hotel, the local club's show is the focus of the entire year's activity and the club's principal source of operating revenue from year to year.

Putting on a respectable and successful show is an art that is passed on to generation after generation by the older hands in a club. When there is a willing group of members to shoulder the responsibilities, things usually go smoothly. If there is a casual attitude among the membership—where few members take any interest in the show until they want to sign up for a table for themselves—then it can be a tough nut to crack. Serving on one or more coin show committee for your local club is a good way to get involved in organized numismatics in your town.

The local club is generally your first opportunity to exhibit your numismatic material competitively. Many coin collectors like the thrill of competition involved in organizing and putting together a display of their coin, notes and other numismatic collectibles—and vying for trophies (Fig. 21-1). It is a natural extension of the pride of ownership that causes most collectors to want to display their treasures for all to see. By exhibiting in competition, you can do this in a relatively safe and anonymous manner. Exhibits are generally displayed in special cases or in custom-made frames that would discourage the casual thief. There is usually some type of security personnel standing nearby keeping an eye on the general public as they study the coins on display.

Most exhibits are on a competitive basis. Collectors vye for trophies, plaques, bowls, and the like. Some collectors really thrive on this; others disdain it.

An exhibition means more than putting a lot of expensive coins in a case. The real purpose behind clubs promoting displays at their shows is to educate the public and to entice others to join the numismatic ranks. Therefore, the awards in competitive exhibition go to the displays that offer the most educational benefits. The points on the judging scale are always weighted toward the informational aspects of the exhibit. Nevertheless, rarity and condition of material do count for a fair number of points. Exhibit judging standards are different for virtu-

Fig. 21-1. Exhibiting numismatic items in competition for trophies usually begins at the local coin club level.

ally every organization. You'll have to study those of the show's sponsor if you think you might like this form of hobby activity.

The social aspects of a coin club cannot be denied. Certain types of persons are likely to be numismatists. There are persons with whom you are likely to share a good deal more in common with than the fact that you all collect coins. For this reason, many clubs have a good share of banquets, picnics, and parties over the course of a year. You will be able to meet fellow collectors on a less formal level.

Beyond the local coin club level, there is likely to be a state numismatic society or perhaps a multistate organization that covers your geographic area. Such clubs tend to change mailing addresses as often as a new secretary is elected. A coin dealer in your area or the members of the local club should be able to help put you in touch with a state group.

While your state coin club might only charge the same $2, $3 or $5 annual membership that your local club gets, you are likely to reap more benefit in the form of a club journal. Nearly every state-wide coin group has a quarterly (or more frequent) publication that usually takes the form of a digest-sized magazine of between 16-64 pages. Besides advertising from many dealers in your immediate area, the club journal is full of information about collectors. Often there are several informational and educational articles.

Many such articles are written about numismatic items of special interest to your home state. Some of the articles are quite scholarly and comprehensive. The magazines of a state numismatic society are often the only place you will find material like this published. The national periodicals often feel that material of limited geographic interest will turn off too large a share of the rest of their audience. Depending on the resources of the sponsoring organization—both in terms of member input and dollars available—these state club journals can be very helpful information sources for the beginner.

In addition to the articles, you will usually find some type of coin show calender in the state journal. This often acts as a clearinghouse for show dates so that two clubs in two cities do not try to hold their shows on the same day. This can be useful to you if you like attending the various coin shows in your area.

The next step up from the state group is the regional organization. These can vary from groups such as the Penn-Ohio that covers only parts of two states, to the Pacific Northwest Numismatic Association that embraces a handful of states and provinces, to the 13-state Central States Numismatic Society that covers the area from Michigan to the Dakotas and Wisconsin to Kentucky.

Such regional coin clubs offer some of the best coin shows put on in the nation. The CSNS show is the second largest in the United States on an annual basis. Their official magazines are generally of very high quality in terms of production and content.

Many of the regional organizations are also actively involved in comprehensive numismatic educational programs. They sponsor the production of slides programs, provide guest lecturer bureaus for coin clubs and non-numismatic organizations, and usually provide support for the grass roots level of local clubs in various ways.

Coin shows sponsored by these multistate groups might have as many as 300 dealer tables and hundreds of cases of exhibits. They are real extravaganzas for the interested collector and the public. The board of governors of these groups generally takes care to ensure that the annual show travels on a rotating basis to all parts of the geographic territory served by the organization. This way all members can attend at least occasionally.

Because their membership is so widely spread, the regional—and to a lesser degree—the state clubs, do not hold regular meetings. Their general membership meetings are usually held once a year in conjunction with the annual coin show. The officers might meet three or four times at various shows around the state or country whenever a quorum can be raised.

Chapter 22

National Organizations

W HILE THERE ARE MANY NATIONAL NUMIS-
matic organizations, none is so general in nature
and so beneficial to the individual as the American
Numismatic Association. No other organization has as its
sole purpose the job of representing, protecting, and
aiding the coin collector. With membership in excess of
30,000, it is evident that many collectors have found the
ANA to be a useful part of their hobby. After reading a bit
more about the association and its benefits, especially for
the beginning numismatist, you will probably agree with
the current members and may want to join.

Membership fees are approximately $15 annually for
adults and $9 for young collectors (ages 11-17). If you
want further information about the ANA or any of its
programs, write to them at P.O. Box 2366, Colorado
Springs, CO 80901, for a membership application and
current dues structure.

The idea of a national numismatic organization was
conceived by George F. Heath, a nineteenth century
physician from Monroe, Michigan. When not involved in
the practice of medicine, Heath studied world history
through his coin collection. The obscurity of his little
town hampered his efforts in gaining knowledge of the
hobby and in obtaining specimens for his cabinet. He did
not have much direct contact with fellow numismatists.

In 1888, Dr. Heath founded, printed, and published a
four-page leaflet that he titled *The Numismatist*. Distributing the pamphlet himself, he listed his personal coin
needs, advertised duplicates for sale, and discussed
numismatic topics of the day.

The little publication found many friends among
hundreds of coin collectors who were, like the doctor, too
far removed to take advantage of the numismatic
societies in existence in Eastern cities like Boston, New
York, Pittsburgh, and Montreal. While these societies
were quite active, their sphere of activity was limited by
geography and the primitive transportation and com-
munication of the period.

As Heath's subscription list increased, it became
evident that there was a growing need for a society
similar to those found in large cities, but one which would
reach the more isolated collector and serve the needs of
the beginning numismatist: a national organization of coin
collectors.

In February, 1891, *The Numismatist* posed the question. "What is the matter with having an American
Numismatic Association? There is nothing like the al-
liance of kindred pursuits to stimulate growth and interest." Aided by Charles T. Tatman, young editor of *Plain
Talk*, a leading hobby magazine, a campaign was begun to

Fig. 22-1. The ANA annually sponsors the world's largest coin convention. The magnitude of the show can be seen in this scene of the 1981 bourse floor, at Cincinnati, where more than 300 dealers gathered.

organize such an association. Numismatists from across the country reacted favorably to the idea of banding together in order to derive greater benefit and pleasure from their avocation.

On October 6-7, 1891, five men, representing 61 charter members, founded the American Numismatic Association at a meeting in Chicago. The five were Heath, William G. Jerrems, David Harlow, J.A. Heckelman and John Brydon. Tatman, just entering Harvard law school, was unable to attend. Heath declined the presidency of the group in favor of his friend Jerrems, but he did accept charter membership No. 1 on the ANA rolls.

The visionary Dr. Heath, summing up the birth of the ANA, said, "The foundation of the ANA was not laid for today alone, but for the long and distant future, as well." Since that meeting in 1891, more than 100,000 persons and companies have been listed on the ANA membership roster.

Heath also originated the idea of a numismatic convention where members could make personal contacts with fellow numismatists, and exchange ideas as well as coins. These small-scale meetings, forerunners of the expansive modern conventions, were held annually from 1891 to 1895, and again in 1901 and in 1904.

In 1907, with the aid of Dr. Joseph M. Henderson, the convention was held in Columbus, Ohio. This convention was so successful that it was determined to hold annual meetings henceforth. This procedure has been followed since that time except for the war years 1918 and 1945.

Present-day conventions include a large bourse room that brings together many of the world's most noted professional numismatists. There are exhibits, educational programs, club and district representatives' breakfasts, spouses' activities, young numismatists activities, meetings and social affairs of members' specialty organizations, and a host of other coin and non-numismatic related activities.

Each ANA convention affords the opportunity to visit with old hobby friends and to make new ones. With a few exceptions, each annual convention has surpassed its predecessor in attendance, number of dealers and exhibits, educational programs, and general magnitude (Fig. 22-1).

Dr. Heath died suddenly on June 16, 1908. President Farran Zerbe assumed the task of editing and publishing *The Numismatist*, and he purchased the publication from Heath's heirs a year later (Fig. 22-2). In 1911, through the generosity of Vice President W.C.C. Wilson, of Montreal, *The Numismatist* was purchased from Zerbe and donated to the ANA. The official periodical has been

Fig. 22-2. Farran Zerbe carried on the development of ANA as its president after the death of Dr. Heath.

owned and published monthly by the Association since that time. Due to the scarcity of most of the volumes issued prior to 1920, many of the more worthwhile articles published prior to that date were reprinted in four books in 1960. Three indexes have been published to the contents of *The Numismatist*. The first was published in

1940, the second was published in 1959, and the last, covering the entire span, was published in 1980.

National prominence was attained by the association on May 9, 1912, when it was granted a federal charter, signed by President William H. Taft, for 50 years. An amendment to make the charter permanent and allow for a larger board of governors was passed by Congress and signed into law by President John F. Kennedy on April 10, 1962. The ANA maintains the distinction of being one of the very few organizations in the United States to operate under federal charter.

In 1961, a National Home and Headquarters building fund was established under the chairmanship of Charles M. Johnson. Sixteen cities in the central United States made offers of sites for the location of the ANA offices. Upon nearing completion of the fund goal, Colorado Springs, Colorado, was chosen and ground breaking ceremonies were held on September 6, 1966. By the end of the year, nearly $300,000 had been collected to build and furnish the national headquarters.

Debt-free, the home and headquarters of the American Numismatic Association was dedicated and officially opened on June 10, 1967. The original building occupied 16,000 square feet and was professionally staffed with an executive vice president, editor, librarian, curator, and various assistants and office personnel on a full-time basis.

One of the first services established in the early years, for the benefit of ANA members, was a numismatic library. It remained small and unpretentious for years, but gained in size with the growth of membership. Today, housed in the headquarters, members have the use of the largest circulating numismatic library in the world. Its 7000 books and 15,000 periodicals and catalogs are listed in a specially designed library catalog given to all members. Most of the items in the ANA library are available to members by mail without charge other than postage both ways. The library has a number of numismatic slide sets that are loaned to member clubs for use as educational programs at their local meetings.

The Association maintains an extensive museum of coins, medals, tokens and paper money at its Colorado Springs headquarters that is open to visitors, members, and nonmembers at no charge (Fig. 22-3).

In mid-1972, the association inaugurated a certification service (American Numismatic Association Certification Service, known hobby wide as ANACS) that examines coins submitted by numismatists for a determination of their authenticity. Subsequently, this department also undertook the grading of coins as to their condition. Staff experts examine each coin submitted for

Fig. 22-3. One of the ANA museum galleries. The Museum is open to collectors and the general public free of charge.

authenticity and condition. If there are questions the staff authenticators cannot agree upon, the association maintains a national panel of expert consultants who will render an opinion. A certificate is issued with each coin. Included are photographs of obverse and reverse, and the written finding of legitimacy and grade.

By Board action, in 1965, a code of ethics was adopted and a coin theft reward fund was established. The ANA Code of Ethics, binding on each member on pain of expulsion, outlines principals of moral conduct that numismatists—whether collector or dealer—are required to follow in their hobby undertakings. The board of governors regularly deals with breaches of the code in an effort to police the hobby.

The ANA's theft reward fund provides up to $5,000 each to persons furnishing information leading to the arrest and conviction of persons responsible for robberies, thefts, or deaths in connection with crimes committed against members of the association.

In 1969, the association initiated a summer seminar that has become an annual numismatic event. Numismatic

educational opportunity of courses conducted in Colorado Springs are combined with a "working vacation" for collectors.Beginning in 1981, the association began to conduct its seminars at locations in other parts of the country. This affords more members the opportunity to take intensive study in such fields as coin authentication and grading, collecting basics, specializing in fields such as paper money, and ancient coins.

The program provides excellent instruction on various popular numismatic subjects and offers tours, food, and lodging at a very nominal cost to students. The first seminar attracted 20 numismatists from 13 states. It now has grown to an attendance of more than 100 participants. This popular membership benefit is made possible through the cooperation of Colorado College, on whose campus the ANA Headquarters is located. Annual highlights of the summer seminar include special tours on the floor of the Denver Mint and sightseeing in the Colorado mining country of the Pike's Peak area near Colorado Springs.

In 1976, the services of the ANA were consolidated

189

at Colorado Springs when ANACS was moved from its previous location in Washington, D.C. It soon became evident that this move and the general enlargement of operations, especially the library, were creating an intilerable crowding of the headquarters building. In its February, 1979, meeting, the board of governors approved the drawing of architectural plans for an addition to be added on top of the existing building. Plans for this new second story were approved in February, 1981, and ground was broken in May. Completion of the addition was expected in late 1982 (Fig. 22-4).

The American Numismatic Association will accept for membership all worthy persons 11 years of age or older who have an interest in the collecting or studying coins, paper money, tokens, medals, and related numismatic items. Memberships must be approved by the signature of two persons, at least one of whom is an ANA member. Because many of the members of a local coin club and virtually all coin dealers are ANA members, it should be no problem for the beginning numismatist to obtain the necessary signatures. They are actually more of a formality than references. If the new collector feels obtaining the required signatures will be a problem, he may request that the ANA Executive Vice President sign the membership application when it is returned.

Junior memberships, at a reduced rate, are available for persons aged 11-17. Those persons 18 and over may apply for regular membership or life membership. There are associate memberships for spouses and family members.

AMERICAN NUMISMATIC SOCIETY

Founded by a group of 12 coin collectors in New York City on April 16, 1858, the American Numismatic Society set forth its objectives as "the collection and preservation of coins and medals, with an investigation into their history, and other subjects connected therewith." Incorporated in 1864, the society continues to pursue the same goals today.

Because of its lengthy history and policy, from the first, of collecting coins, medals, and books in the name of the society, the ANS today owns one of the finest numismatic collections in the United States. It is perhaps second only to the holdings of the Smithsonian Institution.

Parts of this great collection are on exhibit at the ANS Museum located in the same uptown Manhattan building that has been the society's home since 1907. It was constructed through contributions from the membership (Fig. 22-5). Besides the museum, the ANS headquarters houses the offices and libraries of the organization. The museum incorporates coins of all periods and geographic areas, as well as medals and military decorations. In all, the society draws upon the more than 1,000,000 numismatic items in its coin cabinets when setting up

Fig. 22-4. Architect's model for the addition of a second floor to the existing ANA headquarters in Colorado Springs.

Fig. 22-5. Headquarters of the American Numismatic Society in New York City was constructed in 1907 and houses one of the most impressive museums and numismatic libraries in the world.

exhibits for public view. The exhibit halls of the society are open, free of charge, from 9 A.M. to 5 P.M., Tuesday through Saturday, and from 1 to 4 P.M. on Sunday. The ANS building is located on Broadway, between 155th and 156th Streets.

The ANS library is believed to be the country's most comprehensive in the area of numismatic subjects. Covering all branches of the hobby, the library consists of nearly 25,000 volumes. In addition there are countless periodicals, pamphlets, auction catalogs, and dealer price lists.

One of the society's functions has always been the publication of original numismatic literature. Many numismatists actively seek out the current and older editions of *Numismatic Notes and Monographs*. This is a lengthy series of publications, ranging from a couple of dozen pages to several hundred, each on a single topic.

The official journal of the society is *The American Numismatic Society Museum Notes*. Published annually, the most recent issue contains 14 major articles of original numismatic research. Of special interest to numismatic scholars and researchers is the ANS' *Numismatic Literature*. This twice-annual numismatic bibliography lists current numismatic publications with abstracts of their contents (Fig. 22-6).

Numismatic Studies is the top of the line in ANS publications. There now are more than 16 such large-format numismatics books. The *Studies* series is given free to fellows of the ANS. It is made available at a discount to other members.

There are four classes of membership in the American Numismatic Society; fellows, honorary fellows, associate members, and corresponding members. Fellowships are limited in number to 150. Persons or groups who have rendered exceptional service to the society or to numismatics in general may be elected as honorary fellows. Associate membership is unrestricted by numbers and is open to all with an interest in numismatics. Annual dues are comparable to those of the ANA. Corresponding memberships are open to those persons or organizations outside the United States. All classes of members receive the *Notes and Monographs, Museum Notes* and *Numismatic Literature* periodicals.

Government of the society is by a 15-member council elected from among and by the fellows and honorary fellows. The council elects its president and three vice presidents, and appoints the other officers.

The ANS has been conducting summer seminars since 1952, but they are of a different nature than those of the American Numismatic Association. The ANS seminar is aimed primarily at the non-numismatist to provide graduate students in such humanistic fields as the classics, archaeology, Oriental languages, history, economics and art history with an understanding of the contributions numismatics has to make in these areas of study. Grants-in-aid to these university postgrads provide them with sufficient training in numismatics to be of use to them in their future studies or careers.

A more advanced program, graduate fellowships, has been available since 1958. The program offers doctoral candidates in the humanities assistance in preparing dissertations on topics in which numismatics plays a significant part. These graduate fellowships, which carry a $3,500 stipend, are open only to candidates who have attended one of the society's summer seminars.

Additional services of the ANS include the extension of their vast holdings to serious collectors and students through the use of slide presentations, a photographic service, and a casting service, (expert casts are made of items in the ANS Museum).

Information on ANS membership can be obtained by writing the Secretary of the Society, American Numismatic Society, Broadway between 155th and 156th Sts., New York, NY 10032.

SOCIETY OF PAPER MONEY COLLECTORS

For the paper-money collector, there are several national and internation specialty organizations. The largest such organization is the SPMC. Organized in 1961, and incorporated as a nonprofit organization under the laws of the District of Columbia, in 1964, the Society of Paper Money Collectors maintains as its goal the propagation on the collecting and research of paper money and related items from all corners of the world. While membership in SPMC is overwhelmingly situated in the United States, the areas of members' collecting interests are worldwide. Associated with the American Numismatic Association, the Society of Paper Money Collectors holds its own annual meeting at the ANA convention each August.

SPMC works toward its goal mainly through the publication of its bimonthly journal *Paper Money* (Fig. 22-7) and the publication of books on paper-money topics. The society is currently engaged in cataloging all known obsolete currency issues of the United States on a state-by-state basis. Members who are expert in the issues of one state or several prepare manuscripts and illustrations that the society then publishes under its own banner. Approximately, a dozen states and territories have been covered already. The books provide the most in-depth information in this popular collecting area currently available. Besides its state bank note and scrip series, the SPMC also publishes other works relative to paper money such as Peter Huntoon's recent work on territorial national bank notes.

Membership in SPMC is open to paper-money collectors and scholars age 12 and over. Regular member-

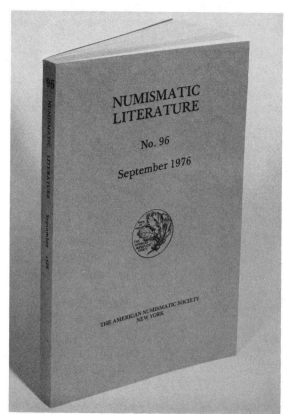

Fig. 22-6. The several publications of the ANS benefit all numismatists. This is an edition of their numismatic bibliography that lists and describes virtually everything written about numismatics on an on-going basis.

Fig. 22-7. The bimonthly journal *Paper Money* is the principal benefit of membership in the Society of Paper Money Collectors.

shortened to Token and Medal Society. In April, 1966, the group was incorporated.

TAMS is a national organization dedicated to serving the interests of those who collect numismatic items outside the realm of officially issued coins and paper currency. The society's principal aim is to promote and stimulate the study of tokens, medals, and similar issues; to encourage research and writings pertaining thereto; and to publish such research in the pages of its bimonthly official organ *TAMS Journal* and in separately published books and monographs (Fig. 22-8).

The *Journal* generally contains feature length articles on tokens, medals, and related subjects. Several times a year, special supplements to the regular *Journal* present lengthier works. Often this includes original cataloging efforts in such diverse collecting areas as American Legion medals, prison tokens, Texas trade tokens, etc. Recent book projects of the society range from the huge compendium *Medals of the United States Mint, 1792-1892*, by R.W. Julian, to the recently issued *Medallic Portraits of Hitler*. The *Journal* and supplements

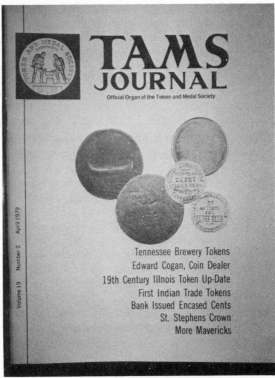

Fig. 22-8. In the pages of the Token and Medal Society's *Journal*, the exonumist will find articles about all manners of noncoin collectibles in the numismatic field.

ships are available to those over the age of 18. Society dues are approximately $12 annually.

Besides the *Paper Money* journal mailed free to members, SPMC membership offers, as a benefit, the use of a lending library of currency related topics. Members are offered substantial discounts on the books published by the society.

Because of the transient nature of officeholders in SPMC and similar societies, interested persons can write for current membership information to the author, Robert Lemke, Krause Publications, 700 E. State St., Iola, WI 54990, for current data.

TOKEN AND MEDAL SOCIETY

The Token and Medal Society, known hobby wide as TAMS, was founded on November 19, 1960, under the rather unwieldy name of the Society of Token and Medal and Obsolete Paper Money Collectors. Even in acronym form, STM & OPMC, it was a mouthful. When the obsolete paper money collectors branched off to become part of the newly formed SPMC, late in 1961, the name was are mailed free to all members. The books are made available at a discount.

Because of the informational value in its *Journal*, the society recently published a comprehensive index to article and subject matter, and has reprinted the first six volumes of the *Journal* for the benefit of newer members. Long out of print and high on the want lists of many members and numismatic researchers, the first 27 issues of the *TAMS Journal* comprised more than 900 pages of original research. This has been bound into the two-column reprint set.

While 1982 TAMS dues were $6, interested readers are advised to write the author at the address above for current information and a membership application.

INTERNATIONAL BANK NOTE SOCIETY

The leading international organization for world paper-money collectors is the International Bank Note Society. This society features joint headquarters on both sides of the Atlantic. There are active branches in the United States and Great Britain.

Organized in 1961, to promote an interest in world bank notes, IBNS began with a small number of members in England. It has grown to a worldwide organization of nearly 1500 active collectors and dealers.

In addition to publishing a magazine-format journal four times a year, the society keeps members up to date with a quarterly newsletter. Libraries of world currency titles are maintained on both sides of the Atlantic for use by members.

Twice a year IBNS conducts a large auction of world paper money entirely by mail. All members are allowed to consign duplicate or unwanted notes to the sales. Only members are allowed to participate in the bidding. The IBNS auctions are particularly attractive to beginning collectors in that they include large numbers of the more common and lower-priced notes, as well as many rare and expensive items usually found in this type of auction.

The society is also working on a highly specialized series of world paper-money reference catalogs. The catalogs are based on a manuscript by Dr. Arnold Keller, that is being revised, expanded, and updated by IBNS members who contribute their input in the areas of their particular speciality. This mammoth undertaking is designed to picture and describe all the known notes of each country by the time it is completed sometime after the turn of the century.

SPECIALTY COLLECTOR GROUPS

Besides the national and international groups outlined above, there are a great number of specialty organizations within the numismatic hobby that are dedicated to a wide range of collecting pursuits. While many of these groups have been around for some time and can be expected to remain on the scene, others are quite transient in nature and might or might not remain viable. Because such groups generally change official mailing addresses when they change officers, it is not practical to give an address here. Interested readers may contact the author at the address given previously in this chapter to inquire of the current status of any of these clubs.

World Coins. In the field of world coins, a number of large, active groups are based in the United States. Among them are the Azteca Numismatic Society, which specializes in the coins of ancient and modern Mexico; the Organization of International Numismatists; Oriental Numismatic Society, with a bend toward the coins of the Far East; Society for International Numismatics; and the American Israel Numismatic Association, a large group with many active local and regional chapters. Formed in 1967 to serve the rapidly growing field of collectors who specialize in the coins, medals, tokens, bank notes and related items of Israel, the ancient coins of the Holy Land and all numismatic Judaica, AINA publishes a popular journal called *The Shekel*, participates in major coin conventions and sponsors annual numismatic study tours of Israel and other Near East locations. Collectors who want to learn more about the association and its many chapters should contact: American Israel Numismatic Association, P.O. Box 25057, Tamarac, FL 33320.

Error Collectors. Those who collect numismatic errors might want to contact the BIE Guild, Collectors of Numismatic Errors or Numismatic Error Collectors of America. Their current addresses and membership information may be obtained by writing noted error specialist and writer Alan Herbert, P.O. Box C, Deadwood, SD 57732.

Tokens and Medals. Many different specialty areas in the token and medal field are represented by their own organizations. Those that have been around for some time include the American Political Items Collectors, for devotees of the campaign tokens, medals, buttons, badges, and other memorabilia associated with American elections since the days of George Washington.

The American Tax Token Society collects the minidenomination special tax payment tokens that were in many states in the first half of the twentieth century. For the collector of bus, train, and related transportation tokens, there is an American Vecturist Society.

Collectors of wooden nickels and other "denominations" might want to become associated with the American Wooden Money Guild or the Dedicated Wooden Money Collectors.

The Civil War Token Society is an active group for the study and collection of the cent-sized copper penny substitutes that were privately issued, on both sides of the Mason-Dixon line, during the Civil War when government-issued coinage was being hoarded.

There are clubs for collectors of the souvenir elongated or rolled-out cents: The Elongated Collectors.

For collectors of the finely re-engraved nineteenth century love tokens, there is the Love Token Society. For collectors of merchant or "Good for" tokens, there is the Merchant Token Collectors Association. And for collectors of coal-company scrip and related currency substitutes, there is the National Scrip Collectors Association.

Those with an interest in the ration tokens and other scrip of the World War II era, can join the Society of Ration Token Collectors. For the specialist in military decorations and orders, there is the Orders and Medals Society of America.

U.S. Coins: A number of specialty groups also exist in the broad spectrum of United States coinage. Among them are the Early Silver Dollar Club, specializing in the cartwheels of the 1794-1803 era, the Early American Coppers Club, who are devoted to the half cents and large cents of the 1793-1855 period, and the Liberty Seated Collectors Club, specialists in the half-dime through silver-dollar coinage of the mid-nineteenth century that featured a common obverse design of a seated representation of Liberty.

Virtually all of these groups keep members in contact with regular, or at least semiregular, newsletters that range from a few photocopied sheets to nicely bound digest-sized journals. These periodicals usually contain articles of interest within the specialty group and advertisements from members. These ads are often the best way for specialty collectors to find the material they need for their own collections or to dispose of duplicates for the best possible price or trade.

Most of the groups hold meetings in conjunction with large national or regional coin conventions. Often such meetings are during the American Numismatic Association convention.

Chapter 23

Security for the Collector

EVERY COIN COLLECTOR SHOULD QUICKLY learn the basics of security. With just a little common sense and some helpful tips, the collector can learn to protect his valuable hobby treasures and, more importantly, himself and his family.

The same liquidity that makes coins and other numismatic items so attractive to investors makes them equally attractive to thieves. Because many coins are very valuable, because they are virtually unidentifiable unless the collector takes special steps, and because the coin market operates largely on a cash basis with few questions asked, thieves are understandably drawn to numismatics. If you can make yourself as uninviting a target as possible, the potential crook will take his business elsewhere.

One of the best ways to protect yourself and your collection is to keep a low profile. Don't advertise the fact that you are a coin collector. The fewer people who know about your hobby, the lesser your chances will be of having that information reach the ears of the thief.

Many collectors are justifiably concerned with receiving coin collecting-related mail at their homes. While you can generally trust your mailman to keep his mouth shut, think of how many other people have a chance to glance at your mailbox the day your copy of the weekly

coin paper arrives. Because of the prohibitive wrapping costs, none of the major hobby papers are delivered in plain brown wrappers. A mailing label is slapped over the front page and the easily identifiable name is out for all to see. If your mailbox is the type that has a rack at the bottom for papers and magazines, your hobby is right out there on public view for the paperboy, the door-to-door salesmen, and other people who might be passing by. The same is often true in many apartment buildings.

Many collectors avoid this situation by buying their paper at the local coin shop each week. While this is a good way to avoid getting it at home, it is also expensive. The over-the-counter price of the paper about triple the subscription cost. If you are like most numismatists, it will be hard for you to get out of the coin shop each week with nothing more than a paper. Besides, the shop might be sold out of that week's *Numismatic News* by the time you get there.

I suggest that you rent a post office box at a convenient location near your home or on your route to work. The cost is much less than buying your paper each week. You can have all your hobby mail sent to the Post Office box. Auction catalogs, dealer price lists, and your mail-order purchases have no safer place to sit than in a post office box.

By filling out the box rental agreement with the provision that only mail addressed directly to you at the Post Office box be put in there, you can avoid having the box filled with junk mail. You can cut down your trips to the box to only those days on which you expect hobby mail.

The use of a post office box is one of the least expensive security measures the collector can take. And it is one of the most effective methods.

Avoid appearances in the local media identifying yourself as a coin collector. While you will be justifiably proud of being elected president of the local coin club, it is probably better not to give the local paper a news release on the subject.

While it is fine to promote numismatics in your town during National Coin Week, for example, by placing posters in stores, samples copies of papers in doctor's offices, and numismatic exhibits at a friendly bank, make sure your name isn't on them. Use the name of your coin club or just don't give credit. The main idea is to keep your collecting interests as quiet as possible outside your circle of hobby acquaintances.

Another good tip is to make sure, if you have numismatic displays at home, they are out of sight of persons passing by in the street. For many years when I was in grade school, I would walk past a house that had several large frames of coin and stamp displays on the back of the living room wall. They were easily visible night and day through the large picture window. While most of us enjoy displaying some of our items at home, we can usually do it as easily on a wall that is not visible from the outsider or to the casual visitor. Use an interior hallway, a basement recreation room, or an upstairs bedroom. Precautions like this wil help you avoid the attention of the coin crook, but your security cannot stop there.

If a professional thief moves in on your town or neighborhood, he will know how to find out who is a collector. He might loiter around the coin shop and follow customers to their homes (especially customers who make a big purchase). Most coin dealers—even the small storefront shops—have private offices where serious numismatic business can be conducted out of the way of general shop traffic.

The dedicated crook might read about an upcoming monthly coin club meeting and decide to attend and keep his ears open. Chances are he'll hear somebody tip themselves off as an easy mark. To help prevent this, make it a point to know your fellow club members. When you see a new face in the crowd, ask around and see if he is known to other members. If not, ask the person to identify himself with a driver's license or other positive means.

The newcomer might be a new collector or a burglar who specializes in coin collections.

SECURITY OPTIONS

Where you keep your coins is actually the biggest factor in their security. But there are tradeoffs to be considered in each case, and the collector must make his own decision on a combination of safety and convenience to suit his individual needs.

A great many collectors keep their numismatic items in the home. Maybe I've been falsely lulled by living in medium-sized cities, stable neighborhoods, and small towns all my life, but I'm not going to knock this system. I'm also not going to give an unqualified endorsement.

A coin collection is just not much fun locked away in a bank vault. I want my stuff where it is easily accessible so that I can flip through my albums or rummage through my 2 × 2s whenever I feel the urge. Because most of my personal numismatic collections are items of more historic than intrinsic or collector value, and because most of them are not irreplaceable, I am willing to trade off the fact that in my home they are not especially secure from fire and theft. I sleep a little easier knowing that I have a good watchdog and a large-caliber handgun with which I am extremely proficient.

When I am going to be gone for extended periods, I can place my collections in the bank safety deposit box where I keep my more valuable numismatic investment items. In this respect, I suspect I am like a great number of fellow numismatists. I keep some of my material at home and some in a safety deposit box. Unlike the relatively inexpensive coins and notes I keep at the house, the material in my bank box cost a great deal of money and constitutes much of my personal retirement program. I would not expose that to the risks of being kept at home.

One collector I know keeps all of his numismatic material in a bank box. Well, almost all of it. Realizing that he may someday become the target of armed robbers or burglars who know he is a coin collector, he has made up a small metal strong box full of nearly worthless junk. There are low-grade, early date Lincoln cents he has pulled out of circulation over the years, a nice box full of expensive-looking foreign coins, and gobs of world paper money taken out of 10-cent junk boxes. Some of it is even housed in surplus plastic cases and other fancy holders he gets free from a friendly coin dealer. My friend looks on this as a kind of insurance policy against amateur thieves. He says he would hate to tell a couple of big masked men holding a gun at his head that all of his coins are locked up in the bank. And he has no intention of starting a shootout.

It is his intention, in the event of a robbery, to quickly hand over this box of junk coins and notes. The amateur thief is likely to be fooled, and my friend says he is only worried about the amateur. A professional coin thief, he theorizes, would easily believe that there is no valuable material lying around the house unless he has concrete evidence otherwise. My friend quickly acknowledges that if he did happen to have part of his collection out of the bank or if he had just received some coins by mail, and he was confronted with an armed intruder, he would hand the valuable merchandise over along with the junk.

The bottom line is that none of your coins are worth the risk of your own or your family's health or lives. Protect your coins as best you can, but not at the risk of life or limb.

HOLDINGS AT HOME

If you have decided to keep some or all of your numis-matic holdings at home, there are several good books available detailing things like burglar alarms, hiding places, and defense against armed intruders. There is one excellent hiding place I'd like to pass along that is little known and doesn't even appear in most of the books. A collector I know has fasioned a hiding place for his coins beneath the bottom step of the stairs leading to the upper floor of his house. He had the actual floor board hinged to swing up. The hinges are hidden by the carpet on the stairs. Instead of tacking the carpet down, he has secured the portion that covers the first step with Velcro strips. This allows him easy access to his hiding place. While such a hiding place is very likely to be missed by even the most thorough burglar, it is little good in the event of fire, flood, or high wind.

As protection against natural disasters, some collectors invest in a safe or other strong box (Fig. 23-1). Several safe manufacturers regularly advertise in the numismatic trade papers. They will send you illustrated

Fig. 23-1. Many collectors feel a good home safe, such as this model that is disguised as an end table, is good security from fire and theft.

literature on their lines upon request. One of the fellows at the office has a nice large old safe at home in which he stores his valuables. He has chosen it well because it required several strong men to get it into the house. It will not be easily carted off by the neighborhood junkie to be cracked at his leisure.

If you decide to buy a safe for your home, be sure to investigate its fire resistence capability. That's the only real value a home safe has. A determined armed robber can easily force you to open your safe by threats or violence. Most home safes are little challenge for the experienced burglar. Shop for a safe more for its resistance to fire and water than as a theft deterrent.

DEPOSIT BOXES

If you have decided that all or part of your coin collection should be somewhere else besides the home, you have the option of choosing two basically different types of security locations for your material: the bank safety deposit box or the increasingly common private safe deposit box. Private vaults have become a major growth industry in the security business. The shortage of bank facilities of this nature in many areas has led to an entire new business in providing security for the individual.

The most common method for stashing valuables remains safety deposit boxes at local banks. While there is a shortage of bank boxes in many parts of the country, it should be possible for you to line up access to a box in a relatively short time. If your bank has no boxes immediately available, ask to be put on a waiting list for when a box holder surrenders his place in the vault. If you have a box that is too small to fit your growing collection, it is usually possible to obtain larger boxes or additional boxes.

Although bank safety deposit boxes do offer a maximum of security for your collection, there are two drawbacks that you should consider before entrusting your valuable collections to such a repository. These boxes are not insured by the bank. If there is a fire, flood, burglary or other loss of the contents of your box, the bank is not liable (except in the case of negligence). If you want your collection insured while it is a bank safety deposit box, you must provide for coverage.

A second drawback is that you do not have absolute access to your box. In the event of the death of the boxholder, the bank is required to seal that box and deliver its contents to a probate court. This eliminates the stashing away of hugh amounts of untaxed income or personal property that can be transferred without tax penalty.

In the unlikely event of another bank holiday, such as the country went through during the Depression, it is possible that you could be denied access to your collection or investment coins at the time when you need them most.

In signing for a safe deposit box with nearly all banks, you give them the fairly extensive privilege of opening the box to various tax and law enforcement authorities. If you are conducting your hobby affairs in a perfectly lawful manner, you should have no problems with this type of restriction. If you don't see the need for the government to get its share of the profit on every coin transaction you make, you might be forced to consider an alternative to the bank safety deposit box.

For many American coin collectors, this alternative is the private safe deposit box. Some companies offering this service do so in quarters that were once large bank buildings. Indeed, a New Orleans firm acquired the old Federal Reserve branch bank in that city and converted its mammoth vaults to a private safety-deposit-box center. Other companies are building such facilities from scratch. They are designed with utmost security in mind.

Unlike the bank safety deposit box, no government agency or tax authority is empowered to inspect or impound your private box. Most owners of these facilities make it almost impossible to trace the owner by providing a system of codes and keys that allow the individual maximum protection while maintaining a low profile. The cost for this type of security is not inexpensive, but it is reasonable.

The drawbacks to the system include the lack of insurance for the contents of the boxes and that there are still too few of these private vaults available to accommodate all who would like to have one.

You should also be very careful about investigating the company before entrusting your valuables to a private safety deposit box. An investment of a couple of hundred thousand dollars in setting up a phony private vault company could well net millions of dollars worth of cash and valuables if a person were to be so inclined.

Don't ever leave gold and silver bullion in the possession of the dealer.

I have seen several once-large bullion dealers go bankrupt in recent years. They took many of their customers with them. Unfortunate buyers of gold and silver coins and bullion who left their material in possession of the dealer "for security," too often found that "their" precious metal or coins had been sold to several other people. The dealer speculated in the market with their money. If that dealer didn't call the market actions correctly, he lost—and so did you. Always take possession of your purchases even if you have to store them at home in the back of the freezer. At least you'll know where your money is.

INSURANCE

One of the best forms of security you can provide for your coin collection is a good insurance policy. While you can ask your family insurance agent about such coverage, you can also find specialty firms dealing in collectible insurance. One of the more financially appealing benefits of American Numismatic Association membership is that the ANA offers a group insurance policy for your collection.

Premiums vary according to where you live, what your collection is worth, and where you store it. If you keep your coins at home, the premium is higher than if they are kept in a bank vault. The ANA policy also provides protection for your material while traveling to a coin show or even when it is kept at home for short periods of time while you are working on it. As a side benefit, ANA members may also take advantage of group insurance plans in such areas as life and health policies.

Chapter 24

Counterfeit and Altered Coins

WHILE THE DANGER OF GETTING STUCK with a counterfeit or altered coin should not be minimized, the beginning numismatist should not be overly concerned to the point of paranoia. It is certainly true that virtually every numismatic item of any intrinsic or collector value has been counterfeited or created by altering another item. The collector can virtually eliminate the risk of accepting such a fake by using a little common sense.

Your single best defense against counterfeit and altered coins—even better than becoming a counterfeit detector yourself—is to know and trust the persons from whom you buy your coins and other numismatic material. It's as simple as that. No legitimate coin dealer is going to risk his reputation, his business, and his freedom by selling bad coins. If you have followed the advise given in earlier chapters on how to choose a coin dealer, you can virtually forget the risk of buying or getting stuck with a counterfeit coin.

Every reputable coin dealer offers a lifetime money-back guarantee of authenticity. For your own protection, if you ever have any doubts about a coin purchase, you should have it authenticated immediately. That way the seller can make a fast adjustment and maybe recover his own investment from whomever sold him the coin in the first place. Don't hold a coin for years, watching its value climb, only to find out you've been taken when you want to sell.

Generally, you can figure that the more an item is worth, the greater the chances that somebody is now, or has in the past, counterfeited it by starting from scratch or altering an existing piece. Dozens of people each year think they have struck it rich when they discover a "1913 Liberty nickel." What they have actually discovered is a 1903 or 1912 Liberty nickel that has been tampered with (Fig. 24-1). It is ironic, but at the very top end of the numismatic rarity scale, you almost never have to worry about fakes. The very rare items, such as 1804 silver dollars and 1913 Liberty nickels, are all so well documented that the appearance of a previously unknown specimen would raise immediate suspicions in all but the most novice numismatist.

FAKED COINS

The beginning collector is likely to find the most abundant fakes in the U.S. gold coin series. For many years, private "mints" in Mexico and Lebanon have been turning our die-struck "U.S. gold coins" in all denominations from $1-$20, dating back to the 1840s, and selling them in the bazaars for a hefty premium over their gold content to

Fig. 24-1. Only five 1913 Liberty nickels are known. All are in proof condition and all in famous collections in museums. Yet, fakers continue to try to peddle altered 1903 or 1912 nickels as the real thing.

unscrupulous importers who try to pass them off as genuine collectible U.S. gold pieces here and abroad.

Huge percentages of the gold coins seen in necklaces, rings, and bracelets are this type of counterfeit. Many coin dealers recognize these modern fakes at first glance and will have nothing to do with them. If you are unfortunate enough to be stuck with one, the best you can hope for is to find a friendly bullion dealer who will pay you the melted down value of the piece.

Probably a greater danger to the average collector than outright counterfeits are altered coins. With the flood of modern technology in the past decade, there is virtually no effect that can't be recreated on a coin (Fig. 24-2). Mint marks can be added or removed with ease. Signs of circulation can be removed and proof finishes restored to circulated or abused coins. Holes can be plugged almost undetectably. All manners of damage can be covered up or repaired.

Your best defense is to know your dealer. Buy only from a trusted local coin shop, a well-known bourse-floor dealer or a mail-order advertiser in a paper that you trust.

If you are not an expert counterfeit detector, you can get badly burned shopping for coin "rarities" at flea markets, junk stores, or in alleyways.

There are several books available which detail the most commonly encountered counterfeit and altered coins. One of the best is by Virgil Hancock and Larry

Spanbauer and it is titled *Standard Catalog of United States Altered and Counterfeit Coins*. Hancock is a former ANA president and was for many years the best friend the coin collector had in fighting fakes and fakers. Both he and Spanbauer have penned numerous articles in the numismatic press warning collectors of new and old counterfeits and alterations.

Their 1979 book is the perfect beginner's course in protecting yourself by learning how to detect fakes. Enlarged photos and descriptions of hundreds of commonly encountered fakes provide the collector with his first line of defense.

Your local coin dealer might have a copy of the book in stock or might be able to obtain one for you. Your membership in the ANA could come in handy because you can borrow the book via mail order. There are several other titles available dealing with the same subject. It wouldn't hurt the collector to have access to one or more of these books when contemplating the purchase of an expensive coin.

CERTIFICATION SERVICE

Luckily for the modern collector, there are places you can go to have a coin authenticated by experts. The best known and most widely used and respected of these is the American Numismatic Association Certification Service (ANACS). ANACS authenticates and grades U.S. coins, and provides authentication services for world coins and nonlegal tender paper currency. The grading of coins by ANACS is detailed in Chapter 25. The authentication of coins was the hobby service for which the organization was formed in the early 1970s.

Fig. 24-2. Collectors must watch for altered coins whenever big money is at stake. The addition of an "S" mint mark on the back of this dime turned a $10 coin into a reasonable facsimile of a great rarity that sells in the high five-figures—if genuine.

The grade or condition assigned to the coin described here represents the personal opinion of one or more members of the ANA Grading Service staff. Although specific grading parameters and suggestions are outlined in 'the official ANA grading guide' and are used by the ANA Grading Service; as the introduction to the book notes, grading is a matter of opinion, and qualified numismatists can legitimately differ from each other on certain points. The intermediate grades of Select Uncirculated or MS-63 (equivalent to a grade midway between Typical Uncirculated and Choice Uncirculated) and Gem Uncirculated, or MS-67 (a grade between Choice Uncirculated and Perfect Uncirculated), are used by the Grading Service following approval by the ANA Board of Governors.

Fig. 24-3. American Numismatic Association Certification Service certificate of authenticity and grading helps assure the collector he is getting what he paid for.

The American Numismatic Association Certification Service is a semiautonomous arm of the federally chartered, nonprofit educational American Numismatic Association. It is the function of ANACS to examine and make nondestructive tests on numismatic items submitted to them and to render a statement of opinion as to the genuineness of those items (Fig. 24-3).

ANACS services are available to ANA members and nonmembers. Members pay a lower fee for ANACS services. The fee covers the costs of the staff and operation of ANACS. Authentication fees are approximately $5.40 ($6 for nonmembers) for coins valued to $125, $13.50 ($15) for coins valued $376-500, and 2.7 percent of value for coins over $500, to a maximum fee per item of $500. Nonmembers pay a 3 percent authentication fee for coins valued at over $500, to a $550 maximum.

Besides the authentication fee, if the owner wants the coin graded, he pays an additional $5 fee ($6 for nonmembers) for coins valued to $500, and then 1 percent of the coin's value, to a maximum of $20. The nonmember maximum grading fee is $25 or 1.5 percent of the value for coins worth more than $500. These fees must be accompanied by sufficient remittance to cover return registered mail. Currently costs range from $3 for items insured for less than $100 to $8.50 for items valued to $10,000. These fees and postage charges are subject to change.

Contact ANACS for current information before submitting any coin: ANACS, 181 N. Cascade, Colorado Springs, CO 80903.

All items received at ANACS are given individual registry numbers, weighed, and photographed for the permanent ANACS files. The items are examined using stereo microscopes and even a sophisticated new scanning electron microscope (Fig. 24-4).

Those items that warrant additional testing receive specific gravity tests. This is a simple procedure to determine the metallic content of a coin. If the item requires further examination by outside consultants for either authenticity or grade, it is forwarded to one of the recognized authorities in the field and the submittor is notified of the delay. These expert consultants serve anonymously and without fee beyond a token $1 annual payment as a service to ANA and fellow numismatists.

All items submitted to ANACS for authentication are returned to the sender with one of the following descriptions.

Genuine. A photographic certification by ANACS will accompany the item.

Cannot Be Certified. This means that the item has been altered, is counterfeit, or is otherwise not genuine. In such cases, any fee paid over $100 is returned to the submitter.

No Decision. Occasionally, because of excessive circulation wear, corrosion, damage, or other factors, a definitive conclusion cannot be reached as to an item's genuineness. In these cases, the entire fee is returned.

Modern Replica. ANACS defines the term *modern replica* to be those items that are made of base metals, sometimes gold or silver plated, and sold as souvenirs or novelties. Only the minimum base fee is charged to make this determination.

In most cases, authentication and/or grading can be completed within a few working days of receipt. A photographic certificate of the item, if genuine, and the item itself are then returned to the sender together. If additional time or expense will be needed to certify the coin, the sender is advised. If the extra time and expense are not agreeable to the submitter, the item is returned promptly, without certification.

All numismatic items, whether genuine or counterfeit, submitted to ANACS will be returned to the sender unless the service receives strict instructions in writing to do otherwise.

The general procedure for submitting numismatic material to ANACS is as follows. Place each item in a suitable holder and prepare the package for shipping in suitable heavy mailers. Include name, address, and the

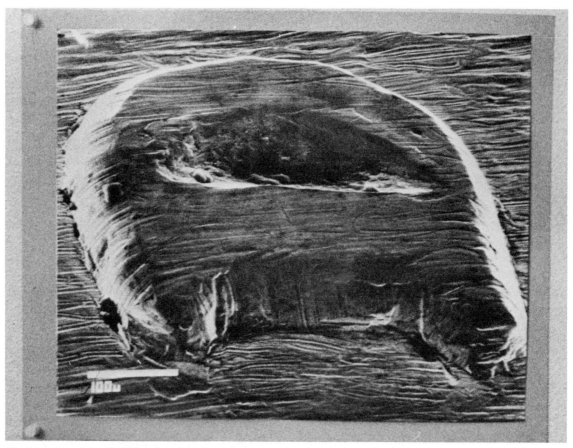

Fig. 24-4. One of the ANACS tools in the fight against counterfeiters is the scanning electron microscope. This photo shows a mint mark enlarged 100 times.

name of the person or firm to whom the certificate of authenticity (if rendered) should be made out to. Describe the item fully by country of issue, denomination, date, mint mark, metals, assayers initials, signatures, and any seldom-seen or unusual characteristics or significant features. Provide the source if known from whom the item was acquired. Place a value on it for fee purposes and for insurance purposes. Submit the item with the correct fee and return postage to ANACS; use registered mail.

Because it is a nonprofit membership service and not commercially involved in the numismatic field, ANACS is the authentication service used for well over 99 percent of the items being authenticated. A private competitor, the International Numismatic Service Authentication Bureau, in Washington, D.C., is headed by a former ANACS employee.

One other service that ANACS provides to collectors is numismatic photography. ANACS has its own photographic facilities and darkroom and can provide photos for research, display, or other educational purposes of those items submitted for certification. Minimal fees, available upon request, are charged for enlargements in any size, up to 8×10 inches, of either full obverse, full reverse, or details photographed through a microscope.

While the ANACS services are certainly all the counterfeit detection assistance most average numismatists will ever need, many collectors take it upon themselves to learn something about counterfeit detection on their own. Many look upon the time and money spent in pursuit of such an education to be a great value in comparison to getting stuck with a phony coin or of paying a fee everytime they want to buy a coin.

AUTHENTICATION COURSES

There are a number of numismatic authentication courses

of study available. Probably the best known and most widely used is that provided by ANACS as part of the annual American Numismatic Association summer seminar. There, students receive a week-long intensive study course in the basics of authentication. The emphasis is not so much of learning to detect counterfeits as it is on how to identify a genuine coin. The theory is that there are numerous ways to fake a coin, but the real thing is made only one way.

In 1978, I completed the ANACS authentication course in the summer seminar. The first day was spent viewing slides of genuine and counterfeit U.S. coins in all series. The emphasis throughout the course was on U.S. coinage; it is the most frequently collected and counterfeited. The thrust of the course was in teaching students how to tell mint-produced coins from those made somewhere else or altered after leaving the mint.

In the course of presenting this information, a large number of identifiable characteristics of genuine and known fake coins were pointed out to the students. Hundreds of slides were viewed during the course. Each slide is used to impress upon the collector the differences between genuine coins and fakes through the study of the minting process and what it does to a coin (Fig. 24-5).

To get a better handle on the mint operation, the class was given a special tour of the nearby Denver Mint. The public never gets this type of tour. Conducted right on the working floor of the mint, rather than overhead walkways, we were guided by knowledgeable supervisory personnel. We were encouraged to get as close as safety will allow to the great machines that turn rolls of metal strip into coin blanks, into milled planchets, and finally into coins. It was a "hands-on" type of tour; we were allowed to handle the coin strip, unfinished coins, damaged and "error" coins, and other educational tools along the way. All of this was under the watchful eye of a security guard. Students are even allowed to visit the die destruction area where worn out or damaged coining dies are melted (a rare treat for any numismatist).

Class sessions for the counterfeit detection students in the summer seminar are longer than for the other classes. We generally met from 9 to 11:30 A.M., and then from 1:30 to 4:30 P.M., and again from 7 P.M. in the evening until as late as necessary to cover the material.

At our session, we were addressed by the mint's chief assayer. He discussed mechanical quirks in the coin manufacturing process that aspiring counterfeit detectors should become aware of. Lab work included learning the use of the stereo microscope and specific gravity weighing. Students work with fake coins that come from

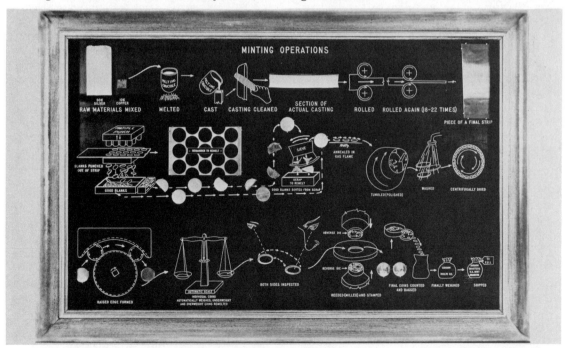

Fig. 24-5. The collector can help protect himself by learning how coins are produced, as simplified in this mint diagram.

ANACS' study collection. Students are also free to bring specimens they suspect are bad.

The "final exam" for the course comes on the last day when students are presented with a group of coins. Some are genuine and some are counterfeit or altered specimens. Then the student really finds out whether or not he is a counterfeit detector.

The beginning collector should remember to look at coins objectively. A little knowledge is a dangerous thing. You will probably get stuck with more bad coins if you have only a rudimentary knowledge of fakes and fakers than if you know nothing at all. A brief course in counterfeit detection should not be allowed to strip you of your wariness in dealing with coins when there is significant money involved. If you are going to learn to detect counterfeit and altered coins, you should be prepared to keep on learning after you leave a counterfeit detection seminar. There are many good articles written by the ANACS staff in *The Numismatist*. Keep up on new trends and equipment in the field. For the serious numismatist, counterfeit detection is an on-going skill that must be used regularly to keep you sharp.

One method of refreshing your knowledge is to attend the occasional mini seminars which the ANACS staff conducts at larger coin shows around the country. Usually two evenings long, for a couple of hours each, these mini courses are a good brush-up for the graduate or a good beginning for the new student.

Adelphi University offers counterfeit detection courses in their extension program of weekend coin courses. Watch the hobby press for details of upcoming classes.

THE BOTTOM LINE

The bottom line in counterfeit detection is not to get stuck with a bad coin. But what if this information comes too late? What if you have already bought a counterfeit or altered coin? That depends on who you bought the coin from. If you know the dealer from whom you buy coins, you will probably come out all right. If you bought from some guy dealing out of the back seat of his Buick, you have no recourse.

Any reputable dealer stands behind the authenticity of the material he sells. It is in your best interests to check out suspected coins early so that you can get your money back quickly and invest it in the genuine article.

If a dealer refuses to refund your money, you have several alternatives. Probably the most effective choice is to threaten to turn the coin over to the nearest U.S. Secret Service office along with the full particulars of where it was purchased. You will never see the coin again if it is counterfeit. The Secret Service will be more interested in finding out who makes and sells the fakes than in getting your money back, but it is a good lever to get a reluctant dealer off dead center in making restitution to you for selling a fake. You can try complaints to the newspaper where the dealer advertises, if you bought the coin by mail order, as well as complaints to the ANA or any other numismatic or trade organization of which the seller is a member.

If you can't even find the seller of the coin, you have little alternative beyond marking your loss down to education. Don't ever try to sell or spend known counterfeit currency. Besides risking prosecution yourself, you are only perpetuating a fraudulent coin in the hobby.

Chapter 25

Overgrading

THERE IS NO SANTA CLAUS IN NUMISMATICS. That truism should be embossed on your wallet so that you can look at it every time you reach for your money to buy a coin or other numismatic item. There are no bargains in the coin market. Yet, the larcenous corner of each soul seems to come to the forefront when a collector sees a coin advertised at a ridiculously low price. Many otherwise sensible numismatists can't resist trying to "steal" a coin for far less than its true value. I'm not referring to cherry picking where you make a good deal because the seller doesn't know what he has. I'm referring to plain old greed.

Far too many collectors loose their common sense when they see an ad offering a popular coin at a seemingly bargain price. When you see a $200 coin being advertised for $75, you're really only buying a $75 coin. It is just another case of overgrading.

Overgrading is the practice, almost exclusively done in mail-order coin selling, of describing a coin as being of a higher grade than it actually is. The practice is almost exclusively a mail-order phenomenon because nobody is going to buy an obviously overgraded coin over the shop counter or at the coin show where they can actually see what they are getting before they lay out their cash. That assumes, of course, that the collector knows how to grade coins. That should be a prerequisite to your spending money on numismatic items (Fig. 25-1).

Overgraded coins are principally the stock in trade of the crooked mail-order dealer. When you see an ad that appeals to you, but you haven't previously done business with the dealer, my advice is to test order first. Instead of sending in the entire amount of money you had intended to spend, send in only part. Wait and see whether the coins he delivers are actually as represented. If not, send them back for a refund and cross him off your list of suppliers. If you do get what you have paid for, then you've probably found a good source.

Don't ever be pressured into buying by thinking the deal is so good they will be sold out before you can check out the dealer. In the coin collecting hobby, if the deal looks too good to be true, it probably is too good to be true.

Under normal market circumstances, there is an orderly wholesale-retail structure for nearly all coins and numismatic items. There are several readily available sources of accurate buy-and-sell prices on coins so that you can rather easily find out about what a dealer has to pay for the coin you want.

If the "Coin Market" section of *Numismatic News* says that the "Buy" (wholesale) price on an MS-65

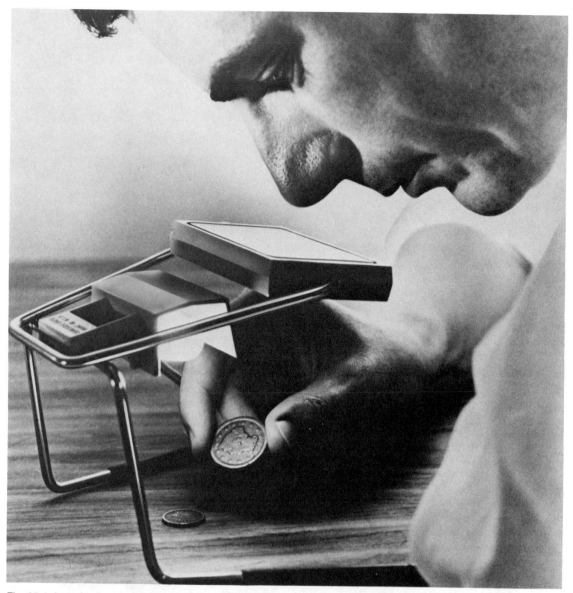

Fig. 25-1. Learning how to grade coins for yourself is the best protection against buying overgraded coins.

1922-P Peace silver dollar is $110, what are you to think when a dealer in that week's *Coin World* is offering "Gem MS-65 1922-P Peace dollars" at only $75? Is he just a nice guy trying to sell you a $155 (retail) coin for half price? No way. He is a crook trying to sell you a $75 coin for full price. Why should any dealer who has accurately graded MS-65 1922-P Peace dollars have to let them go for bargain prices when there would likely be plenty of takers at $110? Because he doesn't really have accurately

graded coins. He is trying to sell overgraded coins. If those coins were "right," dealers would snap them up at wholesale and sell them for retail.

Nobody gives coins away. When you see a $155 coin offered for much less than $110, you should be very suspicious. This is not to say that there is not an occasional good buy in the coin market. Unless you have a penchant for writing letters demanding refunds and threatening legal action for fraud, you are better off to buy your bargains only from those dealers with whom you have previously done business and in whom you put your trust. Doesn't it make you suspicious when you see ads where the dealer offers to buy MS-60 coins, but only has MS-65 examples of those same coins to sell?

If you could sit in front of the Teletype machine at a friendly coin dealer's office for a few hours, you would pretty soon get a good idea of who is overgrading by watching for these messages where people are trying to buy "super sliders, commercial Uncs." or "borderline Unc." Those are all just fancy monikers for overgraded coins.

As a rule, I will give any dealer the benefit of the doubt in a grading situation as long as it doesn't cost me money. If I order a coin from a dealer who is new to me, and that coin doesn't meet my grading standards, I am willing to concede that we just grade by different standards on three conditions. The first is if the coin is not off by more than a full grade (i.e., I order MS-65 and get MS-60 or MS-63, Ok; if I get AU-50, I scream). The second is if I get my money back because I refuse to accept overgraded coins. The third is that I don't order from that seller again.

There are plenty of honest and reliable coin dealers around so I don't feel the need to throw my money away on marginal types or outright crooks. Remember, there are a lot of crooked coin dealers around who are perfectly willing to give you a refund if you ask for it. They make their money on the collectors who are not knowledgeable enough or not bold enough to demand their money back.

There can be a legitimate difference of opinion between buyer and seller on the grade of a coin. It is axiomatic that the buyer always tends to undergrade the piece and the seller tends to see it as being better than it is. For this reason, the American Numismatic Association Certification Service added an impartial coin-grading service to its authentication activities. For a fee of $5 to $20, depending on the value of the coin, the ANACS staff (or outside experts) will assess any U.S. coin and place a grade designation on it on the basis of the official ANA coin-grading standards.

Because the ANACS staff is neither buying nor selling the coin, they can logically be deemed to be objective in the matter. They have nothing to lose or gain because they receive the same fee no matter what grade they place on the piece.

Because coin grading is an objective thing, the ANACS opinion is worth no more than any other person's viewpoint. But they do have the advantage of not being commercially involved in the buying or selling of the coin in question. There has been much controversy recently about the quality of ANACS grading. While detractors of the service point to the fact that the same coin may be graded differently by ANACS on two different days, they are ignoring the fact that an impartial grading authority is still a step in the right direction—even if it is not yet perfect.

Perhaps in the future, a coin grading computer will be developed that will accurately grade—by ANA standards or otherwise—any coin laid down under its sensors. When that happens, perhaps coin grading disputes will cease. But don't hold your breath and don't relax your personal efforts at becoming a proficient coin grader.

Unlike the case with counterfeits, you do not have an indefinite time in which to return an overgraded coin for refund. Most reputable dealers allow the buyer a five day return privilege. For any reason, or for no reason at all, the buyer has five days from receipt of the merchandise to return it for a full refund. Additionally, unless the seller specifically says otherwsie, the buyer is allowed the right to send the coin to ANACS for grading (or authentication) if he so informs the seller within the five days. If the coin is not properly certified as being of the advertised grade, the buyer may return it for a refund, even though more than five days have elapsed.

Dealers who do not follow these rules should be reported to the customer service department of the publication from which you answered the ad. You might also complain to the ANA or other dealer organizations to which the seller belongs.

There is no reason for overgrading except greed on the part of the seller who hopes to widen his profit margin and on the part of the buyer who is trying to "steal" a coin for far under true value. You can protect yourself by learning how to grade coins, by knowing your dealers, and by complaining to the proper authority to shut down those dealers who are crooked.

As former ANA Governor Byron Johnson says of the coin market, "the only thing you get at a fire sale is burnt."

Index

Edited by Steve Bolt